THE MIRACLE MILE

To Ivor,

Hope you enjoy these stories of the 1954 Games — a 'Miracle' Milestone for Vancouver and all BC! Thank you for all that you've done for BC Track & Field.

Yours in Sport,

Jason W

BC Sports Hall of Fame

Caitlin Press Inc.
8100 Alderwood Road,
Halfmoon Bay, BC V0N 1Y1
www.caitlin-press.com

Edited by Betty Keller
Text design and cover design by Vici Johnstone
Images courtesy of the BC Sports Hall of Fame unless otherwise noted.

Front cover image top: Bannister sprints by Landy on the final corner. Image courtesy *Vancouver Sun* photographer Charlie Warner. Bottom left to right: Lorne "Ace" Atkinson, Marjorie Jackson-Nelson, Doug Hepburn, Emmanuel Ifeajuna and Irene MacDonald.
Back cover: Canada's rowing eights seconds after their unlikely victory.

Printed in Canada

Caitlin Press Inc. acknowledges financial support from the Government of Canada and the Canada Council for the Arts, and from the Province of British Columbia through the British Columbia Arts Council and the Book Publisher's Tax Credit.

Canada Council   Conseil des Arts   BRITISH COLUMBIA
for the Arts   du Canada   ARTS COUNCIL

Library and Archives Canada Cataloguing in Publication

Beck, Jason, 1982-, author
    The miracle mile : stories of the 1954 British Empire and Commonwealth Games / Jason Beck.

Includes bibliographical references and index.
ISBN 978-1-987915-00-6 (paperback)

    1. Commonwealth Games (5th : 1954 : Vancouver). I. Title.

GV722.5.B7B42 2016   796.09711'33   C2015-908118-1

THE
MIRACLE MILE

STORIES OF THE 1954 BRITISH EMPIRE
AND COMMONWEALTH GAMES

JASON BECK

CAITLIN PRESS

To Nicole
For your patience, understanding, and sacrifices in the long run
to this finish line. This book is dedicated to you.

CONTENTS

Pages IV-V: Canada's Don McFarlane (right) sprints for the finish in the 4x110yd relay against Edward Ajado.

Pages VI-VII: One of the many billboards in Vancouver promoting the 1954 British Empire and Commonwealth Games.

This page and page VIII: Canada's Ron Miller clears 13ft 9in (4.20m) on his way to winning silver in the pole vault.

Over 35,000 spectators packed Vancouver's Empire Stadium on the final day of the 1954 Games, Saturday, August 7. It was the largest paid crowd in Canadian sports history to that point. Photo by Jack Cash.

ACKNOWLEDGEMENTS

So many people helped in this book's journey in the ten long years since I began my research efforts in August 2006, and I am sincerely grateful for their contributions along the way, large and small. A few individuals deserve special recognition.

I will forever be indebted to Robin Anderson for planting the seeds for this book, as well as for my future job as the BC Sports Hall of Fame's curator.

I must express sincere thanks to nearly eighty individuals who agreed to be interviewed and then entrusted me with their 1954 BECG stories. I hope I did your Games justice. Sadly, several of these amazing individuals passed away before this book was published, and I'd like to pay tribute to them: Bob Ackles, Lorne "Ace" Atkinson, Herb Capozzi, Mario Caravetta, Sir Chris Chataway, Stan Cox, Garde Gardom, Jim Kearney, Phil Kueber, Victor Milligan, Tommy Paonessa, Bill Parnell and Ted Reynolds.

Thank you to Kate Bird of the Canwest Media Library and Andrew Martin of the Vancouver Public Library for allowing me to sift through thousands of Games photo negatives. And to Colin Preston of the CBC Vancouver media library for allowing me to view hours of original Games broadcast footage. Michael Dawson and Ron Palenski generously mailed photocopies of various New Zealand and Australian newspapers. The late Chuck Davis kindly assisted with many obscure Vancouver city details. Author Tom Thurston provided valuable suggestions on the life of weightlifter Doug Hepburn. Jennifer Wadley-Smith shared access to the personal training journals of her father, Jim Peters. Lucy Kenward suggested key structural changes that took my manuscript to the next level. Marin Beck, Bob Graham, Len Corben and Alan Watson each read and critiqued selected chapters.

Three media hall of famers, "Dr. Sport" Greg Douglas, Jim Robson and Jim Taylor, provided unwavering support for this project. Without hesitation each contributed letters of support while I searched for a publisher. I am so honoured you thought enough of this project to back it.

To Doug and Diane Clement—truly BC's "Hall of Fame" couple—for including me among the thousands of athletes, organizations and the sport of track and field itself you have fostered across the country over many decades.

I am truly grateful for the support of the BC Sports Hall of Fame, specifically Allison Mailer and the Hall's board of trustees. The Hall generously granted free use of its 1954 BECG photo collection for this book and based the "A Week You'll Remember A Lifetime" 1954 BECG 60th anniversary exhibition on my work. Thank you for giving me the opportunity to combine my passion with my profession over the past thirteen years.

I must give special thanks to Vici Johnstone and the entire Caitlin Press team for believing these stories are important and deserved to be published. I feel very fortunate to have been placed in your capable hands. To editor supreme Betty Keller, who improved this collection of stories beyond any of my expectations.

I would be remiss if I didn't recognize the ongoing support from the entire Beck and Cerf clans. Thank you, Mom and Dad, for teaching me to always finish what I start.

Without the help and support of three truly special individuals this book would have died at any of a hundred points along the way. When all hope seemed lost, Mike Harling took up my cause to find a publisher and became an unshakeable ally. Mike, you have no idea how much our many conversations figuring out the next step meant to me. Fred Hume read every single word of every single chapter of every single version of this manuscript and provided invaluable suggestions. More than this, Fred, you were this book's biggest cheerleader from day one and you kept me going during the toughest times.

Finally, to my life partner, Nicole Cerf. Through every twist and turn, you've been there, my rock, my strength, my inspiration. Pieces of the love and support you've shared with me shine from every page in this book. I couldn't have done this without you.

Jason Beck
Langley, BC. December 2015.

FOREWORD

I was a member of the silver medal-winning 4x440yard relay team at the British Empire and Commonwealth Games that took place in Vancouver in 1954. It wasn't my first time in international games as I had been on Canada's 1952 Olympic Games 4x440yard relay team in Helsinki, but my experience in my hometown of Vancouver was a bigger thrill. The attention of the entire city was focussed on this event at a level that never existed before. The Games changed the direction of Vancouver's future, introducing the city to the world and the world to the city. They catalyzed change toward the more tolerant, inclusive, diverse and multicultural society it has become, an evolution that was enhanced when we hosted Expo 86 and the 2010 Winter Olympic Games.

Although Jason Beck's book was written sixty years after the 1954 Games, it captures the essence of that long ago experience by reconstructing the events of the time in such detail that it is hard to imagine that he was not present himself. He

Doug Clement, 1958.

has been relentless in seeking accurate information from every source possible to recreate the aura and excitement of being in the front row of Empire Stadium or on the bleachers beside Empire Pool or on the dikes beside the Vedder Canal's regatta site. He has captured the essence of sport by entering into the hearts and souls of everyone involved, and as a result of the breadth and depth of his reach, my own understanding and appreciation of the events I participated in so long ago has been increased.

This book provides a great experience of Vancouver's history through the story of the British Empire and Commonwealth Games of 1954.

—Doug Clement

INTRODUCTION

Among the 27,000 artifacts residing in the BC Sports Hall of Fame's remarkable collection, there exists a small Omega stopwatch. Many items grab your eye with their colour, size or shape, but I overlooked this stopwatch at first. That is, until one day I noticed the hands on the dial were stopped at 3 minutes 58.8 seconds—the winning time for the historic race remembered today as "The Miracle Mile." This race, the climax of the 1954 British Empire and Commonwealth Games, put Vancouver on the world sports map for the first time. One newspaper called the Games "the greatest Canadian sports spectacle ever" while another decreed that it was "certainly Canada's greatest sporting week."

Most British Columbians—sports fans or not—usually have at least passing knowledge of "The Mile of the Century" because it still ranks as one of the great world sports moments of the 1950s and some claim of the entire 20th century. So while that white watch face and the numbers *3:58.8* stared back at me, other questions sprang to mind. What had it been like sitting in Empire Stadium's bleachers that sweltering August afternoon when a race timer halted this watch? What happened leading up to that moment? And what happened after? Since this watch had been stopped abruptly over half a century ago, few had tried to go beyond this one race to understand the 1954 Games as a whole.

Other interesting gems and stories of the 1954 Games had been finding me for years, and in August 2006 I decided it was time to begin research for a book that was not only about the Mile but also about all the events that had been overshadowed by the Mile. As the BC Sports Hall of Fame's curator, I had some advantages: access to the largest collection of 1954 BECG-related material anywhere in the world as well as dozens of key contacts, each of whom had some connection to the Games as an athlete, spectator, volunteer official or coach. I also had a disadvantage: my heavy schedule of duties at the Hall of Fame meant this project must be completed part-time and it would take far longer than if I could work on it full-time.

For the first year and a half I broadened my research, spending many hours in archives around the Lower Mainland, sifting through thousands of documents, photographs and newspapers on microfiche. I analyzed hours of original broadcast footage and ordered rare books from around the world. I also began interviewing the first of the nearly 80 individuals from a dozen nations I would eventually tape who had attended or competed at the Games. Many were eager to help me, and an interview with one athlete often led to interviews with several more of his or her teammates or competitors. In April 2008 I finally felt ready to begin writing. One morning on my daily commute to the Hall of Fame aboard the West Coast Express and Skytrain, I hand-wrote a dozen pages about the marathoner Jim Peters. After that, on every two-hour commute—morning and night—for the next six years I packed my notepad, a pen, various piles of research papers and occasionally several books and diligently scrawled out a few pages of very rough narrative. On weekends I transcribed my chicken scratches onto my laptop.

By the end of this process, I don't think anyone could know more about the 1954 Games or the athletes who starred in them. One of my biggest discoveries was *how many* other significant athletic stories had been overlooked beyond the glare of Roger Bannister and John Landy's historic clash in the Miracle Mile. For instance, just thirty minutes after that race's stirring finish had electrified Empire Stadium's 35,000 spectators, Jim Peters staggered through the stadium gates, and the tragic conclusion of the Marathon had evoked even stronger emotions in those who witnessed both moments in person.

And there was so much more. Crowds were thrilled by the gripping athletic triumphs of New Zealand's all-round track star Yvette Williams, England's perennial runner-up Chris Chataway, and Vancouver's very own "World's Strongest Man" Doug Hepburn. The simmering rivalry between Trinidad rocket sprinter Mike Agostini and hot-tempered Australian world record holder Hector Hogan sparked fireworks that could have lit up the night sky. The sudden rise and tumultuous post-Games life of Nigerian high jumper Emmanuel Ifeajuna might as well have been pulled from the pages of *Ripley's Believe It or Not*. Equally as improbable was the performance of a group of novice University of British Columbia rowers, who engineered what was perhaps the greatest upset in Commonwealth Games history. There was even the dramatic final race in the astonishing career of the fastest woman in history to that point, Australia's "Lithgow Flash" Marjorie Jackson-Nelson. From the shocking controversy surrounding Canada's statuesque shot putter Jackie MacDonald to the homegrown surprise of Vancouver Island high school student Terry Tobacco and the stirring comeback of Vancouver cyclist Lorne "Ace" Atkinson, the 1954 BECG had it all.

Without doubt, Vancouver and British Columbia had never before seen a week like that and quite possibly never will again.

Author's Note

The 1954 British Empire and Commonwealth Games was the first time the word "Commonwealth" was included in the formal title, but it was seldom used at the time, even in official correspondence. Instead, shorter variations such as "British Empire Games," "BEG," "1954 Games," or simply "The Games" were used. To stay true to the 1954 usage, I have used "BECG," "1954 Games" or simply "The Games" throughout this book.

To preserve the flavour of the era, I have also employed the 1954 designations for measurements, names of individual events and nations. For instance, I have used imperial measurements for most events and "broad jump," which is today's "long jump." British Guiana refers to Guyana, Gold Coast to Ghana, Northern Rhodesia to Zambia, Southern Rhodesia to Zimbabwe, and Trinidad to Trinidad and Tobago. As is Games custom, England, Scotland, Northern Ireland and Wales competed as separate nations.

CHAPTER 1
LET THE GAMES BEGIN

In the early evening of July 30, 1954, a fleet of cream-coloured BC Electric buses ferrying hundreds of athletes, representing two dozen nations from the farthest corners of the world, departed from Empire Village on the University of British Columbia campus. By the time they were halfway across the city, the convoy was navigating streets clogged by an unusual number of cars and pedestrians all moving toward Empire Stadium for the opening ceremonies of the British Empire and Commonwealth Games. The athletes peering out at Vancouver and its people were seeing a city at a pivotal moment in its growth, a city bustling with the undeniable energy of new-found postwar wealth and freedom.

The Vancouver they saw was one that would seem foreign today. The Red Ensign fluttered on City Hall flagpoles. Citizens stood at attention when "God Save The Queen" was sung—even in movie theatres. All banks closed at 3 p.m. and were never open on weekends, although a recent civic vote allowed retail stores to be open for business on Wednesdays for the first time. The law allowing restaurants to legally sell alcohol with meals was only two years old, and club-goers at the most happening night spots in the city were still adjusting to drinking freely instead of stealthily sipping from brown-bagged liquor bottles. The Lions Gate and Pattullo bridges were still toll bridges, and on Games event days toll-collecting was about to cause lineups of creeping cars stretching for miles, but the brand-new Granville Street Bridge had opened just months before and it did ease congestion within the city. Canada's first shopping centre had been launched four years earlier at Park Royal in West Vancouver, while the first Grouse Mountain chairlift, built of rough-cut fir logs, was less than five years old.

Sports were still outlawed on Sundays. The biggest team in town was the Canucks, but they only played in the Western Hockey League, and the BC Lions would not play their first football game until a few days after the Empire's best athletes had left town. Radio and newspapers were how most people got their news, although television, viewed on brand-new 15-inch RCAs, was the latest fad taking hold. Residents who hadn't purchased their first "black-and-white" in time for Queen Elizabeth's coronation the previous spring chose the Games as their reason to splurge, and many of them caught the events on the city's first locally based television station, CBUT channel 2. Months earlier, the CBC had paid $50,000 for exclusive world film, television and radio rights to the Games from the cash-strapped BEG Society. The broadcaster then sold sponsorship of their coverage to communications giant Northern Electric as part of a $500,000 package that included Canadian football, marking the largest deal in Canadian television history. This sponsorship allowed the CBC to offer free nation-wide daily Games broadcasts for

Opposite: Vancouver's Lorne "Ace" Atkinson, on a racing bike he built himself during his lunch breaks. Atkinson braved China Creek Park's 45-degree banked cedar corners during the 1954 BECG to produce one of Canada's best international cycling results in decades.

Vancouver's largest indoor boxing crowd was treated to one of the great amateur bouts in BECG history when England's Brian Harper (pictured) fought Canada's Gerry Buchanan in the heavyweight final. Years later as a professional, Harper went on to fight Muhammad Ali.

the first time. They also partnered with NBC to produce North America-wide coverage, and they provided footage to all 24 competing nations as well as such non-competing countries as Germany, Sweden and Spain. Vancouverite Glinda Sutherland recalled "walking from house to house on our street" and getting a glimpse of televised events during the British Empire Games. "It was summertime and most doors were open so you could just walk in. As one moved from living room to living room, one saw children lying on floors with their little faces looking up at the rented or newly purchased television screens and the adults were all watching, too."

While many of the athletes arriving for the BECG were pushing the known boundaries of their sports, much of the world still moved at a slower, old-world pace. A couple of weeks later when *Sports Illustrated* covered the Miracle Mile as the lead story of its first-ever issue, puzzled readers wrote in, confused: How could they possibly be reading a New York-based magazine complete with photographs on a Thursday when the event had only taken place the previous Saturday afternoon thousands of miles away in Vancouver? Disbelief at this speed of publishing prompted *Sports Illustrated* to print an explanation in their September 6 edition detailing how this technological marvel had been accomplished.

The BECG of 1954 were lacking two constants that are unfortunately part of any modern major sporting event: security and performance-enhancing drugs. No physical threats to the athletes or the crowds that came to see them were even contemplated in

Australia's Marjorie Jackson-Nelson (far left), the fastest woman in history, wins the 100yds over Australian teammate Winsome Cripps (third from right) and Northern Rhodesia's Edna Maskell (far right). Jackson-Nelson later ran the final competitive race of her illustrious career on Empire Stadium's new cinder track.

those days, and thus there was no razor wire around the venues, nor were there cameras spying on the crowds or bag searches of attendees. One participant, Jackie MacDonald, remembers security as "two Boy Scouts with a rope." And the idea of using drugs to improve athletic performance was unknown. Scottish swimmer Elenor Gordon, a double gold medalist in 1954, recalled that "the only drug we got was a Horlicks milk tablet. That was supplied free."

☸

As the buses loaded with athletes wheezed to a stop outside Empire Stadium, the young men and women who would be the subjects of so many remarkable stories over the next nine days stepped down and quickly became part of a whirling mob of crisp new national blazers and youthful energy. Most of their exploits, however, would be overshadowed by the deeds of just three men among them, men who largely came to define the 1954 BECG. England's Roger Bannister and Australia's John Landy were already the stars of the Mile and the talk of the Games. Their every move and word made headlines, and the attention upon them would only ratchet up as their race approached. More anonymously, English marathoner Jim Peters was also prepared for the most important race of his life. Although the Games spotlight would shift to other athletes and other stories over the course of the week, it would never truly leave these three as they prepared in the background for their events on the final day.

Of the three, Jim Peters had come the farthest in so many ways. Born in working-class east London just weeks before the end of the Great War, he had been a sickly child, and his father bought him a soccer ball, hoping exercise out in the fresh air would help improve his health. Young Jim fell in love with the game and played throughout his youth, at one point alongside Alf Ramsey, who coached England to the 1966 World Cup. But Peters had discovered he could outpace his teammates on training runs, and by his late teens he was more or less living at the running track. National service as a dispensing optician during WWII derailed his immediate athletic plans, though it did provide him with a lifelong occupation. After the war, at the advanced age of 27, he returned to running and began a surprising rise up the English ranks. Linking up with coach Herbert "Johnny" Johnston proved pivotal as Johnston reinforced the key tenet of Peters' distance running make-up: "You can't take out of yourself in a race more than you have put in during training." However, Peters' initial success was tempered by great embarrassment at the 1948 Olympics in London when he was lapped in the 10,000m event by gold medalist Emil Zatopek. To extend his fading career, he made the jump to the marathon distance, and here he truly blossomed. Under Johnston's guidance and training and alongside fellow Londoner Stan Cox, Peters changed the face of marathoning forever. As he had to shoehorn his training time around work and family, he might only have 30 minutes a night, but he would run for that 30 minutes at unheard of speeds, near or at race pace. When he could spare the time, his longer runs topped 30 miles. His weekly mileage—which was consistently well over 100 miles—became legendary, and it became standard for him to log over 400 runs a year.

No one worked harder, no one ran farther, and no one looked more awkward doing it. Some may have confused him with a clerk dashing for a bus. Peters was the first to admit that he had "a terrible rolling-gait style. They used to say, 'If he's rolling, he's all right'—and my head went back and forth." But hidden below his chaotic, swinging upper body, his legs glided along with perfect economy, and they were powered by an intense focus and iron will. At times he became so intent on the road ahead, he failed to notice that his slashing thumbnails had caused bloody splotches to seep through his singlet. But somehow it all worked for him. Beginning with his first marathon in 1951 at the age of 32 and continuing over the next three years, he produced an unprecedented series of winning results. Running in the only athletic shoes available at the time, canvas and rubber Woolworth's plimsolls, which offered little support and less cushioning, he broke the world's best time on four separate occasions. He was the first man to go under the 2hr 20min barrier and ultimately lowered the world mark by over *seven* minutes to 2hr 17min 39sec, the largest margin by any single athlete—ever. His only setback was another devastating Olympic failure, this time in 1952 when he failed to finish as the gold medal favourite. Thus, the 1954 BECG loomed large for him, one final chance to prove he could rise to the occasion in a big international event.

Like Peters, Roger Bannister was also born in London, but over a decade later, six months before the Wall Street crash of October 1929. An active and exceedingly bright boy, Bannister had an affinity for running from a very young age, but other than winning his school's annual cross-country race, he showed little hint of the great runner he would become. That changed in his mid-teens when his father took him to White City Stadium to see former mile world record holder Sydney Wooderson gamely race Sweden's Arne Andersson. Bannister left the stadium that day with his head and heart aflame. After that, "nobody could have wanted to run more than I did."

While attending Oxford University on an academic scholarship to study medicine, Bannister began coming into his own, drawn to the Mile distance. Using the *fartlek* or "speed play" training method made famous by the great Swedish runners of the 1940s, he soon entered the conversation as an English international. Surprisingly, he passed on the 1948 Olympics, feeling himself not yet ready, and instead began gearing all his efforts toward the 1952 Olympics when he hoped to capture the 1500m gold.

What set Bannister apart as an athlete was that he ran as much with his brilliant, probing mind and fiery heart as with his naturally gifted body. As with his medical research, every race was an experiment to learn from, and he came to relish racing strategy and developed a fearsome finishing kick. He wasn't a running "stylist" in the traditional sense, but no one could deny that he was a man built to run. With arms churning, hair flapping, mouth often agape, he was a furious machine-like blur of many moving parts as he gained momentum, almost like a ferris wheel sprung from its supports and rolling smoothly down a hill. In the ESPN-TV movie *Four Minutes,* Bannister's long-time friend and training partner Chris Chataway said, "There have been very few in my lifetime who I think really had as perfect and fluent a style as Roger's and that he was born with."

England's Jim Peters, the world's fastest marathoner, came to the Games seeking a victory to erase disappointments in past "big" races.

Bannister approached the 1952 Olympics in the best shape of his life, but a last-minute scheduling change forced the 1500m entrants to run three races in three days. Bannister had only trained for two and knew his hopes were all but dashed by the added race. He did qualify for the final, but "there was just no energy in my legs and they felt lifeless," he recalled in *The Four Minute Mile;* he finished an exhausted, shattered fourth. Knowing he couldn't end his running career on such a sour note, he continued training, setting his sights on the elusive four-minute mile and the 1954 BECG, a final target before retiring to a career in medicine. He began training with others, notably Chataway and Chris Brasher. Although coach-less by choice thus far, Bannister

Less than three months before the 1954 BECG, England's Roger Bannister became the first person to run a mile in under four minutes, which made headlines around the world. But some criticized his use of pacers to break the barrier and so Bannister arrived in Vancouver with something to prove.

now allowed Franz Stampfl to advise him. His breakthrough came on May 6, 1954, at a British AAA versus Oxford University meet at Oxford's Iffley Road track. It was a blustery evening, but the rain held off just long enough for Brasher and Chataway to pace their friend Bannister to everlasting fame and glory. In *The Four Minute Mile,* Bannister recalled of the final yards that "I had a moment of mixed joy and anguish when my mind took over. It raced well ahead of my body and drew my body compellingly forward... I felt at that moment that it was my chance to do one thing supremely well." In 3min 59.4sec, he achieved what some had felt was not humanly possible, the first sub-four-minute mile, track's Holy Grail.

While many celebrated his feat, a few felt it barely bordered on acceptability. The use of pacers then "wasn't totally cricket, as the English themselves would say," noted Doug Clement in the 2004 CBC documentary *The Miracle Mile.* Thus, after John Landy subsequently took the mile record, Bannister headed for Vancouver seeking validation. If he could gain victory in the BECG Mile, a true race, no one could say he was just some "test-tube" runner who'd scored the first four-minute mile under artificial circumstances. This man of such great ambition suddenly had something to prove.

Born a year after Bannister, John Landy had been raised in an upper middle class Melbourne suburb in relative worry-free comfort. While growing up, he barely gave running a second thought, preferring instead to collect butterflies or play Aussie Rules football. That's not to say Landy didn't have running potential: in his last year in school he swept the middle distances and took the State of Victoria mile title. Yet running remained something he dabbled in. That changed while he was studying agricultural science at Melbourne University where he joined the Geelong Guild Athletic Club and for the first time began training seriously. From an also-ran in local club meets, he began to emerge onto the radar screens of the Australian Olympic team selection committee.

The remarkable thing about Landy's rapid rise is that it originated solely from his own fierce personal resolve. He loved to run for no other reason than to challenge himself. Like Bannister, he didn't follow any single coach but rather bounced around, listening, learning, taking scraps of knowledge that made sense to his own unique set of circumstances and discarding the rest. He was one of the final athletes selected to Australia's 1952 Olympic team, but he was outclassed and underprepared and ran poorly in his events, failing to advance past the heats.

"I remember the golfer [Gary] Player saying he treasured his defeats because from defeat you get the focus to do something," Landy told the *Melbourne Age* in April 2004. "I was disappointed, and I came back determined to redress that situation." He analyzed what he had learned in Helsinki and adopted a new training schedule. After spending the day in his university classes, he forced himself through brutal workouts late at night on the dimly lit footpaths of the park across the street from his home. He worked relentlessly at smoothing out the kinks of his running form until he ran with a feather-footed, clipped stride that oozed effortless efficiency. Months went by without him missing a session. "He was hungry, a hard trainer," explained Geoff Warren, an Australian teammate, in an interview in 2013. "He realized early on hard work is the only way to achieve."

Australia's John Landy makes yet another gruelling training lap at UBC's Varsity Stadium appear effortless. His discipline and work ethic astounded observers. Just six weeks after Bannister's historic run, Landy had bettered it to become the new mile world record holder. Photo courtesy of Dr. Doug Clement.

Landy's discipline and fitness astounded observers, as did the results it produced. Out of the blue in December 1952 he ran the mile in 4min 2.1sec, shocking the athletic world with the third-fastest time in history. Some called it a fluke, but he produced a string of similar results after that, each time crossing the finish line fresh as a daisy. Suddenly the race for the four-minute mile was on, and he appeared the leading contender. His runs were covered in *Time Magazine* and the *New York Times* and drew Australia's prime minister out to watch.

The only thing outshining Landy's outstanding results was his stalwart character. He was so down-to-earth and approachable that his competitors wanted both to beat him and be like him. He became the most admired runner of his time, and in the process he single-handedly raised the profile and standard of Australian middle distance running from the athletics wilderness, although he was competing on inferior tracks with few rivals fast enough to push him. For Landy, it seemed only natural to go it alone and lead from the front, a trait that seems typically Australian. "If you want to run a world record, go and do it," he explained to Jim Denison, the author of *Bannister and Beyond* (2003). "You can't wait around for someone else to help you. And that's the type of person I was; I think that's reflected in my style and tactics as a miler: lead, go for it."

Ultimately, Bannister crashed through the four-minute mile barrier before Landy did, but just 46 days later Landy went him one better. Chased by Chataway in Turku, Finland, Landy blazed to a new world record of 3min 58sec, destroying Bannister's mark by a colossal 1.4 seconds. For the second time in six weeks, the impenetrable defences of "sport's Everest" had been breached. And then, like something a team of Hollywood's best scriptwriters could not have conjured up, both men were destined to meet on the track for the first time in Vancouver. As Len Johnson so aptly put it in his book *The Landy Era* (2009): "It was as if having conquered Everest, [Edmund] Hillary and Tenzing [Norgay] had squared off for the world heavyweight title."

❂

On Friday evening, July 30, 1954, the largest crowd in BC sport history to that point, a full 29,350 spectators, each paid two dollars to sit on the plank seating of Empire Stadium. As they waited for the Opening Ceremonies of the British Empire and Commonwealth Games to begin, the scent of hot dogs wafted in from the concession stands. Souvenir vendors worked their way through the bleachers, hawking everything from spaceship balloons to BECG pennants, chinaware, kewpie dolls and pork-pie hats. One sly swindler even sold flattened American pennies stamped "I Was There" and charged a quarter for them.

Around 7:30, when the air was electric with anticipation, thirty Mustangs, Vampires and Harvards screeched and thundered overhead in formation, some buzzing the stadium so low that even Royal Canadian Air Force officials looked alarmed. Then as the stadium's northwest gates swung open, the crowd became hushed and in marched an RCAF band followed by a combined Canadian navy, army and air force honour guard. The setting sun caught the gleaming steel of their bayonets pointed skyward.

As the clock struck eight, a powder-blue convertible rolled into the stadium, a burst of gunfire saluting its entrance. A man wearing a ten-gallon pearl-grey hat, charcoal pinstriped suit, and blue-and-white-checkered tie stepped out. As he removed his hat, the crowd politely applauded and cheered, as if welcoming an old friend, which in a way, he was. Earl Alexander of Tunis, or less formally Lord Alexander, had been a World War II hero and served as the seventeenth governor general of Canada from 1946-52, endearing himself to the nation with his lack of pretention. He was now minister of Defence in Winston Churchill's British cabinet. While he was a step down from His Royal Highness Prince Philip, Duke of Edinburgh, the man the BECG Society had coveted for this prestigious opening night, Alexander evoked as much respect and sentiment as anyone in the Empire. He waved casually to the crowd as he walked along the

The Jamaicans salute Lord Alexander and a crowd of thousands while marching during the Opening Ceremonies.

cinder track before climbing the stairs to the royal box on Empire Stadium's west side where a bevy of VIPs quickly surrounded him. They included BC Premier W.A.C. Bennett, the Hollywood gossip columnist, former opera singer and actress Cobina Wright, and American Democratic Party leader Adlai Stevenson.

Attention then turned back to the gate, as a group of New Zealand supporters caught sight of their compatriots marching into the stadium in tight formation and broke out the "Haka" war cry. After them, all the participating Commonwealth teams paraded around the track in alphabetical order: green-blazered Australians, Barbados' one-man team of weightlifter George Nicholls, all 129 English team members with red roses on their blazers, a half-dozen regal Fijians wearing snow-white sulus and pale turquoise jackets, Indians in pale blue turbans with their flag bearer sporting a colourful trailing plume, the team from Northern Ireland in emerald green plaid, Pakistanis in Jinnah caps, 32 Scots wearing sprigs of heather in their lapels, and finally 220 Canadian men and women in brilliant red blazers and white panama hats. Of course, the home crowd saved its loudest roar of the evening for last.

When all the athletes were standing in neat ranks on the infield, the flag bearers formed a semi-circle around a raised podium bearing the golden BECG seal. The RCAF band began a long drumroll, and mistaking it for the opening to "God Save The Queen,"

The navy, army and air force honour guard march past lines of athletes from 24 national teams.

everyone stood up. But embarrassed laughs filled the air as doffed hats were popped back on and people sat down again to watch the white BECG flag—a gold crest with red-and-blue-striped barber pole border—being raised up the infield flagpole. When it reached the top, a battery of artillery guns outside the stadium fired five charges, saluting the fifth commencement of the BECG, and simultaneously flocks of white homing pigeons billowed skyward from infield cages. According to the next day's *Vancouver Sun*, some of the pigeons were spooked by the barrage and deposited droppings on the crisply pressed uniforms of the athletes below.

"Sacre bleu!" cried Montreal cyclist Guy Morin, who was hit.

"That's okay, Guy," said Jim Trifunov, Canadian wrestling manager. "When a pigeon does that to you in the BEG, it means good luck."

"I will trade you the good luck," countered Morin, "if you will pay my cleaning bill!"

Next, Bill Parnell of North Vancouver, the Canadian team captain and defending BECG mile champion, stepped forward to deliver the athlete's oath:

"We declare that we shall take part in the British Empire and Commonwealth Games of 1954 in the spirit of true sportsmanship recognizing the rules which govern them and desire of participating in them for the honour of our Commonwealth and Empire and for the glory of sport."

BEG Federation chairman Arthur Porritt then stepped to the microphone and called on Lord Alexander to open the Games. Alexander began his address with:

National flagbearers, including Canada's Bill Parnell (foreground), stand at attention on Empire Stadium's infield.

Your Honour. Ladies and Gentlemen. For me, it is both an honour and a pleasure to have been invited to officially open the British Empire and Commonwealth Games of 1954... The visiting teams of famous athletes and our friends who have come from all parts of the world to see them perform cannot but be impressed by this fine new stadium, specially built for the occasion... Rome was not built in a day. Neither was this stadium... We are greatly indebted to our host country and its organizing committee under the able leadership of the general chairman. So on behalf of the visitors I should like to express our warm appreciation and sincere congratulation to Mr. Stanley Smith and his staff. Together with all those who have helped to organize and lay on this grand show, a show which, if I may say so, is an excellent example of Canada's genius for organization.

At these words, Stanley Smith, Vancouver's Mayor Fred Hume and businessman Jack Diamond humbly lowered their eyes against the appreciative glances and knowing nods directed their way from those close by. It had been such a long haul to get there. So many obstacles had stood in the Society's way at the outset and so much had fallen into place in spite of those obstacles that it seemed a miracle. After years of endless meetings, thousands of letters and phone calls, press quarrels, bitter disputes and grudging agreements, they had done it, and no one understood this better than these three men who had been charged with pulling off the biggest international sports event held in Canada to that point.

CHAPTER 2
ROME WASN'T BUILT IN A DAY

Yes, Rome hadn't been built in a day and neither had the venues for the 1954 BECG. Alexander had got that right.

The story of those venues goes all the way back to the late 19th century when the British Empire encompassed a quarter of both the world's population and landmass, and to 1891, five years before the first modern Olympic Games were held, when Reverend John Astley Cooper had begun promoting the idea of a "Pan-Britannic Festival." It had taken a full twenty years before his idea became reality as the 1911 Festival of Empire in London, organized to celebrate the coronation of King George V with teams from the United Kingdom, Australia, and Canada competing in various sports. World War I prevented a reprise of this event, but in 1924 Norton Crow, national secretary of Canada's Amateur Athletic Union of Canada (AAU), proposed "taking the initiative in an All-British-Empire Games, to be held between the Olympic Games." His proposal ultimately bloomed as the quadrennial British Empire Games, thanks in large part to the persistent leadership of newspaper editor Melville Marks "Bobby" Robinson of Hamilton, Ontario. For the first BEG, held in Hamilton in 1930 at the height of the Depression, Robinson convinced hesitant nations to send their best athletes overseas by dangling large travel subsidies and the promise of free food and lodging once they arrived. The Games proved such a phenomenal success that the newly created BEG Federation immediately made plans for Games to be held every four years. In 1934 London, England, hosted followed by Sydney, Australia, in 1938. World War II interrupted competition, but the Games resumed in 1950 in Auckland, New Zealand. By the time Vancouver prepared to add the fifth link in the chain, which would be called the British Empire and Commonwealth Games to honour the changed relationships between the countries of the old empire, a strong tradition had emerged.

Unlike other large international sporting competitions where a common climate (the Winter Olympics) or geography (the Pan American Games) are the basis for inclusion, from the beginning the BEG looked toward a common history and language as the ties that bind, inviting only those nations once or currently part of the Empire. The renegade United States, of course, which broke away from British rule in 1776, received no invitation. It was no coincidence either that these games leaned toward spirited but friendly competition rather than the overly intense, win-at-all-costs atmosphere of events such as the Olympics, which occasionally sever rather than strengthen bonds. This idea of "the Friendly Games" remains one of the trademarks of the Commonwealth Games today.

Vancouver's drive to host the 1954 Games had begun in 1938. That year at the third BEG in Sydney, Australia, the BEG Federation allocated the 1942 Games to Canada, leaving the officials of Canada's AAU to designate which city would play host. Subsequently,

Opposite: BEG Society General Chairman Stanley Smith tests out the new cycling track at China Creek Park. Photo by Bill Cunningham, the *Province*.

several BC athletic and tourism groups met at Vancouver City Hall to discuss the possibility of Vancouver hosting with the Hastings Park Oval and Kitsilano Pool promoted as logical venues. Ultimately, eastern AAU officials chose Montreal, but World War II intervened, forcing the abandonment of both the 1942 and 1946 Games.

When regular international competition resumed, the BEG Federation offered Canada first option to host the 1950 Games, and both Vancouver and Hamilton submitted tentative bids. Once again Vancouver sports officials gathered at City Hall to discuss the possibilities, but the tight time frame was a major concern: the city had no proper stadium, no freshwater swimming pool (Kits Pool is filled with salt water), no cycle track, and no plan for how to raise the estimated $300,000 needed to build these venues. So instead, Vancouver officials looked toward 1954. When Hamilton also withdrew its proposal, Canadian officials politely declined the offer, and the BEG Federation awarded the 1950 Games to eager Auckland.

Then late one night in early January 1950 while Canadian athletes and officials were setting sail for New Zealand aboard the RMS *Aorangi*, the *Province* newspaper's sports editor, Erwin Swangard, saw an interesting news item unfurling from the Canadian Press teletype machine: the BEG Federation was set to name Canada as the site for

Fencers engage atop a stage erected in downtown Vancouver as part of an April 1953 Games fundraising blitz.

the 1954 Games, which would make it the first nation to host the Games a second time. But, according to Canadian Press, Hamilton was the most likely host city.

"Screw Hamilton," Swangard reportedly said. "Let's get them in Vancouver."

Then, even though it was the middle of the night, he ordered his entire *Province* sports department to start building support by phoning every major sport and tourism leader in the city. Most of these leaders promised them full backing, and somehow they even managed to get the endorsement of BC's premier, Byron "Boss" Johnson, who was in Ottawa at the time. Meanwhile, Swangard sent instructions to his lead sports columnist, Eric Whitehead, who was en route to New Zealand with the athletes, to rally Canadian officials face-to-face on that front. Around three in the morning Swangard phoned Vancouver Mayor Charles Thompson for the second time that night—Thompson had hung up on him the first time—and strong-armed the mayor into holding a meeting at City Hall the following week to discuss the possibilities.

Swangard's blitz didn't stop there. For the next several weeks, he used the sports pages of the *Province* as his personal pulpit to convince the masses that hosting the 1954 Games was the best idea since the salmon burger was invented. On January 25, the newspaper's editorial praised Thompson and other city council members for supporting the Vancouver effort, "an opportunity to really do something for the youth of our city, province, and nation." In the same issue Swangard reprinted a *Hamilton Spectator* article describing the Steel City's BEG efforts in 1930 and brazenly re-headlined it: "Hamilton Did It Once, Vancouver Can Do It Better."

Pressured by Swangard's relentless bullheadedness, Mayor Thompson had no choice but to fall in line. To his credit, he caught the ball Swangard zinged in his direction and ran with it, lining up any hesitant civic leaders firmly behind Vancouver's bid and organizing a working committee. And after word arrived from Auckland that the BEG Federation had officially awarded the 1954 Games to Canada, Thompson directed his efforts toward convincing the BEG Association of Canada, headed by Major (later Colonel) Jack Davies, to select Vancouver over Hamilton, Toronto or Montreal, which were preferred by the eastern-based Davies. Thompson cabled Davies, who was in Auckland as Canadian BEG team manager, to express Vancouver's hope to host and it was reprinted in the *Sun* on January 28:

> City of Vancouver wishes me to extend to British Empire Games Association a hearty invitation to hold 1954 games in Vancouver. The city is prepared to post a goodwill bond to ensure proper staging of program. We feel that decision regarding site for 1954 should be decided in Auckland so that plans may be started immediately...
> Charles E. Thompson, Mayor.

Thompson also cabled Vancouver businessman Ken McKenzie, who had gone to Auckland to watch his daughter Eleanor compete in the women's sprints. Thompson gave him the task of personally delivering Vancouver's invitation to host, but when Davies could provide McKenzie with no assurances that Vancouver would be chosen and instead remained preoccupied with matters of the current Games, fears grew that Vancouver might be overlooked. Fortuitously, by this time the Vancouver bid had the full support

Bob Osborne (top) and Fred Rowell (bottom) played crucial roles in securing the Games for Vancouver.

of two extraordinarily influential individuals: AAU president Bob Osborne and Vancouver lawyer Fred Rowell. Osborne had been a member of the Canadian basketball team that won an Olympic silver medal in 1936. After the war he had been appointed director of UBC's newly formed School of Physical Education and coached Canada's basketball team at the 1948 Olympics, all the while rising up the ranks of the most important BC and Canadian sports bodies. From his youth Rowell had been one of the most involved men in Canadian track and field, and later while working full-time at his Vancouver law office, he also held down the position of UBC's assistant track coach. Together with Osborne, he had founded the Vancouver Olympic Club in 1949, and as a hobby he kept prolific athletics records.

Osborne and Rowell occupied places high enough within the AAU and the Canadian Olympic Association to orchestrate what amounted to an end run around Major Davies. In order to stifle eastern Canadian bias, Rowell suggested to Osborne the AAU should form a "site selection committee." While Davies remained tied up in Auckland, the two men organized a thirty-member national committee representing every province across Canada, and then Osborne named himself chairman. The four prospective host cities prepared briefs in support of their bids, with Rowell presenting Vancouver's bid. Whereas Toronto, Hamilton and Montreal based theirs on pre-existing venues, Vancouver's bid focussed on the scenery and promises. In fact, Vancouver had a major dilemma: the city needed adequate facilities to win the right to host the Games, yet it also needed the Games to stimulate the funding to build those facilities. Costs to stage the Games were estimated at between $200,000 and $750,000, which for the time was significant. This led to some creative "convincing" by the city's boosters. "It was a con job," Swangard said bluntly three decades later. "My God, we made Callister Park sound like the greatest stadium ever built. We had no facilities, but this was a way to get some."

On the first ballot Vancouver received more votes than all other candidate cities combined and, just that easily, was awarded the right to host the 1954 British Empire and Commonwealth Games. Asked by a *Vancouver Sun* reporter to explain how this city could have been chosen so decisively over the larger, better-equipped eastern cities, Osborne shrugged and said modestly, "We out-briefed them, I guess." Major Davies arrived back in Canada to learn that the decision had been made without him. He had no choice but to acquiesce and recommend Vancouver to the BEG Federation in London.

Once Vancouver secured the Games, the real work began. The preliminary seven-man Invitation Committee set up by Mayor Thompson drafted a skeleton master plan, but Thompson lost in the 1951 municipal elections and departed from the picture. As a result, his contribution is often overlooked, but without his initial approval Vancouver's Games bid would have died on the assembling table. His place as mayor of Vancouver was taken by Frederick "Fred" John Hume, and the Games committee could not have asked for someone better suited to the job ahead.

Hume was a true Vancouver booster, and no opportunity to boost the city ever loomed larger than the 1954 Games. One of his first actions in office was to invite 68 prominent citizens to set up a permanent organizing committee for the Games, and the result was the formation of the British Empire & Commonwealth Games Canada (1954) Society, incorporated under the Societies Act of British Columbia with Hume serving as honourary chairman. Eventually the various committees and sub-committees grew to involve over 1,500 individuals who volunteered their time in some manner. However, when Hume became distracted by mayoral matters, complaints began to grow over laggard Games organization, which a *Vancouver Sun* editorial likened to "a church bazaar." The Society obviously needed an individual who could devote all or most of his time to the Games, and the choice of Stanley Smith as general chairman proved to be one of the best decisions of the entire organizing effort. No other individual came to be associated with the Games more closely and no one devoted more time and effort to their success. "Stan Smith was a great citizen," said long-time CBC broadcaster Ted Reynolds in 2007. "He did a remarkable job, starting with no knowledge at all of what the hell the Games were going to be."

On appearances alone, Smith seemed to be an odd choice for the job: bald and rotund, he wore thick-rimmed glasses and a cigarette was never far from his lips. His preference for sharp business suits and the deep lines around his weary eyes marked him as a bona fide workaholic. As assistant branch manager for the Royal Trust Company, his field was real estate development, especially developing the lucrative British Properties in West Vancouver, but it was a job that afforded him considerable influence among Vancouver's business elite. His involvement or interest in sports appeared minimal, but turn back the clock two decades and Smith had ranked as one of the most involved men in BC sport. Born and raised in Vancouver, he had run track, played baseball and lacrosse and boxed as a youth, but by his early twenties, his deteriorating eyesight and a trick knee had derailed his athletic pursuits. That was when he threw himself into the organizational end, helping to form the BC Basketball Association, becoming the first person in Western Canada to serve on the Canadian Amateur Hockey Association registration committee, and sitting as a director of the Canadian Amateur Baseball Association. He served as president of both the Vancouver Senior Amateur Hockey League and the Vancouver Ice Hockey Association, chairman of the City Athletic Commission overseeing boxing and wrestling, and founding manager of the Pacific Athletic Track Club. He did all this while fundraising on behalf of local athletes to send them abroad to the Olympics. And there were at least a dozen city and provincial sports organizations in which he served as secretary—many simultaneously and some for as long as twenty years. Smith later confided to Mary Frizzell Thomasson, the Vancouver Olympic sprinter he mentored, that she should always become secretary of whatever organization she became involved in because only the secretary truly knows what's going on.

MAYOR FRED HUME

Frederick "Fred" John Hume (1892-1967) was a self-made man if there ever was one. When he was 13, his father was killed in a train accident, and Hume quit school and went to work as a warehouse clerk to support his mother and four younger siblings. A few years later he sold the family piano to start his own business, a shop where he sold and repaired radios; eventually he parlayed that shop into the multi-million dollar Hume & Rumble Company, the largest electrical contracting business in Western Canada with transmission line projects as far away as Africa. "It's quite a remarkable story and all from someone who had a grade seven education," explained Hume's grandson, Fred J. Hume II. "I don't think you could do that today."

But Hume had other interests. Throughout his life he was involved in sports. When young, he played on New Westminster's junior and senior lacrosse teams, then came back to sports in the 1930s as the owner of the New Westminster Salmonbellies lacrosse team and the Westminster Royals soccer team, both of which captured Canadian championships under his watch. (He was not above raiding eastern teams of their best players with the lure of a good job at Hume & Rumble.) Later he owned both the New Westminster Royals and Vancouver Canucks of the Western Hockey League, and in the 1960s he spearheaded the drive to bring the NHL to Vancouver and was a major force behind the construction of the Pacific Coliseum.

In 1924 Hume & Rumble founded BC's second radio station, CFXC (later known as CJOR), and while he was still in his thirties, politics also became a major part of his life. He sat as a New Westminster alderman and later was elected mayor, serving from 1932-41. After the death of his first wife, he remarried, moved to West Vancouver and reentered the political arena, this time as the immensely popular mayor of Vancouver from 1951-58, becoming revered for working tirelessly to elevate the city. "It wasn't a job to him," his grandson said in a 2007 interview. "He just loved doing it. I don't know if he liked the power and authority because he really didn't need that, but I think he liked people."

However, as general chairman of the Games, Smith didn't need to be secretary to know what was happening. On top of his already hefty workload with Royal Trust, he attended countless Society executive and sub-committee meetings, mailed an endless string of letters to all corners of the globe and worked the phones like a magician. This was in the days when computers and email were still the dream of science fiction writers, when a long-distance international telephone call was a luxury, and the good old-fashioned handwritten letter sent by regular mail ruled the day. He attended the 1952 Olympics in Helsinki and kept notes on every organizational trick the Finns employed. Then to keep up with the growing demands on his time, two months before the Games opened, he moved into a suite in the Hotel Vancouver where he regularly pulled twenty-hour workdays. He did all of this strictly on a volunteer basis with most of his expenses paid from his own pocket—an estimated $2,000 by Games' end.

STAN SMITH - MAYOR FRED HUME

Stanley Smith (left) and Mayor Fred Hume (right) led the BEG Society's organizing efforts.

Stanley Smith knew the heavy demands the position of general chairman of the Games would entail before he accepted the role and hence had been reluctant at first to fully commit: he told a *Vancouver Province* reporter in March 1952 that he "needed this job like a dog needs two tails." As the Games approached, he always kept a bottle of Aspirin in his suit pocket; when you host hundreds of athletes competing in a wide variety of sports with thousands of spectators in attendance and you are responsible for making all this happen in an organized, safe and entertaining manner, you're asking for a headache or two. The tasks that came his way included finding an Australian-born cox now living in Canada for the Aussie rowing team, devising a pork-free menu for Muslim competitors, and ensuring a greeter fluent in Swahili was on hand to welcome the Kenyan team's arrival. He had to locate homing pigeons for release at the opening ceremonies, acquire enough taro root for the Athletes Village cafeteria to satisfy the Jamaicans, locate recordings of all the national anthems, then find local bands that could play them at victory ceremonies. And these were just some of the simpler tasks. He maintained correspondence with nearly thirty national sports bodies from all parts of the Commonwealth, each with its own unique and confusing web of rules and practices, and coordinated travel for them all to Vancouver. Once here, their daily transportation had to be organized and interesting activities had to be arranged to fill their down time. That Smith and his company of volunteers pulled it all off seems a miracle.

Mary Frizzell Thomasson (centre) laughs as Major Jack Davies (left) and Sandy Duncan (right) model 1954 BECG souvenir sweaters.

The numbers involved in the organization of the Games were staggering. The Society's key form of advertising to promote the Games outside BC was the distribution around North America of 55 million matchbooks bearing the 1954 BECG name and dates. Countless thousands of paper placemats, five million Dixie cups and close to a million bumper stickers were also circulated. Canada Post declined to produce a Games commemorative stamp but did allow millions of BECG-themed cancellation postmarks to be used at post offices across Canada. Under the direction of Sam Rosen, hundreds of thousands of tickets for the nine sports were printed and organized in a complex filing system. Workspace for 400 press members coming to Vancouver was arranged, filling the entire mezzanine floor of a downtown hotel. Over 5,300 miles of cable connected events by various communications methods. The Society ordered 5,600 flags, 1,800 identification badges, nearly 400 winner's victory medals, and well over 1,000 commemorative participation medals. As the BEG Federation required the Society to create new designs for the 1954 events, the Society commissioned Henry Birks & Sons jewellers for the project. The unity chain link and crown design that appeared on the backs of both victory and commemorative medals so impressed the Federation that it was later adopted as the main BECG emblem. It also became the standard medal design for all Games for the next forty years.

To cope with such details, Smith and his key management team—general vice-chairman Harold Merilees, Sports Committee vice-chairman Bruce Hay and Publicity and

Blair Clerk (left) and Stanley Smith hold a ceremonial $2 million cheque. The Games' budget eventually spiralled up to $2.36 million.

Promotion Committee chairman Jack Bain—were released by their respective employers to work for the Society as full-time volunteers while still receiving their normal salaries. "So, in effect, these companies were financially supporting the Games," explained Bain in a 1980 interview. At the time of the Games, the towering former Canadian national rugby player worked for Seagram's Distillery while chairing both the Vancouver and BC Rugby unions, Merilees promoted public projects for the Greater Vancouver Tourist Association, and Hay worked for Trans-Canada Air Lines.

Like any organizing group of this kind, Smith's BEG Society executive committee, working out of humble headquarters at 658 Hornby Street, experienced its share of growing pains and squabbling. On the whole, though, the Society successfully blended the talents of a who's who of Vancouver business and sport titans. "Of all the groups and organizations I ever worked with," Smith said in a 1973 interview, "that was the most dedicated and hard working committee I ever had anything to do with. They were outstanding—every one of them."

Another key member of Smith's executive group was Ken McKenzie, the owner of the McKenzie Barge and Derrick Shipbuilding Company. Colonel William George "Bill" Swan of the engineering firm of Swan Wooster and Partners became chair of the oft-embattled Facilities Committee. Swan had served with an engineering corps in France during World War I and became chief engineer of Canada's Pacific Army Command in World War II. Between the wars he had been the engineering consultant for

Exactly one year before the 1954 BECG were slated to open, Stanley Smith (left) and Ken McKenzie (right) cut a ceremonial birthday cake.

both the Lions Gate and Pattullo bridges. Bob Osborne, who was UBC's director of physical education, seemed to represent every national sports body simultaneously on the executive. Blair Clerk left his job as district superintendent in the Department of Veterans Affairs to become the Games' hands-on general manager overseeing the actual day-to-day operation of the Society's front office. Businessman Jack W. Pattison, who owned local hotels, cafes and billiard parlours, chaired the Concessions Committee until sadly succumbing to a heart attack just six weeks before the Games were set to open. White Spot Restaurants founder Nat Bailey assisted with the Catering Committee, and UBC physics professor Gordon Shrum organized the athletes' housing.

Fundraising fell to Ralph Brown, who sold insurance for Crown Life, and Jack Diamond, the owner of the Pacific Meat Company, and these two men proved to be indispensable as the Society had quickly built a budget of well over a million dollars. But costs skyrocketed from there: $1.365 million for a new stadium, $300,000 for an international-length swimming pool, $82,000 for an outdoor cycling track, $117,000 for visiting team travel grants, $76,000 for publicity—and the list went on. According to the Mayor's Office fonds in the City of Vancouver Archives, the final budget came to $2.36 million.

From the beginning the Society was playing fundraising catch-up and they knew it, so every source of financial relief had to be considered. In August 1952 the *Vancouver Province* reported on one of the early schemes: it involved forming a limited company that would issue a million public shares at $2.50 each. This company would also collect donations of real estate, cars and televisions and list these as assets, though in reality they planned to distribute them as "prizes" among the shareholders at a later date. But after consideration, the Society wisely rejected the idea on the grounds that it might be illegal—which it probably was.

After that, the Society went to work raising money through slower, more traditional routes. They began by seeking government grants, and the city stepped up right away with a $200,000 commitment. The federal government soon matched it but spread it over two years. The city also agreed to put a $750,000 bylaw before civic voters in the December 1952 election to help cover the new stadium's price tag. From this point on, raising money proved a tough slog. "We had to sweat it out to get contributions and beg, borrow and steal to get enough to go," Smith remembered in a 1973 interview. It seemed a cruel coincidence that the original initials of the Games spelled "BEG" because that's exactly what the Society seemed to be doing every day.

With both the civic and federal governments on board, the Society assumed that W.A.C. Bennett's Social Credit government would also be eager to provide a $500,000 grant. After all, the Games would benefit the entire province immensely. But although Bennett personally contributed $1,000 towards the Games in a showy cheque presentation in January 1953, he refused to commit his government to any financial obligation. The Games were "strictly a Vancouver matter," he said. It took several more months before he came around, but when he did, it was only a contribution of $200,000, far short of the half million the Society was counting on.

Erwin Swangard was among the first to rally support for the Games in Vancouver. Photo courtesy of Paul Swangard.

The Society now hoped to make up the deficit through donations from various BC cities and towns. Some municipalities did offer cash contributions with little prodding: the first was $2,650 from North Vancouver and other contributions soon followed from Nanaimo, Penticton and Kelowna. However, regional rivalries came into play and held other potentially prime donors back. While tiny Usk, located northeast of Terrace—population 108—made a gift of $3, which was the largest per capita contribution from anywhere in BC, the city of Victoria at first refused to give anything at all. Only after the editorial team of Victoria's *Times* newspaper offered to contribute 35 cents each to match the donation of tiny Usk did the province's capital finally buck up with a cheque for $3,500.

At the same time that the Society was approaching various levels of government, Ralph Brown was rolling his Special Names Committee into action. Using his own eastern contacts and those of other Society members, he approached the big banks and large corporations such as General Motors and Ford and single-handedly raised $200,000 in straight cash donations. Then in mid-April 1953, Brown's committee launched 400 canvassers on a ten-day fundraising blitz of 4,000 Vancouver businesses. They erected a large stage on the parking lot owned by Eaton's at Granville and Georgia and decorated it with red, white and blue BECG flags and bunting. Boxers, wrestlers, fencers and weightlifters gave athletic demonstrations while speakers tried to drum up funds. Then Mayor Hume, accompanied by a band, officially opened the campaign by walking down Granville and personally calling on merchants to donate to the BECG cause, arguing that 100,000 visitors would be coming to the Games "and maybe they'll want to buy shoes, too." Within 45 minutes he had raised $24,150, but after Hume's initial boost the drive bogged down. Many Vancouver-based athletes, some of whom later competed in the Games were also called upon to canvass local shops. "Can you imagine? Going door-to-door to pay for the Games? Both sides of the street!" high jumper Alice Whitty-Simicak said in a 2013 interview. "You were expected to do it. We went to baseball and football games and passed the hat."

Ultimately, Brown's Special Names Committee plus the business canvass combined to raise over $343,000—a massive sum for the time but far less than needed. By this time whispers were emerging from Society meetings that the Games might be physically moved to an eastern Canadian city that could actually afford to pay for them. This was partly a Society tactic to scare up local dollars, but Toronto Mayor Allan Lamport indicated he would gladly take the 1954 Games off Vancouver's hands, and columnists such as *The Globe and Mail*'s Bobbie Rosenfeld also jumped on the bandwagon to stir up support for the move.

With all other potential avenues tapped out and no idea where to find the final $200,000 needed to break even, the Society gave Vancouver meat-packing magnate Jack Diamond carte blanche to use any means he could devise to raise the necessary funds through a hastily formed Special Events Committee. Already a mover-and-shaker in Vancouver business circles, Diamond now became the difference maker in the Games' fundraising effort. He and his Special Events Committee held cooking shows, dog contests, fashion exhibits, softball games, bingo nights, carnivals, cattle sales, dinners with celebrities (including one hosted by comedian Bob Hope) and performances by the Bob Crosby Orchestra and the US Army Band. Ten thousand people came to a square-dancing festival at Stanley Park's Brockton Oval, the largest festival ever held in Vancouver to that time. He arranged for the New York Rangers to play the WHL Canucks and New Westminster Royals in pre-season exhibition games and brought in a cool $9,000 for the BECG. The Committee followed this success with golf tournaments, a Harlem Globetrotters basketball game, an alpine skiing event, the Caledonian Games, stock car racing at Burnaby's Digney Speedway, curling bonspiels, a pre-BECG fencing tournament, a professional soccer match between the Chicago Falcons and Westminster Royals, and several charity baseball games. However, the biggest money-maker proved to be horse racing after Diamond convinced the provincial government to allow extra racing days and waive the usual taxes. In a single afternoon of races at Lansdowne Park on Coronation Day, June 3, 1953, the Committee raised $56,000.

However, Diamond's fundraising was not all smooth sailing. In September 1953, Diamond convinced dozens of BC bowling alleys to donate a day of bowling income. They settled on a Sunday, but despite running their plan past authorities months in advance, the Vancouver police under the direction of Chief Walter Mulligan paid them a visit for violating the Lord's Day Act and threatened to arrest Diamond.

JACK DIAMOND

Jack Diamond was born into a Jewish peasant family in Poland in 1909 and at 18 followed his older brother to Vancouver where he found work in butcher shops. Within two years he had opened his own shop on Robson Street, and by the end of the 1930s he owned Pacific Meat, one of the largest meat packers in Canada. He got into horse racing first as a hobby but soon set up his own stable and in 1950 bought and redeveloped Richmond's Lansdowne Park racetrack and later operated Exhibition Park.

A few months later Mulligan became a thorn in his side again when the Special Events Committee sponsored the All Nations Home Cooking Carnival at Vancouver's Seaforth Armories. Twenty thousand people attended and over $10,000 was raised at what was reportedly the largest home-cooking sale ever held in Canada, but Mulligan ordered the police gambling detail to seize raffle tickets on a television offered as a door prize. Apparently the TV was valued above $50, violating the lottery laws of the day. Diamond stepped in and substituted a $29.95 radio as a new prize, but the damage had been done. He threatened to resign and cancel two planned days of racing at Lansdowne Park later in the spring. Mulligan limply promised that no prosecution would result if Diamond's committee agreed to return any money raised from the raffle. But Diamond still felt unfairly targeted by the police, and on February 23 he told the *News-Herald* that "at the carnival that night we had a lot of church people, the finest people of Vancouver, and we were treated like a mob from the skid road. I don't go around looking for plaudits for what I am trying to do, but at least I expect some cooperation. All I get is a kick in the face." Mayor Hume rushed to Diamond's support and hurriedly met with his star fundraiser to convince him to stay on, which he agreed to albeit with some reservation.

Interestingly, the following day Alderman Birt Showler told the *Sun* that Mulligan had recently asked city council for $260,000 to hire fifty more police officers, but Showler reasoned that the amount could be cut materially. "If he can afford three or four men to check a raffle, he has men to spare on burglaries." Showler's comment takes on greater significance in light of events just a year later when widespread corruption was discovered within the Vancouver police department. It seems that gambling operations that had paid off the police had been left alone but those totally honest operations that hadn't paid up—Diamond's TV raffle, for instance—had been harassed. A Royal Commission investigated, Mulligan fled to the US and another high-ranking officer attempted suicide.

Despite the red tape and detours, two months before the Games were due to open, Diamond closed his Special Events Committee ledgers with $200,000 in cash raised in just over a year. His work was done, all BECG bills would be paid, and the Games were still in Vancouver. "Just think—but for Diamond," *Sun* sports columnist Jim Kearney wrote years later, "the Bannister-Landy Miracle Mile would have been run hard by Lake Ontario, instead of Burrard Inlet. Vancouver's biggest moment—make that four minutes—in sport would have been Toronto's." While this is debatable, undoubtedly Diamond sealed the deal on a true community effort to reach a common goal.

"Look out the window," general manager Blair Clerk marvelled to a *Weekly News* reporter on the eve of the Games. "See that woman across the street? I'll bet she contributed in one way or another, and those pedestrians did, too. Everybody in Vancouver contributed because this is their show. What we're trying to do is to stage an epic production, which will be a credit to all Canada." Much of that "epic production" would be judged upon the main stage the Society had constructed—Empire Stadium. That it was later greeted with near-universal praise as a modern marvel both in location and design ranks as a major miracle. In fact, it seems a miracle it even reached completion.

When the Society went to work drafting plans for the four venues they would have to build specifically for the 1954 Games, they had no idea what they were in for. As Bill Parnell said in a 2007 interview, it was not a case of "build it and they will come. It was: they're coming, so now we have to build it. This is what happened for the '54 Games." Every last nail, bolt, rivet and glob of cement that eventually became part of Empire Stadium, Empire Pool, the Vedder Canal rowing course and the China Creek cycling track was slaved over, scrutinized and then scrutinized again on architects' and engineers' drafting tables, in smoky boardrooms, in public forums, and then on the construction sites. Key Society members, politicians, engineers and architects became familiar cast members in a daily concrete-and-steel soap opera played out on the pages of local newspapers, working together as often as they opposed and exposed one another.

Case in point: Empire Stadium. Initially, the BECG stadium was slated for the UBC campus as an expansion of the existing Varsity Stadium. This expansion proposition, which was estimated to cost $350,000 to $550,000, called for seating for 40,000-50,000 persons, thus enlarging Varsity's capacity by some fifteen times. A revamped UBC stadium appeared inevitable until March 1952 when UBC president Norman MacKenzie announced that UBC did not want a large, permanent stadium and would only accept 8,000 permanent seats. Colonel Bill Swan and his Facilities Committee devised a solution that would add some seats with the rest to be rented temporary seating, but the white elephant tag soon attached itself to the project and spelled its demise.

After that, there followed a lively game of stadium location ping-pong. Don Carlson, the new *Province* sports editor, suggested Capilano Stadium, the local 6,500-seat home of the Vancouver Capilanos baseball team. Carlson's lead columnist, Eric Whitehead, suggested developing Burnaby's forested Central Park. The Pacific National Exhibition board nominated Callister Park, the city's 8,000-seat soccer stadium. And the BC Turf and Country Club offered to stable their racehorses to allow the use of Lansdowne Park, even proposing—hopefully joking—that the track's infield pond could be utilized for swimming events.

The only one who truly appreciated the opportunity the Games presented when it came to facilities was Whitehead, who had seen first-hand the value of Eden Park in Auckland during the 1950 BEG and understood that a new stadium in Vancouver could become a sporting legacy for generations. You didn't build temporary facilities to tide you *through* the Games, he told his readers, then tear them down afterwards. His voice brought the focus onto the opportunity presented—a rare moment in time when the impetus and funding for facilities at an affordable price coalesced. In the first of many pointed columns he wrote over the next two years taking the Society to task, on March 27, 1952, he wrote:

> Talk about mad dogs and Englishmen! Here is Vancouver's British Empire Games Committee running about the countryside with a free $550,000 stadium tucked under its arm—and no place to drop it!

It might have just been coincidence or perhaps the final push for a movement already gaining momentum as a result of his published musings, but on October 30, 1952, a day after Whitehead's latest admonishment to the Society, Mayor Hume led the charge with a proposal not yet considered by anyone to that point: "We've looked at virtually everything else. Why not the PNE?" he suggested, referring to the nine-hole golf course and driving range in the southeast corner of the Pacific National Exhibition grounds at the corner of Hastings and Cassiar. The site's natural hollow would lower construction costs as banked concrete seating could be incorporated into the natural slopes. The press coined the instantly popular plan as a "new deal Citizens Stadium" and the public rapidly took to the proposal. The following day Whitehead's influence again appeared in a *Province* editorial, calling the move from UBC to the PNE "sensible and realistic." It would also prove costly. An early survey pegged costs at upwards of a cool $1 million; by late 1952 the price tag had risen another $250,000.

After the PNE board agreed to allow the stadium to be built on their grounds, City Council approved submitting a $750,000 bylaw to taxpayers to cover the rising cost. Fittingly for that paranoid Cold War period, one of the key supporting arguments to council members was that the stadium's design would provide an excellent emergency air raid shelter, civil and national defence headquarters and first aid, troop or equipment storage area. The focus then turned to convincing the required 60 percent of the voting public to support the bylaw. "We'll Never Get It Cheaper," argued a *Sun* editorial, noting that, if paid off over 20 years, it would cost taxpayers less than $60,000 a year or "17 cents a resident or 58 cents for each taxpayer per year." Jack Bain's Publicity and Promotion Committee went into overdrive, appealing to voters on a more emotional basis. Vancouver service clubs and organizations were graced by speakers preaching the virtues of voting for it, and a flag relay carried a Union Jack from the proposed stadium site to the downtown Eaton's parking lot. The bylaw was passed by a 76.9 percent majority. "We could have asked for ten million dollars probably and got it," marvelled Bain, and a jubilant Stan Smith announced, "Passing of the bylaw changes Vancouver from a small-time

Hundreds attended the June 1953 sod-turning ceremony for the new $1.56 million Empire Stadium. Even the stadium model didn't come cheap, coming in at $800.00

centre to a major city insofar as the athletic world is concerned." But no one was more thrilled than backers of the BC Lions because the new stadium assured the fledgling club a comfortable first step into the world of Canadian professional football.

Through the early months of 1953, the Society worked with the architectural firm of Sharp & Thompson, Berwick, Pratt ironing out costs and design specs. The new estimated price tag was set at $1,365,000, which would allow for floodlighting at nighttime events. Plans also called for matching banks of 8,000 permanent concrete seats on the stadium's east and west sides—10,000 of which would be covered—with nearly 10,000 seats at each of the rounded north and south ends.

At the June 1953 sod-turning ceremony, the Society managed to coax a silver shovel into the hands of the reclusive Percy Williams, Vancouver's legendary Olympic gold medal-winning sprinter. A crowd of 1,500, plus thousands more across the country tuning in on radio and television, witnessed the most elaborate sod-turning spectacle in BC's history. Acting-Mayor Rollie Gervin fired a pistol skyward to signal that construction was officially underway. A parade of athletes wearing uniforms of their respective sports marched in, each carrying a shovel. They lined up to turn over more of the finely manicured golf course fairway. Drum majorettes and pipe bands added to the celebratory air. The focal point then shifted to the arrival of a flag-draped crate, which contained a scale model of the new stadium. Even that didn't come cheap, ringing in at $800.

But the stadium problems were not over because there is always trouble when both *costs* and *design specs* of a civic project are set in stone (or at least perceived to be so) without much thought linking one to the other. One of two things occurs and neither is good: costs either inflate out of control and the balloon pops or the dream has to be pared back and the balloon deflates. And bless their unlucky hearts, the Games Society found a way for both to occur. When the construction bids were opened, the *lowest* rang in $450,000 *over* the stated $1,365,000 price tag for delivery of a stadium with all the promised bells and whistles. A *Sun* editorial on August 15, 1953, described the feelings of many in the city. It began:

> Vancouver's dream of getting a first-class stadium is apparently dead... Vancouver seems to be under a curse in this regard. Almost all its public projects begin in a blaze of glory and wind up under a cloud.

So it was back to the drawing board. Colonel Swan suggested a new $400,000 bylaw to be put before taxpayers, but Mayor Hume and City Council flatly rejected that idea. "Ratepayers have already put up $750,000," said Hume. "They've [the Society] got to find some other way." Swan, still annoyed that his UBC stadium proposal had been tossed aside, noted that if his plan had gone ahead, the problem of excessive costs would never have arisen. His would not be the last dissenting voice in the coming weeks as one weird and wonderful solution after another was presented to the Society. One involved renting the "coronation bleachers" used in London, but the cost proved prohibitive. With frustration mounting, the mayor—one of the prime catalysts behind the stadium's move to the PNE—organized a study for the reconfiguration of Capilano Stadium, an idea that had not made sense two years earlier and made less sense now. At this point another offer from eastern Canada arrived to remove the Games from Vancouver, this time to Winnipeg. The Society could bicker amongst itself and agree on nothing, but when an eastern threat appeared, the wagons were circled. Smith chuckled at the offer as "darn nonsense," and the mayor just laughed. "We can handle the Games," he said. But the best response to Winnipeg came from Alderman Jack Cornett: "Champagne ideas and beer pocketbooks." Mind you, he could just as easily have been talking about the mess Vancouver was in.

Meanwhile, the Society had gone back to architect Ned Pratt, who had captured a bronze medal in rowing at the 1932 Olympics, to explore various combinations of design features to axe in order to lower costs. First to go was the floodlighting. Next was part of the roof, then all of it. The public outcry was fierce and debate raged. Once united in its desire for a stadium, the city now appeared fractured under the weight of the issue. BC Lions supporters sprayed particularly strong venom, with club officials announcing that professional football was dead in a city with a roofless stadium and no night lighting. Some thought it odd to modify plans on football's behalf when the stadium was being built for the Games in the first place. After all, football had not even been a consideration in the initial discussions for the stadium. The PNE, the Games Society and City Council appeared divided along similar lines.

In response Pratt and the Society tried to devise compromise plans for different lighting and roofing configurations, but the PNE rejected them all outright. Then, on August 25, Smith warned that stadium construction absolutely needed to begin "no later than two weeks from this date." Delay any longer and contractors wouldn't have time to place orders for steel and then complete construction in the remaining ten-month window before the Games began. (Actually, it was only about seven months when winter weather delays were taken into consideration.) To get the stadium completed on time, it was literally now or never.

With the construction deadline looming, efforts—and tensions—heightened. A series of secret meetings between the Society, the PNE board and city officials took place, often inside Mayor Hume's private chambers, in an attempt to hammer out a deal. What that deal was, no one could—or would—say. In a revealing quote in the *Sun* on August 27, PNE president Jack Moffitt summed up the collective feeling of utter frustration: "I haven't the faintest idea how they are going to get this stadium built and I don't think anyone else has either." Two days later the *Sun* ran a more optimistic headline: "Stadium Decision Coming Up Monday." On Monday, however, the newspaper reported: "No New Answers For Stadium Yet."

Throughout the entire 39-month stadium evolution, Eric Whitehead, from the *Province* newspaper served as a good barometer of progress and public opinion. With no end to the debacle in sight, on August 29 he again weighed in:

> With all respect to the great amount of hard work these gentlemen have put into the Games organization—much of it, unhappily, completely wasted— they have, by all evidence, come up with a miserable failure. The current panic is merely a result of mishandling and misdirection over the past several months... Many a time over the past year or more, we have heard and brushed off the cry: "Fire the whole BEG executive and get some men with gumption in there." For the first time, although this would be an injustice to certain men on the executive who have done a sound, conscientious job, we herewith publicly subscribe to this idea—probably too late.

Perhaps by coincidence—perhaps not—mere days later the dispute was settled. In hindsight, it seemed a remarkably simple solution for a dispute that had dragged on for so many months. Posts. Steel posts. Sixteen of them, eight spaced approximately 50 feet apart on both east and west grandstands. The posts would support a truss roof, replacing the "post-less" cantilever beauty envisioned from the beginning. Not as aesthetically pleasing with poorer sightlines for a few unlucky folks, the posts would, however, allow a full grandstand roof on either side as well as floodlighting, the key components at the crux of the dispute. (Savings would also be derived from reducing dressing room and plumbing facilities.) Most importantly, the changes would allow a stadium to be built on time—relatively—and on budget—relatively. Those pesky posts would also hatch a delightful little myth involving one of the prime stadium architects. Legend has it this unlucky fellow showed up for the Games' Opening Ceremonies only to discover his seat was obstructed by a 12-inch-thick steel girder. Pity.

In February 1954, Empire Stadium's west grandstand was under construction. After endless planning delays, construction was rushed to completion in under ten months.

Devised by city engineer John Oliver, Facilities Committee head Colonel Swan and architect Pratt, the steel-posted stadium concept was plucked from a mysterious "package deal" proposed earlier by two unnamed construction firms and now adopted as the committee's own. It was presented to the PNE board and then City Council on September 1, and within three days all parties had officially approved the plan in meetings described as "jovial," a far cry from the bitterness only days earlier. With these revisions, the final cost of the new 35,000-seat stadium rose to $1,557,613, which was

$192,613 above the $1,365,000 budget figure, and that had been revised upward from the original $1.25 million. At the unveiling of the Oliver-Swan-Pratt solution, Mayor Hume spoke for the urgency and relief felt by all: "I'm prepared to stake my whole reputation on [this plan]. Let's all be friends and work together on this."

Little choice remained in the matter. Just ten months now remained until the Games. Crews worked long hours and employed time-saving methods wherever possible—a few of which would cause the stadium to age well before its time. Even with minor hiccups involving seating, erosion and a colder than expected winter that forced construction delays, by December the roof was up and by spring the cinder track was down—all seven layers of it. To save on time, different soil and cinder combinations had been tested during the winter in the horse stalls of the PNE's livestock building. Then donning spikes, Track and Field Committee members Fred Rowell and Lloyd Swindells, as well as local track athletes Bill Parnell and Bob Hutchinson, dashed up and down 400-foot-long lanes of different compositions before settling on a mixture of coke breeze (BC Electric oven-toasted cinders) and clay. Then the Reverend Bob Richards, Olympic pole vault gold medalist in 1952 and 1956, tested the committee's best combination and gave approval during his annual visit for the Vancouver Olympic Club's big spring track meet. By early July the largest permanent sports stadium in Canada was complete, and the keys were turned over to the Society on July 12. At this point only one crucial detail remained unresolved: the stadium's name. Only one thing was certain about that: for the duration of the Games it would be known as Empire Stadium.

Choosing a site for the stadium and constructing it was not the only problem for Colonel Bill Swan and his Facilities Committee. The earliest plans had called for the BECG pool to be included in a $2 million open-air "all-purpose coliseum" modelled on London's Wembley Arena and built on PNE land at Hastings Park. This plan was scrapped in early 1952 when the funding could not be obtained. The Society then selected a location at Hillcrest near the Capilano Stadium, but the Park Board refused to allow it, citing the already dense concentration of athletic facilities there. At that point UBC's director of physical education, Bob Osborne, threw the university's hat into the ring: an outdoor pool adjoining the War Memorial Gymnasium would benefit UBC's large student population and could be built affordably using the gym's existing heating and plumbing systems.

FULL VOLUME

One night in early July before the keys to the finished stadium were handed over to the Society, the consulting electrical engineer on the project brought his crew in for a lighting test. Up in the enclosed control booth, they flicked the floodlight switch and the place lit up. Everything worked perfectly. Then they noticed a record on the turntable and flicked that switch as well. Hearing distant, muffled music, they continued on with their work oblivious. It was not long before a police officer burst in with the order: "Turn off that dang record or cut the volume!" Apparently the loudspeaker sound system playing "Red Hot Jive" worked just fine as well. Complaints had been received from as far away as Port Moody.

Enter Percy Norman of the Vancouver Amateur Swim Club (VASC), a man who had been the face of swimming in Vancouver for decades. Under his watchful eye at the old Crystal Pool thousands of youngsters had learned to swim and more than a few had gone on to international success. The VASC owned land at Riley Park near Capilano Stadium—not far from the coveted Hillcrest site—and had an option to purchase more from the neighbouring Sicks' Capilano Brewery. At first glance, it appeared to satisfy the Society's lust for a Hillcrest-Little Mountain pool site as well as answering the question of the pool's post-Games future since the VASC clamoured for an international standard pool from which to base its operations. However, the VASC site was too small to accommodate both a pool and the required seating, and questions also arose about the club's shaky finances. This resulted in Riley Park being ruled out, and by default the longshot UBC entry became the front-runner. To sweeten the pot, the university confirmed the pool would be enclosed after the Games and guaranteed public access. For the Society it wasn't the ideal location, but they were running out of time and options, so the swimming pool was formally awarded to the university in March 1953.

That should have settled things, but it didn't. The *Province* called it "the pool that got away," and Percy Norman opposed it on geographical grounds. "Why the city of Vancouver wants to build a pool outside of the city is amazing," he complained to reporters. "It's just not fair for 180,000 Vancouver children who can't get near water. How can the kids get all the way out to UBC to swim for a couple hours? It's absolutely disgusting." The newspapers were flooded with letters pelting the UBC site or floating a more centralized location. Eight members of the provincial legislature submitted a joint letter to City Council urging them to build a pool of "the greatest public use." Then Norman, who represented 13 swimming clubs, organized a "Citizen's Committee for a Central Vancouver Swimming Pool," bringing together individuals from business, trade union, political, ratepayer, parent teacher, community and athletic groups with the sole purpose of moving the pool back to Riley Park. After they made plans to storm meetings of the Park Board, BECG Society and City Council, the Park Board agreed to reconsider the Riley Park site and even handle post-Games operating costs. The Society then agreed to shift the pool but only if City Council agreed to come up with some cash. Faced with this public outcry, Council caved, and just over a month after the Society had awarded the pool to the university, the decision was overturned. Riley Park was now the new pool site.

Throughout the spring and summer of 1953 planning went ahead at Riley Park. Surveying ceremonies, complete with Society officials smiling for cameras, were staged. Architectural drawings were completed, and a late August date was set for submission of construction tenders by local firms. A month later the pool saga exploded like "a misguided missile." Construction bids were in and—*surprise!*—the lowest was $140,000 over the $300,000 budgeted for the pool. In response, Stan Smith called a meeting of a Joint Swimming Pool Committee consisting of principal members of the Society, City Council and the Parks Board. It produced fireworks that only ended when Smith proposed that they allow Paddock Incorporated, a Los Angeles-based contracting firm, to construct the pool at the $300,000 budgeted price. Paddock had not submitted a formal bid, so the idea was met with caution mixed with a pinch of skepticism, and Mayor Hume and Alderman Halford Wilson were openly concerned about the impropriety of the step

No Games venue experienced more bitter disputes than Empire Pool, which was built at UBC. Photo by Jack Cash.

being taken. Smith countered by suggesting they invite Paddock owner Philip Ilsley to present the company's proposal in person. This was a plan the more cautious members could live with.

Ilsley is considered the father of the affordable backyard pool as he had perfected the process of "guniting" for his pool building—pneumatically spraying concrete onto a wire-mesh base to eliminate the use of costly forms and supports. A brilliant engineer, cutting-edge designer, shrewd businessman and convincing salesman—he had convinced both Bing Crosby and Bob Hope to install Paddock pools—Ilsley cut a formidable figure, and he wanted the BECG pool contract as another feather in the Paddock cap. He received an icy reception from the assembled joint committee, but shrugging it off, he outlined the Paddock proposal, which included many design features that were not included in the submitted bids. The cost? $300,000, take it or leave it, predicated on an immediate award of the contract.

Two days later a local company, Beaver Construction, submitted a matching bid, also contingent on the awarding of the contract on a "sight unseen" basis, and after the Joint Pool Committee debated the merits of both proposals, the vote went to Beaver. Smith and McKenzie, infuriated, fought back by drafting a "minority report," and submitted it to the mayor and council the same day the Joint Pool Committee's Beaver

Construction recommendation was tabled. After hearing both reports, City Council shocked everyone by officially awarding the pool contract *sight unseen* to Paddock for $287,000. City engineer John Oliver warned about the "dangerous" precedent being set, and as the Council meeting broke up, the dominoes began to topple. The Parks Board members announced that they were withdrawing from the whole scheme and were taking the Riley Park site with them. The architects, Gardiner, Thornton & Partners, pulled out a day later. Beaver Construction representatives were equally outraged and sought legal advice "to see justice done."

After over a year trying to settle the pool question—and only ten months away from the Games opening—the Society had no confirmed pool site, no architect, a construction firm that refused to provide clear design specs, and everyone catching wind of the situation was calling for the committee members' necks. At this late stage there appeared to be only one possible option left: move the pool back to UBC. There was some support for the idea, emanating mostly from the campus itself. Venerable UBC hockey coach Frank Fredrickson, a 1920 Olympic gold medalist and captain of the 1924-25 Victoria Cougars, the last BC team to have won the Stanley Cup, wrote an eloquent and impassioned letter listing six advantages to placing the pool at UBC, and it was published in all the local papers. After that, the pieces to the pool puzzle rapidly fell into place. Negotiations between the Society and UBC resumed where they had been cut off five months earlier. The university again agreed to open the pool to the public after the Games, as well as to roof it at a later date (something that never did occur). The Society also turned the awarding of the construction contract over to the university, which would choose between the existing Paddock and Beaver bids.

Of course, the battle couldn't end that easily. Percy Norman's Citizens' Committee demanded a meeting with the mayor and planned another large-scale petition in favour of Riley Park. Letters of protest flooded Vancouver newspapers in the largest wave yet. The *Province* published an editorial headlined "Vancouver Loses Central Pool." As City Council called a conference with all concerned parties to discuss moving the pool a fourth time, momentum appeared to be gaining in Riley Park's favour. The Citizens' Committee was determined to change the Society's mind once more, in what many were billing as the *final* final pool showdown—finally. In the end, the meeting proved anti-climactic. As the familiar arguments for and against were trucked out and shot down, Smith sat contentedly, armed with an explosive secret. When everyone had said his piece, he revealed the fact that the Society, UBC and Paddock had signed a binding agreement at a private meeting *the previous day*. It was a done deal. Stunned silence swept over the room. Someone had finally stepped up, made a firm decision, and stuck to it. Wherever the pool was built and by whomever, large numbers of people would squawk. That fact had to be swallowed or the problem would never go away. For all intents and purposes, a pool at Riley Park was now dead, officially put to rest after eight of the most tumultuous and preposterous months in the entire organization of the 1954 Games. Within two weeks, Norman's most resolute supporters grudgingly conceded. Beaver Construction's lawyers dropped all scare tactics and no lawsuit was ever filed.

On October 13 construction officially began next to UBC's War Memorial Gymnasium. A month later Paddock unveiled a scale model replete with many of the most modern pool accessories: racing lane markers made of a newly developed plastic that was

Empire Pool's diving tower with signature spiral staircase became a UBC landmark beside War Memorial Gymnasium.

completely buoyant in water; underwater "niche" lighting that allowed the pool to be used after dark, and a special turquoise blue tile design that "coloured the water." The water, which was to be completely recirculated every eight hours, would maintain a temperature of 68-72 degrees. The bottom and sides of the pool, which was built to Olympic standards (55 yards in length and 50 feet wide), were made principally of 50 tons of reinforced concrete, and the designers boasted that the water would be so clear and still on a windless day that "ripples" would have to be created to guide divers to the water. The Society boasted that the pool would be the most modern of its kind in Canada, a swimmer's dream that would stack up against any pool in North America. Despite methods and ethics, Empire Pool did arrive on time and on budget—the only specially built BECG facility to do so.

❂

Ironically, for a coastal city surrounded by waterways, Vancouver could not find a two-kilometre stretch of water that was fit to host the Games' two-day regatta. In early discussions Colonel Swan's Facilities Committee and local individuals with vested rowing interests favoured Burnaby Lake. A large, calm waterway capable of hosting a wide variety of aquatic events, it was accessible and centrally located amid untouched natural surroundings. The one massive stumbling block was the estimated $1.35 million it would take to dredge it and free its congested waters of lilies and other plant life. A slightly cheaper alternative involved dumping countless tons of heavy sand over the lake bottom's entire length to kill off future growth. But even with the reduced cost of sand over dredging, Swan declared Burnaby Lake dead as a possibility, and the committee began looking at alternative sites: Port Moody, at a wallet-friendly $10,000 to prepare it; the ever-unpredictable, high-traffic waters of Coal Harbour; the calmer albeit more removed Deep Cove area; and the even more distant Cultus Lake, a placid cottage hotspot near Chilliwack. Perhaps the most intriguing bid came from Nelson on Kootenay Lake in the province's southeastern corner; the virtually wind-free lake had already been used for local regattas and would require little investment. Plans called for bleacher seating built on the 2,000-foot airstrip alongside the lake and a unique flatcar railroad for spectators beside the race course.

But then Colonel Tommy Taylor, incoming president of the Vancouver Rowing Club (VRC) and a member of the BECG rowing facilities sub-committee, took up Burnaby Lake's cause. Since the 1930s, Taylor had dreamed of turning the site into a rower's paradise, and irrespective of cost he began a fanatical quest for its development as a long-term Games legacy. First, citing the incompetence of the Facilities Committee head, Colonel Swan, he wrote letters to the newspapers demanding the man's resignation. Swan brushed this off as little more than misdirected gusto, and he was backed up by Erwin Swangard, now sports editor for the *Sun*, who said in his column on August 14, 1952:

Enthusiasm is a wonderful thing, and much needed, particularly in sport.

But quite frequently irrational enthusiasm can make you look awfully silly, especially if you don't think twice before you use your nature-given megaphone... Tommy Taylor finds himself in just about that position at this hour... if there have to be resignations... I would suggest... his would be preferable when measured in the interest of the overall cause.

Taylor's response was to begin touring "rowing experts" around Burnaby Lake, and without exception, his hand-picked experts reported their glowing support to local newspapers the following day. A local speedboat enthusiast also claimed the lake could top "all of Europe's sculling courses." However, the *Sun* painted a more realistic picture by running a photo of lily pads and very little water above a slightly sarcastic caption: "This Is Burnaby Lake's Famous Lily Course."

Early in 1953 a new contender for the rowing course entered the fray. VRC charter member John Wickson, who had rowed for Canada at the 1912 Olympics, recommended the Vedder Canal, the arrow-straight, man-made waterway that had been created in the early 1920s to drain Sumas Lake near Chilliwack. According to the *Chilliwack Progress* of January 7, 1953, Wickson deemed it "a rower's dream course" that was "better... than England's Henley." Short of some minor dredging, the canal's prepping costs were minimal, the dikes on either side would provide ideal viewing for spectators, and the more central location—closer to Interior cities but not far removed from Vancouver—would lead to higher ticket sales. Five Fraser Valley communities rallied behind the proposal.

The Vedder now seemed a logical choice, but logic was a fleeting commodity in the great BECG venue dance. Part of the problem was that Taylor wasn't the only one gunning for a permanent rowing site on Burnaby Lake. There were other prominent VRC members on the BECG Rowing Committee, including Nelles Stacey, Frank Read, Jack Carver, and Sedley Campbell "Bimbo" Sweeny, the celebrated rower, rugby and squash player, who saw locating the BECG rowing site at Burnaby Lake as the perfect opportunity to move the VRC from the unpredictable waters of Coal Harbour as their primary training waterway. The longer the selection process dragged on, the better Burnaby Lake looked.

To buy themselves more time, Swan's Facilities Committee now claimed that the Vedder's six-foot summer depth made it too shallow for international rowing. The response of Vedder supporters was that if the Society felt compelled to change the rules, their efforts must not be wanted, and all Fraser Valley rowing committees immediately disbanded. Meanwhile, Taylor was pulling out all the stops to meet a Society-imposed

Ironically, for a city surrounded by water, Vancouver organizers were forced to hold the rowing events 80 km east of the city on the Vedder Canal near Chilliwack.

April 30, 1953, deadline, knowing that if he could raise the funds required to dredge Burnaby Lake by then, the rowing events would be held there. When his funding drive appeared doomed to fall short, as a last-ditch assault he fired off a tersely worded letter to Colonel Swan regarding the rowing site decision, arguing that "only at Burnaby Lake were the essential requirements for a championship rowing course waterway satisfied... under International Rowing Federation requirements" and any consideration of other sites was "directly defeating the main object of the British Empire and Commonwealth Games." If this had been just another swing in the personal battle between Taylor and Swan, the letter likely would have been ignored. However, Taylor sent carbon copies to Stan Smith, Mayor Hume, thirteen prominent Society members, Major Jack Davies in Montreal, BEG Federation secretary Sandy Duncan in London, the International Rowing Federation in Switzerland, eleven local and provincial politicians, five separate rowing clubs, and then to sports editors of every major newspaper in British Columbia from Victoria to Nelson. This was a giant leap over the line, and Stan Smith's patience had been finally worn out. He convinced Fred Carter, secretary of the Toronto-based Canadian Association of Amateur Oarsmen, to lead a new "Special Rowing Committee," which was empowered to immediately settle on a rowing site. Smith also announced publicly that Burnaby Lake was most definitely, once and for all ruled out as a potential site.

The Special Rowing Committee began a province-wide investigation, viewing every possible location. Most sites were eliminated through one glaring defect or another. However, a chance meeting midway through the tour changed everyone's plans. John Wickson, the man who had initially suggested the Vedder Canal, caught wind of the tour and persuaded the committee to give the canal another long look on their way through. Standing on the Vedder's dikes and scanning their surroundings, the committee members could see the possibilities. Meanwhile, the Society's application to the minister of Lands and Forests for permission to use the waterway was leaked to the press, and Vancouver papers prematurely reported the canal was all but approved as the BECG rowing site.

In reality everything rode on a second Vedder inspection. On the morning of July 23, Society general manager Blair Clerk drove out to Chilliwack and found Wickson waiting for him along with Sumas reeve Alex Hougen and *Progress* sports editor Ron Gray. The four clambered into Hougen's rowboat and began drifting downstream. The boat's underside scraped bottom on a couple occasions, causing some pensive glances to be exchanged, but Clerk seemed unconcerned. Wickson periodically plunged one oar downward until hitting bottom to demonstrate a minimum seven-foot water depth throughout, and as the boat returned to shore, Clerk gave his approval.

Taylor and the Burnaby Lakers had one final card to play. He and the South Burnaby Board of Trade secured a meeting with provincial cabinet ministers to discuss the development of the lake. Delegates representing 21 interested groups attended and everyone, including the ministers, agreed on the proposal's potential merits—but no one had the resources to fund their grand scheme. That finally made it official: the Commonwealth's best would row on the Vedder Canal. After dragging its heels and holding out for an eleventh-hour miracle, the Society gave in and publicly announced that the waterway that had been deemed too shallow, too fast and too far away would be the official BECG rowing course.

As the Vedder was the only venue located outside greater Vancouver, a unique arrangement to organize and manage events there was devised. The Fraser Valley Rowing Committee (FVRC), under the leadership of newspaper publisher Cecil Hacker, would handle hands-on operations while answering to the Vancouver-based BECG Rowing Committee governed by Nelles Stacey. Eager to host the event, the five Fraser Valley communities were willing to foot more or less the entire costs. Organized, motivated and with something to prove, they effectively made a huge problem disappear for the Society.

Local contractors hammered away at spectator seating and floating walkways, then built a boathouse, reviewing stand, press box, a tower for CBC television coverage and a Bailey bridge to allow honoured guests to cross the canal. The surrounding gravel roads were paved, farmers' fields were groomed for parking, and spectator pathways were "oil flushed" to keep down the dust. Most agreed that the rowing events were the biggest thing to happen to the eastern Fraser Valley since the disastrous flood of 1948.

The cycling track was the one BECG venue that avoided all the pre-Games controversies that plagued the others. Empire Bowl was built in China Creek Park, which had been named for the Chinese gardens that once bloomed on the banks of the creek that ran through the site. The 31-foot-wide yellow cedar track, which featured steeply banked 45-degree corners, was delivered on time—even early—although it was over budget with a final cost of $81,303. And when the Society could not find the funds to add floodlighting, local cyclists simply staged special "all-comers" cycling exhibitions to cover the extra costs. Problem solved.

The remaining BECG event venues were all pre-built. Lawn bowling was held at the West Point Grey Club and the New Westminster Bowling Club. Fencing found a home at Lord Byng Secondary School in Point Grey. Wrestling was staged at the Kerrisdale Arena. Boxing was held at the Exhibition Forum and weightlifting at the Exhibition Gardens, both on the grounds of the Pacific National Exhibition.

Located at Broadway and Clark, the Empire Bowl cycling track—or China Creek Park as it was popularly known—and its treacherous 45-degree corners offered picturesque views of downtown Vancouver and the North Shore.

CHAPTER 3
SATURDAY, JULY 31, 1954

One of the great myths of the 1954 BECG was that every event was a sell-out with not a solitary seat to be had anywhere. Far from it. On opening day, Saturday, July 31, only 10,091 of Empire's 35,000 seats were filled for the Games' marquee sport. Although it was a near-record crowd for a Canadian track event, it nonetheless stunned seasoned observers, none more than Joe Binks, who wrote for London's *News of the World* and had attended every Olympics and BECG over the previous 52 years. "This is the first one I have seen with any empty seats on opening night," the former Mile world record holder told a *Vancouver Province* reporter as he gestured to the barren sections of the stadium.

But for those who did attend that day, the effort was well worthwhile. The BECG men's 100yd heats, semi-finals and final were all run that afternoon, and all eyes were on two very confident sprinters. One was Mike Agostini, a 19-year-old from Trinidad. Boxing fans will be familiar with the expression "the mouth that roared" that was applied to Muhammad Ali, but Mike Agostini was the mouth that *ran*. Many other words come to mind when seeking to accurately describe him: handsome, intelligent, honest (cuttingly so when it suited him) and quotable. He *never* met a microphone he didn't like. He was also brash, colourful, arrogant, controversial and undeniably memorable. Quite simply, the irrepressible Mike Agostini may well have been the grand character of the 1954 Games. Although a newcomer to this level of competition, he had compiled an impressive athletic resume: he held the 60yd and 100yd world indoor marks at 6.1 and 9.6 seconds respectively, the 220yd high school world best in 21.1 seconds, and the 100yd high school mark in 9.4 seconds.

His primary competition in Vancouver was Hector "Hec" Hogan, one of the darlings of the track world. The stocky 23-year-old refrigeration mechanic from Brisbane, Australia, had recently equalled world records in the 100yds (officially) and 100m (unofficially). Many in the press were calling him the world's fastest human. Others preferred his battery of alliterative nicknames: Hurryin' Hogan, Hurricane Hogan, Hoppin' Hogan, Hustlin' Hogan and Hurtlin' Hector Hogan. He came billed as one of the Games' stars and knew it. The *Vancouver News-Herald* reported that at one reception, as Hogan stood surrounded by female admirers, he winked slyly at a reporter and said in his slow Australian drawl, "I'm just an old man, whom no woman seems to go for." He was clearly enjoying the perks of sprinting fame.

In the days leading up to their anticipated collision, bubbling vitriol brewed between the two men, and reporters who were disappointed to find no hatred between milers Bannister and Landy discovered what they sought when the young upstart Agostini and established favourite Hogan became embroiled in a heated public war of words. In an interview 56 years later Agostini recalled that, as soon as he blew into town a few

Opposite: Handsome and ever-quotable, Trinidad sprinter Mike Agostini may have been the grand character of the 1954 Games.

Australian 100yd world record holder Hector Hogan found himself in a heated public war of words with rival Mike Agostini. Photo courtesy of Doug Clement.

days before the Games started, a reporter had asked him, "How do you think you'll do?" And he had answered boldly, "I've come here to win the gold medal." Then he was asked, "What do you think of Hogan?" His reply was "Who the *heck* is *Hogan*?" Actually, he could have instructed the reporter on many of his opponent's finer points, but his comment was intended to sting Hogan's ego. Minutes later he was busy telling reporters from both the *Sun* and *Province* newspapers just how much he knew about the Australian. "Hogan was in top shape six months ago in the Australian track season when he set his 9.3-second record," Agostini began, "but no man can be in top condition to run the distance in 9.3 seconds at different times of the same year."

Of course, the Vancouver newspapers lapped up the quotes Agostini fed them like thirsty puppies. "I was being cheeky," Agostini recalled, "but I'd been taught how to use the media to ruffle my opponents. I was playing the game that my mentor, Mal Whitfield, taught me. Mal used to say, 'Man, you just get out there and tell 'em whatcha gonna do and then you gotta do it.' That's what I did."

Agostini's opening volley worked like a charm. The *Province*'s Don Brown scurried to Hogan for his response. Had he heard what Agostini said? "Who's *Agostini*?" Hogan fired back. "Don't make it sound as though I'll slit Agostini's throat, but I'll thrash the pants off him. Agostini is to be beaten along with the rest of them. I don't worry about any competitor in the race—just one fellow—me!"

Meanwhile Agostini walked around Empire Village asking everyone, "Who is this guy Hec Hogan?" Word filtered back to Hogan, infuriating him. When Agostini saw Hogan in person, he made a point of never speaking directly to him, only laughing at him. Hogan's Australian teammates considered Agostini a rank amateur talking outside his weight class, and several of them and their coaches exchanged heated words with the brash Trinidadian, which only seemed to fuel him to be bolder. "I really enjoyed this Australian vendetta against me," Agostini said, "because they didn't know that I was putting it on and they were taking it seriously." So seriously, in fact, that at one point Kevan Gosper, the 440yd gold medalist, spat at him. But Agostini's pre-race foreplay did have a serious purpose. He had mastered the art of obliterating an opponent's mindset with his antics. "If the guy was moody or temperamental, I'd tap my forehead every time he looked at me," he explained to Fil Fraser, the author of *Running Uphill*. "Soon he'd start trying to avoid me, but I'd hunt him out, and by the time the race was ready to go, he wouldn't be prepared. With another guy, I'd build him up and then unexpectedly chop him off with some slurring remark just before the race."

Agostini also grated the Australians in another way. "It was rumoured—and probably true—that I had lots of interest in the feminine gender," he recalled slyly in a 2010 interview. "I was supposed to be the Casanova of the Games. I had four, five, six, seven, eight dates a day." However, once he set up his dates too close together, and two attractive young women waited for him at Trinidad's Village hut at the same time. He considered escaping out the bathroom window until Trinidad's team manager, Sir Leonard Hannays, blew his cover and he was caught. Another time, Hannays returned from a team managers' meeting to confront Agostini about rumours the runner had been visited by a young lady after hours. Male and female athletes, of course, lived in segregated quarters. "*Oh no*, Sir Leonard," replied Agostini, feigning ignorance, "that must have been one of the Fijian athletes. The men wear sulus that look like skirts, you know."

Hannays only rolled his eyes.

Agostini defended his extracurricular activities as beneficial to his athletic performance, pointing out that since ancient times there has been a correlation between athleticism and virility. "We expect our great sports people to be saints, which is ball dust. They're just normal, over-sexed people. There's no hornier place than the Games village once people have finished their competition." And he continued his defence by saying, "Dutch Warmerdam, my coach at Fresno, used to say, 'It isn't the doin' it that gets ya, it's the chasin' after it.' On the other hand, intercourse is very relaxing and can be beneficial for an athlete. I used to say [to girls I'd meet], 'How would you like to help me break a record?' It enabled me." Because of Agostini's love of the ladies, he may have been the only person in Vancouver who had a ticket to get into Empire Stadium on the final day of the Games to see the Miracle Mile but missed the race entirely. His explanation? "There was this lady I was seeing out in Kitsilano and I'd spent part of the morning with her. I tried to make my way to the stadium, but I couldn't find a cab!"

While growing up, Michael Agostini hadn't even been the most famous athlete in his family. His Portuguese mother was a top field hockey player, while his father captained the national soccer team. In school his eldest brother, Sedley, often broke records before the next eldest, Colin, set a new mark. The Agostini brothers always seemed to be running in the streets, around the block, and even down to the Queen's Park Savannah horse racing stables, where they'd chew some hay and go off running like horses. During butterfly season, they'd be out all day with their nets, sunrise to sundown, running through the hills.

At age 14, Agostini picked up two debilitating injuries. One was a vestibular inner ear problem that affected his balance, leaving him dizzy, nauseous and prone to falls. The other was an injury to his left knee that caused it to lock up at the most inopportune moments. During a routine check-up decades later he learned that he had a completely torn anterior cruciate ligament. Remarkably, neither injury hindered him significantly, and for a five-year period he remained among the fastest sprinters in the world.

Agostini had taken Trinidad's national sprint championship by his late teens, but officials refused to send him to the 1952 Olympics, claiming he was too young and unproven. Just months later he went to Kingston and defeated Jamaican star Herb McKenley, who had returned from the 1952 Olympics with silver medals in the 100m and 400m. In April 1953, Agostini returned to Jamaica and ran the 100yds in 9.4 seconds, a world junior record that broke the legendary Jesse Owens' old mark. Left in his wake was 1952 Olympic 200m champion Andy Stanfield, who was so impressed that he gave Agostini his AAU All-American badge. Next Agostini travelled to Dayton, Ohio, for the 1953 US national championships where he finished a credible eighth in the 100yd final in 9.7 seconds. This impressive string of results put him on the radar of top US universities, but James "Jumbo" Elliott at Philadelphia's Villanova University proved to be the best salesman. This Catholic university meshed with Agostini's strict upbringing, although he had already drifted from the religion and leaving home had only accelerated the trend. "I went to confession once and an Irish missionary priest said to me, 'My son, you're not confessing, you're boasting!'"

The improved training regimen under Coach Elliott and stronger competition brought immediate results. On his 19th birthday in January 1954, Agostini broke the 30-year-old 100yd indoor world record by two-tenths of a second at the 172nd Armoury in Washington, D.C., running it in 9.6 seconds while wearing flat shoes on a board track. At the US nationals in June he finished fourth in the 100yds and sixth in the 220yds. When he came to Vancouver, his sights were firmly trained on BECG gold.

Hector Hogan was born in Rockhampton, Queensland, and grew up in Brisbane where he attended Marist Brothers College. He quickly made a name for himself as an explosive sprinter and a capable rugby player. After graduating, he worked as a refrigeration mechanic, riding his bicycle 24km to and from work every day. He surged onto the sprinting scene in 1952 by defeating John Treloar, Australia's top postwar sprinter, and he was now on his way to winning his first of seven straight 100yd national titles. He became known for his lightning starts, bursting off the blocks faster than anyone on the planet. Some claimed he was the fastest starter since double Olympic gold medalist Eddie Tolan. In his book *Great Australian Athletes*, long-time Australian athletics writer Robert Solomon claimed he had seen no runner with Hogan's "pick-up over the first 30 yards" until Ben Johnson arrived on the scene in the 1980s. "He was very laconic, very laid-back," explained Australian Olympic historian Harry Gordon, "but once he got down on the blocks to compete, he just exploded. That was his trademark, this astonishing jump

Canada's Harry Nelson (far left) edges out Australia's Hector Hogan (second from left) at the finish line in the first 100yd heat.

when the gun went off. The way he could synchronize his start with the gun was amazing; his instincts were superb."

In March 1954, Hogan ran 9.3 seconds at the Sydney Sports Ground to tie American Mel Patton's 100yd world record. Not long after that, he unofficially equalled the 100m world record, running 10.2 seconds in a handicap race. Based on such form, his confidence going into the race in Vancouver was understandably sky-high. "There will be no holding me," he predicted.

Unfortunately, an injury *would* hold Hogan back. While competing in the broad jump at a meet in California later that spring, he pulled a left thigh muscle. Three days later he pulled it again. In June he pulled up lame after 30 yards in a race in Stockton. The injury lingered right up to the Games in Vancouver, his first serious test since it happened. "The leg feels splendid now and I just hope it holds up," Hogan told a *News-Herald* reporter upon arrival, and after several punishing workouts at UBC's Varsity Stadium, he told the press his leg felt fine. Some felt he ran cautiously at the BECG warm-up meet in

Aldergrove just days before the Games, yet he still won the 50yds in 5.4 seconds to equal the Canadian record set in 1922. Time would soon tell if he was on form or not.

There was no question about Agostini's health and mindset. He looked formidable in training sprints, and 18-year-old Horst Dassler recognized him as a budding star and sought him out. Dassler's father, Adolf "Adi" Dassler, had developed a new design of track spikes that had impressed everyone who saw them. His shoe brand with its trademark three stripes wasn't as widely familiar then as it is today—Adidas—but Dassler had discovered that giving away free footwear to potential champions was excellent advertising. At the 1952 Olympics in Helsinki he had used this tactic on a small scale for the first time, forging relationships with such high-profile athletes as Emil Zatopek. Horst Dassler was in Vancouver to make connections with top athletes on a slightly larger scale, a dress rehearsal for the event usually cited as the worldwide launch of the Adidas brand, the 1956 Melbourne Olympics. With his sack of free spikes slung over his shoulder, he became a familiar sight in Vancouver wherever athletes were training, and he convinced many soon-to-be gold medalists to wear Adidas. The free advertising came when they were photographed crossing the finish line wearing *"die marke mit den drei streifen."* Horst gave Agostini a bright blue pair with white stripes while Chris Chataway accepted a white pair with dark stripes. Others, such as miler John Landy, gladly accepted a free pair and wore them for training but for actual races remained true to a more broken-in pair. Kevan Gosper claimed in his autobiography, *An Olympic Life*, that he had been given the first pair of Adidas spikes (red ones) in North America when Horst met him at Michigan State University on his way to Vancouver. Said Gosper: "Putting on the Adidas shoes was like having wings put on my feet. They were magic."

Like most athletes, Doug Clement saw his first pair of Adidas spikes when Derek Johnson won the 880yds wearing a blue pair. He was blown away by their look, much improved fit and replaceable, screw-in spikes—all dramatic improvements over traditional leather track shoes—and the fact that they felt comfortable right out

Canada's Doug Clement wearing an early pair of Adidas track spikes and an Australian singlet he traded for in 1958. Photo courtesy of Doug Clement.

of the box. In a 2007 interview, Clement explained that before Adidas one of the few types of track spikes available was "a black shoe with replaceable spikes on a metal plate made by Converse or Wilson Sports. It was heavy and not particularly—in quotation marks—*fast*. But if you were serious, you would stand on a piece of cardboard, trace the shape of your feet, and then mail it to one of two competing London shoe companies—Foster or Law. They would hand-make a leather pair with non-replaceable steel spikes that you couldn't screw in or out. You'd get your shoes in the mail some months later." But the process didn't end there. "You'd soak them in a bucket of water and, while still wearing them, let them dry to mould them to the shape of your feet. Then you'd go through several weeks of blisters and literally tearing the skin of your feet apart. Once you had them *broken in*, they were ready to compete in." After all that work, athletes were lucky if their track shoes gave them a season or two of use. Cinder tracks quickly wore the metal spikes down or the leather sides blew out. Then the entire horrendous process began anew. Adidas changed all that, revolutionizing athletic footwear with shoes that were visually attractive, extremely comfortable, much lighter and more versatile, while also holding up to the demands of durability on the track.

But Horst Dassler's small favour of presenting Gosper with that first free pair of "magic" spikes paid massive dividends for the Adidas empire down the road, especially after Horst assumed control of the company from his father, because within a few short years Gosper had risen through the ranks of the International Olympic Committee to become its vice-president. Through similar gifts Dassler soon held great influence and some level of control over the IOC, FIFA and the IAAF, as well as a horde of smaller international and national sports organizations, without ever actually becoming politically entangled within any of them. By the time he died in 1987 Dassler had pushed annual Adidas sales figures into the billions.

❂

In heat number one of the BECG men's 100yd heats—the first foot race ever run at Empire Stadium—Hector Hogan, perhaps still dogged by his thigh injury or lack of training, offered up a rather underwhelming first impression by finishing second in a time of 9.8 seconds. New Westminster's Harry Nelson edged out the Aussie world record holder by half a foot. Nelson's surprise effort ignited the hometown crowd and gave the 19-year-old freshman at Long Beach Junior College a healthy dose of confidence.

Agostini proved he was more than just bold talk when he won the second heat easily in 9.8 seconds, nearly jogging the last ten yards. But instead of Trinidad's colours or name on his singlet, he wore the AAU All-American badge given to him by Andy Stanfield the previous year. In a 2010 interview Agostini explained there had been good reason for this:

> Trinidad gave their athletes nothing, no support, no clothing or equipment. When I asked the Trinidad team for my singlet, they gave me a little eight-inch long strip with "Trinidad and Tobago" in black ink on it. "What do I do with this?" I said. "Get one of your girlfriends to sew it on, man!" they said. I happened to have the AAU All-American badge and that's what I wore in Vancouver. I could have been disqualified.

Heat three saw the 100yd event's first upset. Jamaica's Les Laing, who ranked as one of the world's top 200m sprinters, had been expected to challenge Agostini and Hogan in the 100yd final. But Laing had recently become a father for the first time, significantly disrupting his training, and he bowed out early, finishing well back in sixth place in a glacial 10.4 seconds. Instead, it was Nigeria's Edward Ajado, a 1952 Olympian who had recently clocked 9.5 seconds in training, who won the heat in 9.8 seconds, becoming the race's dark horse. Two-tenths behind Ajado was Welshman Ken Jones, one of the biggest names in European rugby and later the most capped player in Welsh history.

Two solid journeymen sprinters, Canadian Don McFarlane from Burlington, Ontario, and Englishman Brian Shenton, duelled at the front of the fourth and final heat, with McFarlane edging out Shenton by a yard in 9.9 seconds. The Canadian had won the national 100m title three years straight and run at the 1952 Olympics. Heavy on his mind was whether a pulled thigh muscle picked up in training less than a week earlier would hold up over the course on this afternoon.

All of these competitors had needed to balance their speed and endurance in the heats because less than 90 minutes later, the 12 semi-finalists were back on the cinder track. With only the top three from each of the two semi-finals qualifying for the final, the stakes now rose significantly, but those eager for the much-anticipated Hogan-Agostini clash had to wait as the two runners drew different semis. In semi-final number one, Hogan laboured through another unconvincing run, while the spectacled Nigerian Ajado

Trinidad's Mike Agostini (centre) wins this 100yd heat comfortably. Photographer Harry Cantlon, the *Province*.

proved he owned a higher gear, catching up to Hogan in the final yards to snatch victory by two feet in 9.7 seconds. As a result, doubt continued to swirl whether Hogan was still suffering from the thigh injury or just saving himself for an all-out assault on Agostini in the final. McFarlane thrilled the partisan Canadian crowd by nipping in for third just a yard behind Hogan. As his leg was holding up nicely, McFarlane liked his chances for the final. "I thought I had a chance at a medal, but Agostini was the man to beat," he recalled in a 2013 interview. Agostini owned the second semi, leading wire to wire. Easing up in the final yards, he drifted in at 9.7 seconds. Trailing just a tenth of a second behind were the hometown bolt-from-the-blue Nelson and the spritely 32-year-old Jones.

Now the final six were set, ready to singe Empire's cinders less than 45 minutes later, their third race within two-and-a-half hours. Most of the competitors stayed warm on the infield grass doing light exercises. In his trademark floppy fisherman's hat, Hogan killed time doing handstands to the crowd's amusement. Confident after his easy heat victories, Agostini oozed calm self-assuredness. The *Vancouver Sun* reported that somebody had called, "What about it, Mike?" to him while he was warming up on the infield. "Bet me," he had answered decisively.

As the final ticked closer, audible crackles of anticipation festered through the bleachers. The six 100yd finalists busied themselves behind the starting blocks.

Some gathered around a wooden picnic table, lacing their spikes, while others undertook final strides and stretches before discarding sweat suits to the Boy Scout volunteers. Seeing his opportunity, Agostini pulled one final trick from up his sleeve to deliver the psychological *coup de grace* to Hogan. He approached the Australian with an intentionally exaggerated smile, stuck out his hand, and said: "Best wishes, Hogan. May the better man win." Agostini recalled that the Australian had paused uneasily before shaking Agostini's hand. "He was just flattened. Flabbergasted. Because I'd removed the tension on *my* terms."

In an event that would be decided by fractions of a second with as much pre-race posturing as actual racing, if one competitor could shake up his opponent even slightly, it could make the difference between victory and defeat. "Look your opponent straight in the eye, never let him unnerve you: you unnerve him," Agostini is quoted as saying in his 1962 book *Sprinting*. More than any competitor in Vancouver that day, he had mastered this art.

While Hogan must have been agonizing over his tender left thigh, surely Agostini had jarred his focus with this tactic even just momentarily. The opposite occurred for Agostini. He suddenly felt so relaxed he may as well have been on a cruise back to the homeland, *mon*. Shutting off his mind, he had found *the zone,* long before that term had been coined. Later he said, "I don't recall a thing about the race until about 45yds in when I realized I was thinking about some damned silly economic theory. I was majoring in economics at the time."

The race starter, Sergeant "Cookie" Ryan of the Vancouver City Police, brought the six finalists to their marks. Each checked his spikes for clinging cinders and walked forward to the starting blocks. The crowd went silent. It all came down to this.

Two false starts, including once when Hogan jumped at the click of a photographer's shutter, forced the nervy field back to the line. On the third try, Agostini stepped purposely past his blocks in lane five, bent his hands to the dirt, set his feet and leaned forward in his crouch. Hogan was to his far left in lane two. Nelson in lane three and Ajado in lane four separated the two rivals. To Agostini's right were McFarlane in six and Jones on the outside nearest the crowd in lane seven. Lanes one and eight lay empty.

"Get set!"

At this third blast from Ryan's gun, they were away cleanly. Hogan sprang from the blocks first, a split second ahead of the others. Each accelerated swiftly, spikes pelting the cinders. The evening sun's bright glare cast six spindly, whirling-dervish silhouettes onto the track. By the 20yd mark, the shadow of the west grandstand had swallowed up the field.

Ajado moved into the lead by a foot, striding furiously, his glasses wobbling on his nose. Hogan stayed with him, finally looking like the world beater as advertised. Agostini and Nelson were just behind, both running smoothly, the former's mind apparently drifting off somewhere between Adam Smith and John Maynard Keynes. McFarlane trailed the pair, though he was picking up speed, while Jones dropped back, never really factoring after that. Thin puffs trailed in the field's wake, each spike kicking up the dry, flaky cinders with every powerful stride. At the halfway mark, Ajado was still leading by a hair over Hogan, and he was in front of Agostini by several feet. Nelson fell back, while McFarlane was still making up ground with each charging step.

Agostini recalled with a cackle that "at that point I looked around and thought, 'Shit, you're supposed to win this!' and I started running like hell." He set about closing the gap, focussing on driving his arms, which in turn spurred higher knee lift and lengthened his unusually long stride for a man only 5ft 6in in height. He moved up inch by precious inch through the field, slowly, almost indiscernibly until—*bam!*—there he was at the forefront.

The race's turning point came at 75yds. Ajado stumbled ever so slightly, catching his foot in a soft spot on the track. It was just enough to break his rhythm. He righted himself instantly, but the difference between winning and finishing out of the medals in this tight race proved to be that one small pothole for the unlucky Nigerian. Unfortunately, Hogan no longer looked in control either. He had tightened up noticeably and was now fighting to maintain his speed. This race settled things regarding his health. He wasn't the same man who had equalled the world record just four months earlier.

Ten yards from the finish line barely two yards separated the top five competitors. Only Jones in sixth had lost contact three yards behind. Agostini drew in front of first Ajado and then Hogan and pulled away. But the surprise was McFarlane—he wasn't just going with Agostini, he was gaining ground. At the line, each man lunged and grimaced, stretching for that little something extra. So tightly bunched were they that a blanket could have covered them.

Then while the field waited anxiously, the officials compared their watches and waited for a photo of the finish to develop. McFarlane, seeing his coach from the 1952 Olympics, Bruce Humber, who was a race judge here, said between gasping breaths: "I think maybe I snuck in for a medal." Ajado knew he'd come up short even though a gold medal had seemed to be his for the taking, and he remained utterly dejected until a teammate gave him a sympathetic hug. The pack of officials pored over the photo finish to discern positions. And then there it was in black-and-white: with a wide smile plastered on his face, Agostini had cut through the tape four inches in front of McFarlane. On Agostini's chest was that AAU badge, certainly an odd sight at a Commonwealth Games. "I'm the only person to my knowledge ever to have won a major Games event not wearing his national colours, emblem or country name," he said years later. He was also the first-ever BECG sprint gold medalist from the Caribbean, a region that later dominated the discipline.

The photo also showed Hogan making a desperate lunge to hold onto third a scant two inches behind McFarlane. In fourth, Ajado was three inches back, eight inches in front of Nelson in fifth. Remarkably, less than 18 inches separated first from fifth place. Agostini's winning time of 9.6 seconds tied the BECG record but couldn't be made official due to a stronger than acceptable tailwind. McFarlane, Hogan, Ajado and Nelson all finished in 9.7 seconds, while Jones lagged a further tenth behind.

After accepting his gold medal on the infield podium, Agostini's smile lit up the concrete dressing room. Photos circulated around the Commonwealth showed the man of the hour holding aloft his blue three-striped Adidas spikes in one hand and his gold medal in the other—about as good a product placement as you could find in 1954. The moment and the day belonged to the young Trinidadian, who had talked big and won big. "I knew I was going to win three days ago," he buzzed to reporters. "I just felt it."

Mike Agostini (second from left) wins the 100yd final, just holding off Canada's Don McFarlane (far left) who took silver, while Hector Hogan (far right) could only manage third. Photo courtesy of Vonna McDonald.

"A young amateur with the attitude of an old pro," the *Sun*'s Dick Beddoes deigned him. "What is important is that he called it in advance. Of such chips-on-both-shoulders kind of guys are Olympian gestures made."

And what of Hogan?

"Champions are made to be beaten," Agostini told a *News-Herald* reporter with little concern. "I've run against record holders before. They can be beaten."

To Hogan's credit, he offered no excuses for his disappointing performance. "I just didn't have any oomph," he told the *Sun* dejectedly. "I just didn't have it. I got a good start. But at sixty yards I didn't think I had a ghost of a chance. Today Agostini was a better runner than I was."

In the post-race scrum McFarlane revealed a detail that made his improbable silver-medal run even more impressive. "I got a sharp pain ten yards from the tape," he related, referring to the thigh muscle he'd pulled in training. "I faltered slightly but kept going." That momentary faltering may have been enough to prevent him overtaking Agostini. Regardless, some were calling McFarlane the most underrated sprinter in the Games. One headline read: "Mc-Farlane Surprises in Century." When one considers that only three Canadian men—luminaries Percy Williams, Harry Jerome and Ben Johnson—matched or bettered McFarlane's 100yd silver medal in eighty years of Commonwealth sprints, it certainly adds lustre to his accomplishment, surprise or not.

For both Agostini and Hogan, the rest of the Games proved a mixed bag. True to recent form, Hogan disappointed once again in the 220yds, finishing a distant fifth. And before he left Vancouver, he became involved in another embarrassing situation that somehow remained hushed up. One night he and five Australian teammates went out on the town and drank heavily. They returned to Empire Village well past curfew, but the RCMP officer posted at the Village gate promised to turn a blind eye. Unfortunately, Hogan took a liking to the Mountie's red serge jacket. "I'll trade you for mine," he said, indicating his green team blazer. The Mountie politely declined, but a clearly inebriated Hogan barked back, "Okay, we're going to take it off you then!" The Australians were tackling the officer when three other Mounties arrived and hauled them off to jail for the night. All hell broke

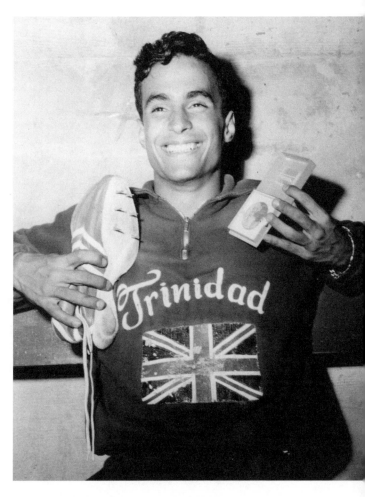

Beaming in post-100yd victory glow, Agostini holds up his gold medal and Adidas spikes. Photo courtesy of Vonna McDonald.

loose the next morning when Australian officials had to bail them out. The story never made the papers, although many athletes in Empire Village were aware of it. In a 2013 interview, Canadian marathoner Barry Lush recalled a red-faced Hogan entering the cafeteria the next morning. "You don't tackle a Mountie," someone scolded him. "I know, I know, I know," Hogan replied, ashamed.

The evening after his victory, Agostini also went out on the town to celebrate.

"I got rotten drunk," he recalled in a 2010 interview. "I got up the next day and I had a hangover, which normally I never got, and I thought, 'That's impossible! How can I have a hangover? I'm a gold medalist!' Not to compare myself to Alexander the Great, but I was reminded of when he was dying and he said, 'How can I die? I'm God. God cannot die.' Because we were brought up to believe the gold medal was the be-all and end-all of everything."

Agostini may have been out carousing and dealing with his new fame, but he still had one event to go. When the 220yd heats and semi-finals occurred three days later,

Canada's 4x110yd relay team (left to right): Harry Nelson, Don Stonehouse, Bruce Springbett, Don McFarlane.

On the last day of the Games, McFarlane played a crucial role in winning Canada's only track and field gold medal in Vancouver. The 4x110yd relay field, although small, was deep. Australia, England, Jamaica and Pakistan all looked tough, and the surprising Nigerian quartet, led by Edward Ajado, boasted four ten-flat men or faster. In the semi-final heats, the Nigerians sprinted away from everyone and suddenly stood as favourites. The Canadian team was comprised of McFarlane and Nelson, Bruce Springbett of Vancouver and Don Stonehouse of Waterdown, Ontario, who had been an eleventh-hour addition after teammates lobbied to have him included. "The four of us had become really good friends. We were really tight," McFarlane remembered.

The day before the final, the Canadians worked on baton exchanges for several hours and moved their marks back, a risky move but one they felt necessary to challenge the Nigerians. It may have made the difference. In the final the Nigerians and Canadians traded the lead back and forth, one nosing ahead and then the other. But the Canadian hand-offs were noticeably smoother and Nelson's strong third leg thrust Canada into the lead. In the last leg McFarlane and a gaining Ajado lunged for the finish line, and at first it seemed too close to call. After five minutes of waiting, a photo of the finish finally arrived down a wire from the stadium roof to officials. Only then could they discern the Canadian victory by mere inches. Both teams were timed in an identical 41.3 seconds, a new BECG record.

As the four Canadian sprinters stood tightly together on the infield podium to receive their gold medals, the band played Canada's national anthem, the only time spectators heard it that week. As the final was run in the hour window between the Miracle Mile and the Marathon, even Canadian accounts provided only brief mention of the Canuck triumph, perhaps Canada's most overlooked victory of the entire Games.

the favourite barely felt ready for them, and in later years he admitted that he hadn't handled them as well as he could have because he was still celebrating his 100yd victory. The event started off well enough. Agostini won his opening heat easily and later that day when he ran in the semi-final things also looked good for him—until the last 15 yards. He wrote in *Sprinting:* "I was tiring somewhat, and through fear and a desire to conserve strength I eased up slightly and looked round to see where the closest challenger was. I looked left and there was no one, and when I turned right I was shocked to see Harry Nelson giving his all and going ahead of me to the tape... I was too surprised and too near to the finish to do anything about it."

It is a cardinal rule in sprinting that you never look around at your competitors in a race, and Agostini paid the price. Nelson squeaked past by an inch or two at the line to move on. In a space of days, the New Westminster lad who had been tearing up southern California college tracks could now claim heat wins over both the 100yd world record holder and the newly crowned BECG 100yd champion. Not bad. And to the shock of everyone, Agostini, the newly crowned fastest man in the Commonwealth, was out. In some ways, the moment typified his all-or-nothing career: a peak of dizzying height followed by a soul-searching low. There didn't seem to be much in between for him. One thing remained certain, though. Love him or hate him, win or lose, Mike Agostini was always unceasingly memorable: the fastest man and fastest mouth in the West Indies and the grand character of the 1954 BECG. They say sometimes it is better to be memorable than great and there may be some truth to that. Yet hearing that, Agostini would likely scoff, "Why not be both?"

✸

On Empire Stadium's infield, the other enticing opening day match-up pitted Toronto's Jackie MacDonald against New Zealand's Yvette Williams in the women's shot put. They were two of the best throwers you could find outside the Iron Curtain where the sport's powers resided, but that was where the similarities ended.

MacDonald had emerged after a little over a year in the sport to become the greatest female shot putter Canada had known. Soon after winning the shot and discus at the Canadian BECG trials earlier that summer, she had smashed her own Canadian record by almost three feet, heaving the shot 43ft 10in. It marked the fifth time she had broken her own Canadian record in less than two months. In Vancouver the press and photographers couldn't get enough of "Jackie Mac," who quickly became a household name as the belle of the Games and one of its most photographed athletes. Tall and fit, with short platinum blonde hair and a winsome smile, she was a stunning beauty and often compared to Marilyn Monroe. From a historical sense, she may have been Canada's most captivating female track and field athlete since Ethel Catherwood, the "Saskatoon Lily," who had won the hearts of Canadians (and broken a few as well) with her high-jumping ability and movie star looks when she won gold at the 1928 Summer Olympics.

Following pages: New Zealand's Yvette Williams (right) and Canada's Jackie MacDonald (left) embrace after finishing 1-2 in the women's shot put.

Williams was New Zealand's best-known athlete and one of the best all-round sportswomen in the world. She had been a gold medalist at the 1950 BEG in Auckland, her home city, became New Zealand's first-ever female Olympic gold medal winner in 1952 and was now the newly minted broad jump world record holder at 6.29m. She approached the 1954 Games in the greatest form of her illustrious career, determined to end it with one final crowning achievement that would dwarf anything that came before.

Leading up to the women's shot put, Williams was heavily favoured, especially after she flung the shot over four feet farther than the outdated Commonwealth record in unofficial practice throws. However, MacDonald believed challenging for gold was not out of the question either and held back nothing. The competition stuck to the predicted plot, with perhaps the biggest surprise being that the two women quickly became good friends.

Despite MacDonald's best efforts, New Zealand's pride proved untouchable, and Williams won with a 45ft 9½in toss on her third of six attempts. As this was the first time women's shot put had been held, this distance measured a BECG record. Each of Williams' first two attempts—both over 44ft—were also good enough to win the competition. Unfortunately for MacDonald, only the day before the event she had learned that she must compete with a shot thirteen ounces heavier than she normally used. She finished second with a best throw of 42ft 7in on her first attempt; although it was over a foot short of her unratified Canadian record, it may have ranked as the best effort of her short career. Afterwards, Williams and MacDonald embraced for a warm congratulatory hug captured by photographers and run in the *Province* under the caption "Spirit of the Empire Games." The photo became one of the Games' signature shots. New Zealanders back at home were thrilled with Williams' strong start, and Prime Minister Sidney Holland sent a telegram in which he singled her out for praise:

> Warmest congratulations to all members of the team on their fine performances on the first day, and particularly to Miss Williams on her magnificent achievement.

In the first of 29 medal ceremonies held at Empire Stadium over the coming week, Williams, MacDonald and bronze medalist Magdalena Swanepoel of South Africa collected their medals atop the white plywood infield podium from BEG Federation chairman Arthur Porritt. After that, the respective weeks of Williams and MacDonald went in about as different directions as one could possibly imagine.

Not satisfied with just one gold medal, the determined Williams trained for up to six hours daily at UBC's Varsity Stadium. In the tattered and patched running shoes she had worn winning the 1952 Olympic long jump, she focussed on her form for the 80m hurdles and the discus. Impressed observers quickly crowned her the hardest-working athlete of the Games. "There is a sort of intelligent, calculating earnestness about everything she does," confirmed the *Province*'s Alf Cottrell. Others noted how polite and likable she was, unofficially anointing her the Games' most charming athlete.

Raised in the relative isolation of Dunedin, New Zealand, at a time when few New Zealanders travelled abroad and few even ventured to other parts of the country due to petrol restrictions, Williams was the product of a simpler time and place. As a young girl she had learned to leap over her grandfather's garden hedges, often accompanied by a stern warning from him—all the more reason to clear them untouched. "He had perfectly manicured hedges and didn't want me to touch the sides, so I learned to jump a long way," she told the *New Zealand Woman's Weekly* in 2012. She may have inherited some of her jumping ability from her mother, a talented Highland dancer in her youth, noted for the heights she could effortlessly spring.

However, the makings of a potential champion remained largely dormant through school as few organized sports existed for girls, and at the annual school sports day she fought off nerves to win a skipping rope race. But after graduating, she craved some sort of fitness away from her office job, and a co-worker suggested she try athletics. One night Williams rode her bicycle down to the local track and found a meet in progress. Organizers didn't know what to make of the newcomer. "In those days, it was all handicap events," she said in a 2007 interview. "I was put out at the farthest mark in front for some running events because they didn't know anything about me. I won easily." It was the same with the field events, which she had at least tried before. Gradually they moved her farther and farther back until she started at the scratch marker. And she continued to win. She was a blinding natural. In 1947 she went to her first national championship in Wellington and finished second in the long jump, missing first place by a half-inch. She also won the shot put, setting a New Zealand record. For the next six years she won both events as well as the javelin and discus. A few years later she tried the hurdles and became national champion in that, too. (The heptathlon didn't exist for women in those days, otherwise that title would have been Williams' to lose. The women's pentathlon was added to the Olympics in 1964 and to BECG events in 1970; the BECG then replaced the pentathlon with the heptathlon in 1982, and the Olympics added the heptathlon two years later.)

It was Yvette Williams' good fortune to attend a coaching school in 1949 where she met Jim and Emilie Bellwood. Jim, who had survived a brutal childhood in a foster home, had served with the army in North Africa where he had been captured by the Germans and spent three years in a POW camp in Greece. After the war he had studied in Britain to become a physical education specialist in order to devote the rest of his life to guiding youth in sport. Emilie had been a gymnast in her native Estonia and competed at the 1936 Olympics. In New Zealand, both coached and taught physical education, and at the first national coaching school held in Timaru, they instantly recognized Williams' tremendous potential and encouraged the unpolished teenager to move to Auckland to train with them. "Jim was very quiet, very encouraging," Williams told a *New Zealand Herald* interviewer in 2012. "He wasn't loud, didn't shout 'do this' or 'you have to do that.'"

The Bellwoods quickly became like family for her, although even years later Williams still addressed Jim as "Mr. Bellwood" and never challenged their methods even at their most punishing or when the application to track and field appeared thin. Youthful arrogance simply didn't reside within her. Combined with her own tireless work ethic, the Bellwoods' subtle support transformed her into a humming training machine and a bona fide star. Her daily training schedule involved three workouts totalling seven hard hours squeezed around an eight-hour workday at her secretarial job. "My friends didn't

Yvette Williams won the shot put competition on this throw of nearly 46 feet. Photo courtesy of Vonna McDonald.

Jackie MacDonald took silver in the shot put with a throw approaching 43 feet.

Displaying her world-class athleticism, Yvette Williams (in black singlet) lunges for the finish line in an 80m hurdles heat. Photo courtesy of Vonna McDonald.

see me much," she recalled in 2007. "I was probably training harder than anyone else then—not much time for pleasure. It was a matter of deep desire to perform the best I could as there were no financial rewards in those days. You do it for the love of your country and the sport."

From her gymnastics background, Emilie Bellwood offered eastern European training methods that focussed on building strength and improving flexibility. But as facilities and equipment were hard to come by, the Bellwoods had to be innovative. "They had me lifting concrete blocks for weight training. I looped sandbags over my feet and, lying on my back, lifted them up to strengthen my legs and abdominal muscles. He would often have me running up and down Auckland's hills in army boots to strengthen my legs." Bellwood even had her lie on her back and lift his two young daughters with her legs.

At other times she ran miles along the beach on the soft, strength-sapping sands, and she used the nearby sandhills to work on her broad jumping technique, taking great leaps downhill to gain the extra airborne split seconds critical to refining her form. Jesse Owens became an inspiration for her own technique: the hitch kick. "It was a continuation of running in the air," she explained. "Your legs are continuing to do running [movements] before you land and it would extend the jump." Williams became the first woman to adopt the hitch kick successfully and quickly outdistanced all her rivals. At the 1952

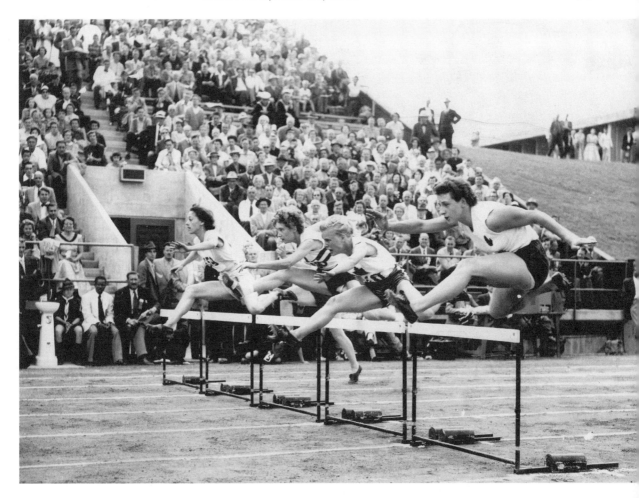

Northern Rhodesia's Edna Maskell (left) leads over the first hurdle on her way to victory in the 80m hurdles.

Olympics, she soared to New Zealand's first-ever Olympic gold medal won by a female athlete with a 6.24m winning jump.

Five days after winning the shot put at the BECG, Williams contested the 80m hurdles for the first time in a major international meet. People knew she could jump and throw, now she proved she could also run: she finished second in her semi-final heat in 11.3 seconds, a time bettering the existing BECG record by three-tenths of a second and qualifying her for the final later that day. There Williams placed only sixth in 11.4 seconds, although that final ranked among the fastest 80m hurdles races ever run to that point. With a driving lunge, Northern Rhodesia's Edna Maskell took the gold in 10.9 seconds. It matched the existing world record and would have been good for a gold medal if it had been run at the 1952 Olympics. Afterwards, Maskell created a stir when she was photographed with Prince Philip because palace protocol dictated that only the Queen was to be photographed alone with him. After she retired from international athletics, she and her husband moved to South Africa where they ran a massive game farm that became a national heritage site.

Yvette Williams (top of podium) receives her discus gold medal, while silver medalist Suzanne Allday (left) and bronze medalist Marie Depree (third from left) watch.

For Williams, the loss in the hurdles meant that she could not attain her personal goal of taking four gold medals at the Games, but she could still win three, and she went for numbers 2 and 3 on the Games' final day just ahead of the Miracle Mile. The broad jump—her specialty—and the discus—a new BECG event for women—were being held at the same time at opposite ends of Empire Stadium. For most, it would have been a scheduling nightmare to avoid, but Williams saw it as an opportunity to push herself further, and the spectators became as engrossed in whether she would miss her next turn in either event as they were in her actual performance. "I had to run between the discus circle and long jump runway right across one side of the field," she recalled. "I had different spikes for each, so I had to keep changing them and keeping the order in both competitions. I had to concentrate on one event and then the other." And while it is one thing to contest two international events simultaneously and be competitive, it's quite another to run away with two gold medals in the process. Yet that's exactly what she did, setting BECG records in both events. In the discus Williams' best throw measured 147ft 8in, over 16ft beyond England's Suzanne Allday, the next closest competitor in the small field. Although this was an event Williams was still learning, her winning toss landed within four centimetres of the 1952 Olympic gold medal distance. Her next two best throws were also good enough to win the competition comfortably.

To complete her gold medal hat trick, Williams put on a broad-jumping clinic. She essentially won the competition on her first attempt, soaring over 19½ft. Rather than letting up, she nearly matched it on two further attempts and ended up extending her lead by another five inches on her fourth. Her best jump officially measured 19ft 11½in—seven inches past her own existing BECG record—and it would stand unbeaten for another twelve years. On her final jumps, the crowd applauded to salute the career of one of the world's great all-round athletes—a true ambassador of sport exhibiting all the grace, dignity and respect you hope for in an athlete but rarely see. After having proved herself the Commonwealth's best in a discipline demanding strength, power and coordination, she had then matched that in another that required the altogether different elements of speed, agility and spring. Although Marjorie Jackson-Nelson would also win three gold medals in the 1954 BECG, one of those came in a relay event, so Williams' three gold medals ranked as the best individual performance of the Games, an exclamation point on a career already punctuated with highlights. For Williams it was the perfect ending.

After Jackie MacDonald's shot put silver medal earned on that first day of the Games, the rest of the week was anything but perfect for her. At first she went quietly back to preparing for the discus. Of course, "quietly" had become a relative term for her. For weeks before the Games, almost every other day a new photo of her had appeared in the newspapers, and the male-dominated press trotted out every well-worn sexist line of the era when describing her. Even some of the more balanced writers noted her physical measurements in the same sentence as her shot put and discus distances. She began to resent the fact that the respect she deserved as an athlete was in such short supply. "I had certainly never thought of myself as glamourous," MacDonald said in an interview sixty years later. "On the one hand it was flattering, but I found a great difference of attitude between the press in Great Britain—where I was taken

Jackie Macdonald was one of the most photographed athletes of the 1954 Games with many reporters comparing her to Marilyn Monroe. Photo courtesy of Jackie Macdonald.

more seriously as an athlete—and the press in North America." In many ways MacDonald truly was an athletics trailblazer for Canadian women in throwing events, which emphasized power and strength, but in her case these also served to highlight her attractive physical features. As a result, she represented an interesting dichotomy for the press and public: could grace and femininity exist side by side with power and sheer brute strength? The answer today is yes, of course, but many then were still grappling with such a fresh juxtaposition.

Jackie MacDonald had grown accustomed to people not knowing what to make of her. Her coach, Lloyd Percival, had instructed her to increase her overall strength by weight training, something very few women did at that time, and by 1955 she could shoulder press 132lbs, clean-and-jerk 150lbs, and press 300lbs with her legs, and likely stood as the strongest female athlete in Canadian history to that point. But when she had phoned her local YWCA to inquire about the weight training equipment available there, a puzzled YWCA staffer had asked, "You mean that you want to lose weight?"

"No, I want to *train* with weights," MacDonald replied.

"Ladies don't do that!" was the startled response.

MacDonald was one of the first Canadian woman athletes who lifted weights as part of her training. Photo courtesy of Jackie MacDonald.

MacDonald had encountered similar reactions when riding her second-hand 1948 Harley 45 motorcycle. "Are you a girl or a boy?" people yelled from rolled-down car windows. "It may have been because I was tall and had short hair," she explained, "but could also have been because nobody expected to see a woman driving a motorcycle." An *Ottawa Citizen* story in 2007 told how nearly every time she went out riding, the police stopped her. One officer was shocked that she did indeed have a driver's licence, a motorcycle permit and even a job. While writing her a speeding ticket, he stopped short and said, "We had better just forget about this. If I went in and asked for a ticket to be issued to a woman schoolteacher driving a Harley-Davidson, the boys would laugh me out of the station."

However, MacDonald had long ago stopped caring what others thought. Born in Toronto, she had studied ballet, martial arts, acrobatic dance, swimming and diving, and had won the Ontario junior diving championship in 1948. But since track and field for high school girls didn't exist in Toronto then, athletically inclined girls like MacDonald were forced to settle for girls' rules basketball and volleyball, and one day the unfairness of it all hit her. Everyone in school was expected to attend the season's final track meet at Varsity Stadium. The boys would compete. The girls could only watch. MacDonald walked out. "The attitude to physical effort reminded me of the old saying, 'Horses sweat, men perspire, and ladies glow,'" she recalled. "They might have added, 'But don't glow too hard, dear, it isn't seemly.'"

Prevailing attitudes did little to deter her. At age 15, she joined a "real" women's basketball team in the Toronto and District Women's Basketball Association and set several scoring records, once dropping 38 points in a single game, but women's basketball at that time went no farther than the city level. MacDonald craved a higher level and individual women's sports were the only way to get there. In high school a teacher, noticing her size and athletic ability, had suggested she try the shot and discus. She declined then, but as she approached 20, she reconsidered. There was just one problem: she needed a good coach and soon if she was to compete nationally and internationally in her best years.

In the spring of 1953 she boldly phoned Lloyd Percival, whom she knew only by reputation, and by the end of the conversation, he had agreed to take her on. As well as demonstrating the benefits of weight training, he taught her the "O'Brien Glide," a revolutionary shot put technique perfected by the American Olympic champion and world record holder Parry O'Brien. It required the thrower to face the back of the throwing circle and turn 180 degrees using a tight spin to generate more speed and power. She progressed rapidly, but this was hardly a surprise for an athlete training under Percival.

Using methods years ahead of his time, Percival coached many top Canadian athletes at the Toronto Track and Field Club. A born self-promoter, since 1944 he had also been hosting the weekly *Sports College on the Air* program on CBC Radio, dispensing views on fitness and training for athletes and coaches, and the media could always rely on him for a juicy quote, particularly when it came to challenging slow-to-change sports governing bodies to discard outdated or wasteful methods. As a result, Percival was managing to live off coaching-related activities—in essence a professional at a time of staunch amateurism—which made the established track fraternity view him with suspicion and outright contempt. However, over the years he also built an impressive cadre of believers, and his knowledge was sought out and utilized by the likes of the US Council on Physical Fitness, the Detroit Red Wings, the Soviet national hockey team, several NFL coaches including Don Schula, Olympic medalists such as Roger Jackson and Steve Podborski, sports legends from Gordie Howe to George Chuvalo, and countless university athletes who earned athletic scholarships. Some called Percival a visionary, while others treated him like a pariah. Rarely has a more divisive figure existed in Canadian sport.

Unbeknownst to MacDonald, Percival had made a few more enemies leading up to the 1954 Games. For several years, although growing numbers of his athletes appeared on Canadian Olympic and BECG teams, officials had avoided naming Percival as a national coach. However, the 1954 Canadian track team was dominated by Percival-trained athletes with fourteen ultimately qualifying to compete, including MacDonald, miler Rich Ferguson and pole vaulter Ron Miller. As a result, officials were finally poised to name him coach of the Canadian track team, which would have suited him just fine, until he learned that they had downgraded his position to co-coach. In a drawn-out soap opera that included several misunderstandings exacerbated by Percival's stubborn pride, he ended up playing no role whatsoever.

Instead, he came to Vancouver as a CBC Radio commentator, while also penning articles for the *Toronto Star* and conducting several Sports College clinics. Fearing Canadian team officials would threaten his athletes if he was viewed as getting too close, he kept his distance from his athletes, although no one understood what they needed for peak performance better than he. "When I told athletes from other countries that my regular coach was at the Games," MacDonald recalled, "but the team officials didn't want me or his other athletes to have anything to do with him, they thought this was crazy, which it was." A few days before the start of competition the entire Canadian track and field team was summoned together for a strange meeting. "A certain man has come to town and we are concerned that he might try to interfere with your training" was the gist of the message delivered by team officials. "Of course, we all knew they were talking about Lloyd," MacDonald confirmed. "I can't remember if we were warned not to talk to him or what, but it was really bizarre." Meanwhile, the dissension between Percival and Canadian officials continued to bubble beneath the Games' surface.

On Friday, August 6, the day before the women's discus event, an innocent-looking advertisement ran in the *Vancouver News-Herald*, promoting Percival's Sports College and its sponsor Orange Crush. It featured MacDonald holding a Sports College pamphlet in one hand and a bottle of soda pop in the other and was captioned "Sports College Graduate." The ad noted MacDonald's silver medal shot put performance, that Percival coached her to "medal winning efficiency" in just fourteen months, and that "Orange Crush is the only soft drink chosen for the BEG stands." The same ad ran in the *Sun* and the *Province* the following day.

This ad was hardly unique. Earlier in the week a New Westminster milling company had advertised its supply of New Zealand grass seed in the *News-Herald* with a photo of the entire New Zealand BECG team. A photo of Roger Bannister had appeared in a shoe store advertisement, while on the same page Pakistan's entire BECG team was pictured for a Persian rug store. Unfortunately for Jackie MacDonald, the Canadian Track and Field Association (CTFA) saw things differently. The day the ad ran, Canadian team general manager Hy Herschorn and women's track and field team manager Margaret Lord summoned MacDonald to Canada's office at Empire Village. Rather disconcertingly, Herschorn locked the door after she entered, then putting his lawyer's background to use, he subjected her to a "blistering interrogation," suggesting her appearance in the ad "reeked of professionalism." Most of his questions, however, revolved around Percival. "I said that I talked to him as a friend from Toronto and that it would seem strange to refuse to speak to someone you knew. I was determined not to let [Herschorn] twist what I said into anything that could be interpreted as Lloyd having 'interfered with' my training—something he never did."

On the morning of the discus event, MacDonald arrived several hours early to begin her warm-up, but less than two hours before the scheduled start time, Canadian track team manager Bob Calder delivered shocking news: officials had barred her from competition. MacDonald was out of the 1954 BECG because of a pop bottle, and now her future amateur athletic career appeared to be hanging by a thread. Even more heartbreaking for MacDonald was having to watch from the stands as the competition she had trained months for went ahead on the oval below.

Scratching a medal contender is usually reserved for serious offences, so the press erupted over this one. As she had become such a public figure during the Games, MacDonald's plight played out on the pages of newspapers right across Canada and beyond. Brief mention of her situation even made it into *Sports Illustrated*'s inaugural issue. The *Toronto Star* claimed the situation had worked the AAU into "their biggest tizzy since Barbara Ann Scott gave back her Buick," in reference to the infamous instance when the renowned Canadian figure skater was presented with a new car after winning her 1948 Olympic gold medal then forced to relinquish it. "They took my picture with a pop bottle in my hand," MacDonald explained, still sounding distraught in a *Maclean's* article published a year later. "I didn't know how they were going to use it. I thought it was the usual newspaper picture. I certainly didn't receive any money for it."

Lloyd Percival told reporters, "This is a terrible testament to our so-called right to be considered innocent until proven guilty." But he also made one more thing clear:

"This is another attempt by AAU officials to get me." In a 2007 interview MacDonald conceded, "I was very naïve in letting myself get involved with this. I thought that if I weren't paid and I didn't endorse the product that I was okay." And she should have been. The New Zealand and Pakistani teams didn't discipline their athletes for similar advertisements, and English officials certainly did not take Bannister to task for his. MacDonald, however, had been snared in a big-time political power play by holier-than-thou Canadian officials who towed the amateur line to its utmost. Maybe her lawyer, Harold Bradshaw, had it right when he told reporters that "She doesn't need a lawyer. She needs a Machiavelli."

In fact, what she had done was not half as blatant as the BC AAU president's car, plastered with signs promoting a Vancouver car dealership, parked outside Empire Stadium's main gate on opening night. Or those Canadian athletes—many coached by Percival—who had competed at the Canadian BECG trials wearing t-shirts that bore the logos and names of products such as Orange Crush. The shirts had been supplied by the AAU's Central Ontario branch, which had obtained money from the soda company to send athletes to the trials. Fred Rowell, chairman of both the AAU's Public Relations Committee and the Canadian Track and Field Association, had assured officials no problem existed with the shirts. So why did they single this one athlete out and ignore the others? Referencing IOC president Avery Brundage, the long-time zealous advocate of an often unreasonably strict amateur code, the *Sun*'s sharp-penned Dick Beddoes wrote in his column of August 10, 1954:

Canadian officials removed Jackie Macdonald from competition over a harmless-looking Sports College Orange Crush newspaper ad. Photo courtesy of Jackie MacDonald.

> If Miss MacDonald's photograph with a beverage smirches amateurism, what of the parties who are sponsored by business firms? It follows that athletes wearing such advertisements on their jerseys [*sic*] as Quadra Club or Arctic Club or Glotz's Laying Mash are endorsing a product same as Miss MacDonald.
>
> Oh, Hy Herschorn, manager of the Canadians, has learned his lesson well from Slavery Brundage, the high priest of amateurism... [who] has long boosted athletics to new heights in hypocrisy.

The public response from CTFA and AAU officials proved rather weak. In effect, they said they feared that if MacDonald was indeed a professional, the amateur status of the athletes she competed against could be jeopardized, and this could lead to protests from other teams, something that had rarely, if ever, occurred in BECG history. This would have been the same as the Australians protesting Bannister running the Mile because of the shoe ad.

MacDonald refused to be bullied, and on August 8 she released an official statement to the press:

> I wish to state emphatically... that, not having accepted remuneration, not endorsed the product in the picture, I have not at any time violated in any manner the amateur code... A cloud has been placed over my amateur standing and I want a hearing to present the facts of the case.

The press condemned the AAU's handling of the entire situation and sympathized with MacDonald. On August 9, *The Globe and Mail*'s Jim Vipond called it "one of the most high-handed operations we've come across in years on the sports beat." He also demanded the resignation of any officials "guilty of using this girl to further their petty jealousies" and a full investigation of "this ill-conceived, hasty and panicky action." But officials refused to grant MacDonald a hearing.

Two days after scratching her from the discus, the AAU held a lengthy in-camera meeting to discuss the "Orange Crush Affair." She wasn't invited to this gathering. Instead, one of the AAU's own—Fred Foot, president of the Central Ontario branch—was designated to represent her. Although he was the coach of the East York Track Club that MacDonald later joined, at this time she neither knew him nor knew he was representing her. She spent the day holed up at her lawyer's house while her future was decided. A day later the AAU announced its verdict: MacDonald had not violated the amateur code. She was free to continue competing as before, her future athletic dreams intact. Though it was a great relief to her, it came at the loss of a BECG discus medal and the opportunity to stand as one of Canada's top individual performers of the Games.

The AAU and CTFA succeeded in driving Percival from coaching for a brief time, but if their intent was to set an example and permanently drive professional coaching from amateur ranks, they failed miserably. Beyond that, it's still not entirely clear what the CTFA and AAU hoped to accomplish. By the time Percival returned from a short hiatus, coaches employing professional methods were considered more the norm than solely amateur coaches anyway.

As the only 1954 Games athlete forcibly removed from an event for any reason other than injury, illness or rest, MacDonald could be forgiven if she looked back on the Games through a negative lens, but remarkably, she held no hard feelings. In fact, she remembered the opportunity to compete at the international level as exhilarating. "The wonderful opportunity to meet people from such a variety of countries, cultures and languages who shared my passion for sport greatly expanded my horizons and enriched my life." You can't help but admire someone with that outlook. Yes, she won a silver medal and lost the chance at another, but if you had to assign a colour to her character, it would have to be gold.

Jumping with one foot bare, Emmanuel Ifeajuna won Nigeria's first-ever international gold medal in any sport.

✵

In spite of the drama surrounding the Agostini-Hogan 100yd race and the Williams-MacDonald shot put contest, the real highlight of the opening day proved to be the men's high jump. Ultimately, no event better epitomized the BECG's growing cosmopolitan trend. Sixteen jumpers from eight nations began the competition on the infield while track events whirred past on either side of the wooden bar and standards, the sawdust-filled landing pit and the grass runway. But after two-and-a-half hours of trials the track was deserted except for the four jumpers who remained alive as the bar rose to 6ft 6¼in, just above the existing BECG record. New Zealand's Peter Wells, Uganda's Patrick Etolu and Nigeria's Nafiu Osagie and Emmanuel Ifeajuna each failed to clear the bar on their first two attempts. The daunting height seemed poised to thwart all four jumpers. Then 19-year-old

No 1954 Games athlete had as dramatic a post-Games life as Emmanuel Ifeajuna. Moreover, no athlete has been more wrongly maligned by the forces of history within his or her home nation. At university he became friends with many of Nigeria's top academics while at the same time becoming very politically conscious and leading protests against Queen Elizabeth's 1956 visit as well as several federal government causes. After graduating in zoology, Ifeajuna became a teacher at Ebenezer Anglican Grammar School in Abeokuta, where he worked near his university chum Christopher Okigbo, who is today regarded as one of Africa's great poets. But disenchanted with the country's corrupt ruling elite, Ifeajuna dreamed of a strong, united Nigeria, where all the diverse cultures within its borders would live free and equal. It was probably Okigbo who encouraged him to join the army in order to carry out their revolutionary aims, and Ifeajuna went to England where he trained at Mons Officers Cadet School in Aldershot. After returning to Nigeria, on January 15, 1966, a group of officers including Ifeajuna, the group's ideological and intellectual inspiration, staged the coup code-named Leopard, that targeted strongholds of political power all over the country. He oversaw actions in Lagos, where according to a disputed police report, he personally assassinated Prime Minister Tafawa Balewa after breaking into his house and kidnapping him; others claim the prime minister died of an asthma or heart attack. Operations in the north and west were equally successful as the rebels effectively lopped off the head of the nation's ruling elite in one cold-blooded swipe. However, troops loyal to the government rallied and forced a quick surrender. Helped by Okigbo, Ifeajuna fled to Ghana, disguised as a woman.

Ironically, rather than uniting his nation, the coup started a bloody civil war that tore it apart because the oil-rich eastern Igbo territories took this opportunity to separate and, calling themselves the Republic of Biafra, battled Nigeria from 1967 to 1970. Millions died. The nation has never fully recovered from the violence.

Forced out of hiding a year after the coup, Ifeajuna returned to his home in eastern Nigeria and served in the Biafran army as a lieutenant colonel and the first chief of staff of the Midwest Liberation Force 101 Division. However, during a failed invasion attempt he allegedly tried to negotiate a ceasefire with Nigerian leaders to save lives and reunite his broken homeland. The Biafran leader, General C. Odumegwu Ojukwu, considered this the ultimate betrayal, and on September 25, 1967, Ifeajuna was tied to a stake in front of a vicious mob at an army base in Enugu and executed by firing squad. "Nigeria's great sporting hero died a villain's death," wrote Nelson Ottah in 1980 in *The Trial of Biafra's Leaders*.

When the war ended in early 1970, Biafra ceased to exist and the victors shaped the popular history of the conflict to their own ends. Ifeajuna was a convenient scapegoat, blamed for a bloody civil war he never intended and then tried to end. Scattered voices occasionally suggest he be given his due place in Nigerian history. Henry Onyeama, a Lagos-based writer, believes the man once called "Emma Vancouver" was a patriot; in the September 2011 edition of *The African Bulletin*, he wrote: "Whatever may be the truth, Ifeajuna stood for a new, united Nigeria... he was a pan-Nigerian revolutionary to the core. Maybe that was what cost him his life in Biafra." Regardless of his role in the January 1966 coup, Ifeajuna's lightning-in-a-bottle high jump gold medal in Vancouver stands as a landmark trailblazing achievement for Nigerian sport, and all of Africa for that matter, but don't expect recognition any time soon. Whereas other revolutionary individuals with truly heinous crimes to their names are celebrated, Nigeria's only international gold medalist until 1966 remains condemned to a place of infamy in the shadows, a victim of being on the losing side of history.

Nigerian high jumper Emmanuel Ifeajuna on a boat cruise of Burrard Inlet during the Games.

Ifeajuna broke the stalemate, sailing over the bar. Etolu and Osagie matched his effort. Wells sent the bar clattering and settled for fourth.

With the bar raised to 6ft 7in, higher than any of the trio had ever jumped before, it once again appeared they had reached their limit. Even the thoroughly engaged crowd providing loud support wasn't enough to propel them over cleanly on any of their first two attempts. For his third and final try, Osagie launched himself vertically, but the bar slapped his hip and fell. The crowd groaned and applauded politely. Osagie was done but had a bronze medal as some solace.

Next came Ifeajuna. Using a traditional angled approach from the left side, he gracefully loped toward the bar. Though he normally competed barefoot, this time he was wearing one shoe. Cat-like, he deftly planted his single shoe, launched himself skyward and rolled with his stomach closest to the bar as he reached the apex of his jump. He cleared easily with inches to spare. The amazed crowd erupted in applause. The bar hung over a foot above Ifeajuna's head when he came to his feet. Osagie raced over and jubilantly hoisted his Nigerian teammate in one massive bear hug. When slender Etolu missed on his final attempt and claimed silver, Uganda's first-ever international medal, a second round of unabashed celebrations broke out and carried over into the crowd.

Ifeajuna had secured Nigeria's first-ever gold medal at a major international games. In the same instant, he went into the history books as the first black African athlete to claim a BECG gold medal while at the same time breaking a Games record. Ifeajuna then took a "victory lap" with the bar set at 6ft 8in. His first attempt sent the bar rattling to earth. On his second the crowd hung on every long stride to the bar. Powerfully planting his shoed foot, Ifeajuna lowered his centre of gravity to generate tremendous thrust and lift. He shot up like an uncoiled spring, twisting his hips sideways. His shorts grazed the bar on the way over, which shivered ever so slightly but remained in place.

And just like that, he had the world's fifth-best jump for the year. He had also accomplished something never before achieved in high jump history: no athlete had ever leapt so high (13½in) above his own height (5ft 6½in). "At the time I attempted the record jump I did not think I had enough strength to achieve the success which was mine," he said later.

Several people, including Aussie sprinter Hector Hogan, hopped the bleacher railing and rushed to congratulate him. The crowd, now on its feet, rained more adulation down on the young Nigerian. A star had been born before their eyes. People shook their heads in disbelief. It didn't matter that he had gone on to attempt 6ft 9in and failed on all three attempts as the fatigue from four-and-a-half hours of competition finally caught up to him. Suddenly Emmanuel Ifeajuna was a name on the lips of the thousands filing out of Empire Stadium, and the following morning it was passed across breakfast tables all over the world.

While not a single reference to him can be found in any Canadian newspaper prior to his victory, it was a different story afterwards, with writers scrambling to fill in his back story. As a member of the Igbo people in eastern Nigeria, Ifeajuna had grown up in the bustling commercial town of Onitsha on the Niger River. He played soccer while attending Dennis Memorial Grammar School but had not begun high jumping until 1953 and was not taught any technique until three months before the 1954 Games. The man who later became his coach, Harding Ekperigin, an advisor to Nigeria's Minister of Education, had discovered him at a high school track meet. On one of Ifeajuna's first jumps after being taught to roll, he cleared 6ft 6in, a height only a handful of the best jumpers on the planet could then match. "I used to tease him that he was the most natural hero in sport," remembered Chief Emeka Anyaoku, a friend of Ifeajuna's, who later rose to become secretary-general of the Commonwealth Secretariat. "He did no special training. He was so gifted, he just did it all himself."

Ifeajuna was offered a high-jumping scholarship to study science at Nigeria's leading post-secondary institution, University College of Ibadan in Lagos, beginning in the fall of 1954. In the interim he had qualified to compete in Vancouver, although some felt his spot on the team was wasted on someone so young and inexperienced. On the long journey to Vancouver, the Nigerian team stopped in London where he competed in the AAA championships, but a wrenched knee in training permitted him only a sixth-place finish. The discomfort kept him awake at night until an injection allowed him to resume jumping just days before the Games in Vancouver.

Returning home to Nigeria by boat with his gold medal in hand, Ifeajuna, now nicknamed "Emma Vancouver," was paraded through the streets of Lagos, showered with awards, and toasted at formal dinners as a pioneer for Nigerian sport and a rising star in world athletics. A pencil sketch of him sailing over a high jump bar was embossed on a popular exercise book used by young students all over Nigeria.

And then, as quickly as he had rocketed to athletic stardom, it was over. "He simply stopped [training]," remembered Chief Anyaoku. "He seemed content with celebrating his gold medal." Within a month after thrilling Vancouver crowds, Ifeajuna retired to focus on his studies. The 1956 Olympics, where he would have been a medal favourite, apparently held no interest for him.

Two years after the BECG in Vancouver, Patrick Etolu led Uganda's first-ever Olympic team. Later he became a teacher and coached athletics in the town of Soroti, but like many African athletes at that time, what he had done was soon forgotten by his countrymen. When he retired from teaching, he lived in a leaky grass-thatched hut, farmed a small garden and kept a few goats; injuries from athletics and a vicious attack by thieves had left him able to do little more.

Then in 2006 IOC president Jacques Rogge met with former Olympians in Kampala and learned about Etolu's impoverishment. Etolu had been unable to attend the event because he could not afford a suit or the fare to the city. Two years later Rogge purchased a new house for him, and this attention gave Etolu a second round of celebrity status as his country honoured the accomplishments of this sports pioneer once more.

The final notable event of opening day was the first competitive appearance of any of the "big three"—Bannister, Landy and Peters. Along with his training partner and teammate, Stan Cox, Jim Peters prepared for the marathon by using the Six Mile race as a supplement to his daily training—sort of a speed workout with medals on the line. Both men approached it seriously, but they felt none of the pressure of a typical marathon. Technically Cox had not even qualified for the event, but the officials allowed him to run as a guest entrant.

THE MESSAGE

Jim Peters had been beset by anxiety since a particular training run early in July. He had been training that day on London's Hainault Forest trail where the damp air had soothed his skin as he ran. His white singlet and cotton shorts clung to his pale body, a combination of rain and sweat soaking him, and the white Woolworth's plimsolls on his feet were caked with mud. As always, he was running fast. He never had the time or patience to train like other marathoners who stuck to the accepted slow and steady training methods of the day. Especially not now. Not when he was just a month away from two top-class international marathons within three weeks, the toughest marathon double he had ever attempted: Vancouver's BECG on August 7 and later that month the European championships in Berne, Switzerland. By his own admission, he believed marathoners should rest four to five *weeks* between races before attempting another. If he was to pull this off, he would have to be very fit—that much he knew. He was now averaging over 115 miles a week—more at race pace than any international runner of his time—and had come to know every path and pothole, every road and rut near his home.

And that is why what happened next surprised him so much.

As he swung tightly around a blind curve in the forest trail, his attention became momentarily diverted by, as he put it, an ominous "message" in his mind. He felt a distinct premonition that he would fail to finish the upcoming races in Vancouver and Berne, "that some tragedy would happen but all would end well." Moments of doubt are not uncommon for any athlete, even one of world-beating calibre, but this was different and more urgent. At the same moment as these thoughts jousted in his head, he forgot about an exposed section of gnarly roots on the trail. His right heel hit a large one and down he went. He paused for a second, then over the shock of his fall he returned to this premonition. Quickly he jerked himself to his feet and brushed the dirt from his shorts and singlet. His heel screamed with sharp pain, but no matter. He laughed quietly, reassuring himself against his silly worries. *Get a hold of yourself, Jimmy. You're going to be fine in the big races...* As he continued on with his run, the odd feeling retreated somewhat and he regained his familiar rhythm.

Peters recorded the injury in his meticulously kept training journal: "July 1... Fell on RT leg just after Hog Hill," but there was no mention of his premonition. In fact, he told no one of it. Not his wife, Frieda. Not Johnny Johnston, his coach. Not Stan Cox, his close friend. Even after the events of Vancouver transpired far worse than even his imagination had conjured possible, he hesitated to tell anyone. It would be well over a decade before he would speak publicly about it.

The race had its share of surprises as the runners circled the Empire Stadium track. Canada's Doug Kyle, a UBC student who was well up with the leaders as they neared the five-mile mark, suddenly staggered off the track and collapsed on the infield turf. On the 22nd lap, New Zealand's Lawrie King barely broke stride as he pulled off his track spikes and tossed them into the infield. Accustomed to running shoeless on grass tracks back home, he continued barefoot on the cinders to the amusement of the crowd. Thirty-five-year-old Peters led for the majority of the race, his head wagging characteristically from side to side in time to his running gait, and he unexpectedly found himself still leading as they approached the bell lap. Based on past results, he knew that his English teammates,

Peter Driver and Frank Sando—both 13 years his junior—should be ahead of him by that time, and he decided to spur the young bucks into action. "You know, you're hanging about too much!" he yelled to them over his shoulder as the last-lap bell rang. "If you two boys don't have a go, the old man is going to beat you!"

That is all it took. Driver and Sando sprang ahead like startled colts, putting on an impressive sprint over the final 440yds to finish one and two. A visibly pleased Peters trotted around the final bend eight seconds behind in third place. When Cox jogged home in fifth place, it meant England had swept the medal positions and four of the top-five placings. Peters could not help feeling proud in aiding a strong English start in these Games, and he beamed as he stood on the podium while "Land of Hope and Glory" played, his chest puffed out as he admired the three red-and-white St. George's Crosses fluttering in the breeze above the scoreboard.

CHAPTER 4
SUNDAY, AUGUST 1, 1954

The muffler rattled on Jim Kearney's dented 1950 Pontiac Streamliner as it sat idling at the stoplight. He fidgeted behind the wheel, growing more impatient by the second for the light to turn green. It was Sunday, August 1, 1954, he was running late for an interview at Empire Pool, and he still had to negotiate Empire Village's clogged roads, a swirling epicentre of youthful activity. With no sports events permitted by law on Sundays, the British Empire and Commonwealth Games had paused for the day, and the athletes were free to entertain themselves.

A veteran of the newspaper business, Kearney had just returned to Vancouver from a two-year stint in London where he had acted as the "Canadian department" with Reuters and the British Information Services. He had been lured back a few weeks earlier to report for the *Province* on the Games with the promise of the fledgling BC Lions beat afterwards. But Kearney had landed in the midst of a pitched newsprint battle with crosstown rivals—these were the days when rival reporters yanked the wires from public telephones after filing their stories in order to gain a scoop on the next guy. If Kearney wanted to hold onto this new job—and he needed it with a wedding in the offing—he must deliver the goods. It was no wonder his patience was wearing thin when he found himself stuck in traffic.

Finally reaching the checkered archway to Empire Village, he flashed his press pass at the RCMP officer on duty and blew his Pontiac through. But just around a blind corner, a shiny Austin Healey 100 motored directly towards him in an unexpected game of chicken. He instinctively hit the brakes, as did the oncoming car, and both vehicles screeched to a halt mere inches apart. Kearney looked through the opposing windshield and was dealt an even greater surprise. Who sat behind the steering wheel but one flaming-haired Chris Chataway, and who occupied the "death seat"—as Kearney liked to emphasize in telling the story decades later—but one ashen-faced Roger Bannister. Kearney broke the awkward silence by leaning out the window to yell with a toothy grin, "Hey, we drive on the right-hand side of the road here!"

As the two cars slowly passed window-to-window, Chataway sheepishly replied in his crisply accented English: "Oh, sorry about that!" As Kearney drove on, he couldn't help envisioning the headlines that would have ensued if not for his swift reaction: "Reporter Ruins Miracle Mile—Bannister Never to Run Again!" In a 2007 interview he said, with the slightly twisted sense of humour common to journalists, that he could not help thinking: "Now that's a story people would read!" Vancouver's Deeley car dealership had loaned the English runners the Austin, feeling it would be good publicity if two of the most famous runners on the planet were seen driving it. Of course, if they *had* crashed, the Deeleys may have had second thoughts.

Opposite: Northern Rhodesian javelin thrower Terry Fisher brought the most unique team mascot to Vancouver: a live galago named Kafupe.

There was a good reason for Bannister and Chataway to be in such a hurry. They were on their way to their final training session before their respective races later in the week and wanted no one to know. Bannister ran a brisk 1:54.7 half-mile that day to cap weeks of build-up, but few outside his inner circle were aware. Since arriving in Vancouver on July 24, he had been using creative and at times deceptive methods to dodge headline-hungry reporters and cameramen. Occasionally, with training partners Chataway and Chris Brasher, he would announce where they were training and then go somewhere else entirely. The day before Kearney's near collision with the runners, *Province* photographer Bill Cunningham had noticed Bannister in the Village wearing dark sunglasses and a panama hat pulled low over his face. Bannister had hopped into the Austin with Chataway and sped off, but Cunningham had followed the duo to Balaclava Park, about six miles from UBC, and managed to snap the first photograph of Bannister running on a Vancouver track. The next day the photo appeared in both the *Province* and the *Victoria Daily Times*, although the latter misidentified the location as UBC's stadium.

✪

Weather-wise, that summer of 1954 had proved one of the coldest recorded to that point, and July had been the coolest ever, with an average temperature of only 20 degrees Celsius, and a top temperature only 22 degrees. Luckily the rain held off during the actual Games, but like many people from warmer climates, Peter Renner, the coach of the team from the Gold Coast (which became Ghana in 1957), worried that his athletes' unfamiliarity with Vancouver's cool summer temperatures could affect their performance, and on one particularly nippy day, he only allowed them outdoors for a short time to train. "We nearly froze to death," he said later in mock seriousness. Other team organizers took weather precautions, too. Rain capes were allotted to each Canadian team member. The *Province* reported that Fiji's athletes brought heavy coats, "thick navy blue affairs which would make one sweat in Siberia in December." Even the BEG Federation's honourary secretary Sandy Duncan stepped out of his Trans-Canada Air Lines Northstar holding aloft his umbrella, eliciting nervous chuckles from the Vancouver officials waiting below. As the *Sun* said the next day, "This is Vancouver. And he has been here before."

As this was still the early days of mass air travel, the journeys of many athletes to Vancouver had proved challenging and eventful. A group of New Zealanders endured the roughest plane trip: an exhausting and tense 52-hour marathon that ended with their four-engine plane operating on two engines. White-knuckle flyers like Yvette Williams noticed from their windows that the propellers had stopped turning. Officials at YVR, fearing the worst, mustered every available fire truck with lights flashing and sirens blaring to await the plane's arrival. Luckily the pilots brought it down without incident.

For Australian boxer Steve Zoranich what would have been a 50-hour flight from Sydney to Vancouver turned into a round-the-world excursion after American authorities refused to grant him a visa to land in Honolulu while en route. Officials remained vague whether Zoranich had been barred on "political grounds," but there was certainly a whiff of McCarthy-era Red Scare paranoia permeating the situation. Born in Czechoslovakia,

Zoranich had moved to Perth in Western Australia with his family when he was 11 and lived there for 15 years. While he admitted he had acted as a bodyguard for a Communist public speaker at political meetings in Perth years earlier, by 1954 the boxer had no political affiliation of any kind. The *Vancouver Sun* reported that when his visa was refused, to get to Vancouver he was forced to go the long way via Singapore, Calcutta, Cairo, Rome, London, Iceland, Greenland and eastern Canada—approximately 20,000 miles over nine exhausting days.

Australian wrestlers Fred Flannery and Malcolm Cowdrey were two of the earliest foreign competitors to arrive, a full month-and-a-half before the Games opened. Flannery, a hotel receptionist, and Cowdrey, a trucking business operator, both stopped off in Japan to compete at the world wrestling championships then sought a boat to Vancouver. After Japanese steamships refused to accept their currency, a sympathetic Aussie sea captain allowed them to pay for their passage by working aboard his cargo ship, the *Angus Glen,* which was bound for San Pedro, California.

The widowed mother of Welsh discus champion Hywel Williams deserved a medal even if her boy didn't win one. When it appeared Williams would not gain his release from his Royal Air Force duties in Kenya in time to make his flight from London to Vancouver with his Welsh teammates, team officials dropped him from the squad and added another athlete in his place. Meantime, he not only obtained his release but borrowed money for the flight from Kenya to London, joining his teammates unannounced. Though his seat on the plane was now taken, the team officials declared there was still a chance he could compete for Wales if he paid his own way to Vancouver. They also promptly left him behind. Up stepped Mrs. Williams to the rescue, dipping into her savings to cover the $800 plane fare for her stranded son. He flew directly to Vancouver, arriving three hours ahead of his teammates and was waiting for them on the tarmac. Williams then had to face a Games technical committee, who fortunately accepted his late entry on the grounds that he had been entered originally and didn't want to "quibble about what happened in between." His mother's faith—and deep pockets—allowed him to finish a solid fifth in the discus.

Many teams brought mascots—the New Zealanders chose a plush kiwi bird, the Kenyans a stuffed lion, the Indians an ivory elephant, the South Africans a furry springbok named "Bokkie." But the most interesting mascot of the Games belonged to Terry Fisher, a javelin thrower from Northern Rhodesia (which became Zambia in 1964). In her jacket pocket she carried a squirming eleven-week-old male galago named "Kafupe." A nocturnal animal, the galago or "bushbaby" resembles a squirrel with larger eyes and a longer, bushier tail. They are known for their ability to leap over 25ft, but most are quite ferocious. Fisher had won Kafupe over with bananas, chocolate and nuts, a delectable menu compared to the typical green leaves and insects galagos normally eat. However, anyone other than Fisher putting a hand near Kafupe's pocket "home" could expect to be bitten. When Fisher stepped off the plane with Kafupe, customs and immigration officials could say little in protest and fast-tracked the animal through as "meat" to avoid quarantine problems. Kafupe was the only "boy" allowed to live in the women's dorms.

New Zealand diving coach Doug Freeman took a boat to New York and then rode his motorcycle across the continent for six weeks to reach Vancouver. After coaching at the Games, he sped south on his motorcycle to Mexico where he booked passage for home aboard another boat.

Expecting the eight-member team from Trinidad to arrive in Vancouver on a CNR train at noon on July 20, Games chairman Stan Smith stood patiently on the platform with a welcoming police pipe band. After the surge of disembarking passengers cleared, no Trinidadian athletes were to be seen. The *Sun* declared the team "lost," while railway officials frantically launched a nationwide search. They were located a day later in Montreal, where their ship from the West Indies had arrived late. They were completely oblivious of the frenzy their "disappearance" had caused.

The three-man team from the Bahamas also went missing. Like the earlier scare, what was once lost was found a week later as three smiling Bahamian tradesmen—a tailor, a carpenter and a watchmaker from Nassau—stepped down from a plane at Vancouver's airport. The reason for their delay? Failure to get plane reservations. They were the last athletes to straggle into Vancouver for the Games, just two days before the opening ceremonies.

A third Caribbean nation, Bermuda, would not have made it to Vancouver at all if not for last-minute donations from the Bermudian and Canadian national associations. And the BEG Society, which aided the travel costs of most nations winging it to the Games, provided the final $1,000 necessary to get Bermuda's athletes to Vancouver.

❂

Although every athlete was welcomed upon arrival, the biggest welcomes had, of course, been reserved for Landy and Bannister. Landy's arrival at Vancouver International Airport on July 14 had heralded the onset of the BECG hysteria that gripped the city and surrounding environs for the next month. Nearly a thousand curious locals, 37 members of the media and a dozen BECG officials turned out. With no security to speak of at YVR in those days, the enthusiastic crowd simply surged closer and closer as the Australian's TCA North Star taxied to a stop and the passenger door popped open. Down the stairs bounded Landy, somehow still smiling on three hours sleep after an exhausting 72-hour journey that started in London and included stops in Montreal, Toronto, Winnipeg, Regina and Calgary. At about that moment, the assembled mob advanced, shouting to get Landy's attention, extending hands to shake or papers to sign, and shoving him in the direction of this camera or that official. Flashbulbs popped and newsreel cameras whirred. Sensing impending disaster, Stan Smith took matters into his own hands, roughly shepherding Landy through the crowd and into Mayor Hume's waiting green Cadillac. Landy climbed into the back seat as the milling throng nearly engulfed the car, but unfortunately, someone rolled down a window and cameramen tried to sneak shots. Then one of the doors opened and kids began handing him comic books and cards to sign.

Eleven minutes after touching down, Landy was on his way to Empire Village where Society officials quickly organized an impromptu 20-minute press conference, although only seven of the original 37 pressmen made it there in time. Naturally, media criticism of the mile world record holder's botched arrival was fierce. Australian newspapers called it "shocking." The *Sun*'s Dick Beddoes cracked: "Stanley V. Smith hustled

Just minutes after arrival at Vancouver International Airport, John Landy (centre) faces a mob of press and interested locals.

[Landy] to Empire Village with the fervor of a weasel scuttling through a henhouse. If Landy and Smith are ever matched, I'm betting on Smith."

Bannister's arrival as part of the 129-member English contingent—the second-largest at the Games—on July 24 was an even bigger event, but airport officials were confident that they were better prepared for the swarm of 3,500 welcomers. Fearing outright chaos, they had set up rope barriers to keep the crowd at bay, which for those times represented a significant tightening of airport security. But the crowd simply hopped the barriers and bounded across the tarmac and right up to the plane's wingtips, shouting greetings and cheering as the English athletes marched down the plane stairs, while above the din of the ever-present police pipe band, car horns honked. The *Province* claimed "Vancouver had seldom seen such a welcome—not for dignitaries, world leaders or even Marilyn Monroe." One of the last to emerge was Bannister. With his complimentary TCA bag and a camera slung over one shoulder and his team-issued fedora in his hand, he gazed down upon the massive crowd, caught momentarily in silent awe. *Province* photographer Eric Cable broke the pregnant pause when he called out in a clear cockney accent, "I say, is there a doctor in the house?" The newly minted medical doctor smiled widely as a gust of wind tousled his sandy hair. The crowd roared. Eager reporters hollered out questions. Clusters of bobbing and weaving photographers yelled to get his attention. Children called out his name while waving autograph books. Bagpipes droned

Roger Bannister (left) and John Landy (right) meet for the first time in Vancouver at UBC's Varsity Stadium track, while Chris Chataway (centre) looks on. Photo by Brian Kent.

in the background. It was pandemonium.

A group of reporters, including CBC Radio's towering Bill Good Sr., waited at the foot of the stairs, and though on Vancouver soil for all of five steps, give or take, Bannister happily obliged with an impromptu press conference right then and there. Afterwards, officials whisked the entire English team away to the Village in a twenty-car convoy. As the motorcade worked its way up Granville Street after crossing the Marpole Bridge, it morphed into a spontaneous parade. People waiting for buses waved happily. Homeowners galloped across front lawns to call greetings. A Little League game paused as infielders turned towards the road and waved their baseball mitts. Motorists pulled over and hopped out to catch a glimpse. Others honked their car horns, an echoing cacophony of goodwill.

Landy's workout on July 25, the day after Bannister's arrival in Vancouver, made headlines around the world. Paced by Aussie teammate Kevan Gosper, he ran a searing three-quarter mile time trial of 2:59.4. When he finished, he was hardly puffing. The message to Bannister seemed clear: *You have a fast finish, but will it matter if I'm too far ahead to be caught?* To reinforce this, three days later, Landy reeled off a 4:14.4 mile in a relative jog and after a brief rest sprinted three more laps in 2:59.5.

Bannister, on the other hand, avoided the cinder tracks where most of the athletes trained and instead jogged on the University Golf Club course, which was off-limits to the

A MEETING OF MILERS

The day of Bannister's arrival in Vancouver, Landy had been striding one more quarter-mile on the track when he spotted two familiar figures approaching. Recognizing Bannister's unmistakable gait and Chris Chataway's shock of red hair, Landy sprinted across the grass infield and met them halfway. Those lucky enough to witness this summit of the world's two premier milers couldn't help but notice how starkly they contrasted when standing face-to-face. Hawkishly alert, shorter by several inches, curly-haired, tanned, well-defined and wearing only a pair of white shorts, Landy looked as if he was just back from an afternoon at the beach. With his long hair and slight slouch, the ghostly pale Bannister in his English team sweater and slacks seemed more suited to the bookish confines of the university library. Each man smiled self-consciously.

They hadn't seen one another in person since 1952 when they had participated in at least one training session together at London's Motspur Park then ran in the same 1500m heat at the Helsinki Olympics. Days after the Olympics, they also ran together on a British Empire 4x1-mile relay team alongside two other 1954 BECG mile competitors, David Law and Bill Parnell. At the time they barely made an impression on one another, but once the chase after the elusive first four-minute mile commenced and their respective attempts made world headlines, neither had been far from the other's thoughts.

The *Sun's* columnist Dick Beddoes and photographer Brian Kent arrived just in time to record the first Landy-Bannister encounter in Vancouver for posterity. When interviewed nearly sixty years later and asked how they had greeted each other, neither of the milers could remember. However, Chataway, the human link between the two men, having raced in both their historic, barrier-breaking runs, eased the tension. As they made small talk about Landy's father travelling to Vancouver for the Games, the sunny weather—"smashing," they both thought—and Empire Stadium's cinder track, they avoided any talk of the one thing that really mattered at that moment—their impending mile showdown.

press, although he was risking beanings by golfers' wayward drives. The Australian press corps criticized him for supposedly hiding. "Where's Roger the Dodger?" a *Melbourne Herald* piece had demanded on July 30. Although Landy's training times and distances were a matter of public record dutifully reported in all the daily papers, Bannister's were all but impossible to locate in the ten days preceding the Mile. And Bannister wanted it that way in order to keep Landy guessing. He alone could draw true comparisons between Landy's training times and his own, a definite edge in choosing race tactics. In *The Four Minute Mile* he explained:

> I wanted Landy to remain quite confident until the last minute. As his times were faster than mine, he was automatically the favourite, and with his splendid public training performances, the odds on his winning increased daily. This did not disturb me—I do not regard being the favourite as an enviable position.

In truth, Bannister's final few training runs and races, although not as impressive as Landy's either in time or quantity, did prove he was in excellent condition. In the AAA championship Mile the previous month Bannister had run a comfortable first three-quarters before bursting all out for the line and running the last lap in a scorching 53.8 seconds. He was intentionally sending a message to Landy on his strategy for Vancouver: *you want to avoid a sprint finish with me. You don't have my kick.* In a CBC "Breakaway" interview in 1983 he recalled, "I wanted to persuade John Landy he needed to run a fast first three laps—if he wanted to win. That if he dawdled, then he wouldn't win."

It was the Balaclava Park training session caught on camera by Cunningham that produced Bannister's most "satisfying" work. By the end of that session, his race strategy—as well as that of Chataway's for the Three Miles—was undeniably decided. After running a number of 60-second quarter-mile repeats, before the final one, Bannister and Chataway discussed using it to simulate where they planned to engage their respective finishing kicks. In *The Four Minute Mile*, he wrote:

> [Chataway] suggested that I should lead for the first 220 yards in 31 seconds, and then he would sprint past me at exactly the place where he intended to take the lead in his own race. I said I would hang on and try to overtake him again at the beginning of the final straight. This was the point where I was hoping to wrest the lead from Landy. Chris overtook me as planned, and despite a hard day's training I found I had enough speed left to shoot past him before the finish. Our time for the last 220 yards was 25 seconds. It was a good speed, and I felt well prepared.

As Chataway possessed one of the fastest finishing bursts in the world, it was no wonder Bannister felt confident. His race strategy for the Mile against Landy was set. However, the apparent secrecy of his training runs was drawing the ire of a few contemporaries. "We thought they were snobs," said New Zealand's Bill Baillie, when interviewed in 2007 about Bannister and the other Oxbridge athletes. "Bannister would never come down to the track and jog around with the boys, ya know? They were a lot like a secret little clan of their own. We used to call them the toffee boys. You'd say, 'G'day' to them and they'd ignore you. They wouldn't officially recognize you until you were officially introduced to them." Baillie's teammate Murray Halberg agreed: "If you saw them in the Village, you'd say, 'Good God, I saw them!'" Most times Bannister did project an air of unconcerned calm, and some of the athletes from other countries chalked it up to a class rift in the English team between the stuffy "University Brigade" Oxbridge athletes and the more common working class "Club" runners. But in an interview in 2007 Chris Chataway insisted:

> We certainly did not have any feeling of social superiority. Both Roger and I had attended university on scholarships and came from very ordinary backgrounds. The way we geared ourselves for major races was, however, a solitary business. Our training was very light by the standards of today and even by the standards of some of our contemporaries. A hard race was very painful indeed. Gearing myself up for such an effort was a solitary, introspective affair and it was this, I think, that made me unsociable.

Bannister's solitary training methods were also seen by some as arrogance, but this is what it took to maintain his single-minded focus. This didn't stop rumours from flying about his training—or lack thereof—and it drove some of Landy's teammates to attempt reconnaissance to aid his cause. "I spied on them to try and get some clues on what they were doing," Geoff Warren recalled. "Rumours said he didn't train much. We didn't believe this. I snuck out and watched a couple of his sessions and found Roger actually trained quite hard."

✪

Village accommodations for the athletes at UBC were simple yet comfortable, and Marjorie Jackson-Nelson rated them "at least the equal of those in Helsinki" at the 1952 Olympics. Men were housed at Acadia Camp, the nucleus of which was a group of tar-paper-sheathed "huts" that had been built in 1937 by the federal government to train Depression-era youths as forestry workers. The huts had been taken over by the army during the war then sold to UBC for student use at war's end. The university, facing an enormous enrolment of veterans, had augmented the camp by barging in another 20 Department of National Defence huts. But there still weren't enough beds for all the BECG's male athletes due to a higher number attending than expected, so Gordon Shrum's Athletes Housing Committee also commandeered several campus buildings that had housed dogs used in scientific experiments and converted them for housing; the locals nicknamed them "the dog houses." Women athletes were accommodated at Mary Bollert Hall, built on the far side of the campus in 1950 for women students. Men and women athletes were provided with separate lounges, cafeterias and Village commandants—Major-General J.P. MacKenzie for the men and BC's first female Olympic medalist, Mary Frizzell Thomasson, for the women.

Despite a 10 p.m. curfew, whether they were staying in the men's or women's camps, the athletes' lives were pretty good. Free Coca-Cola and hot jazz records greeted athletes on arrival. There were five TV sets, a big deal then when even developed nations such as South Africa or New Zealand had little or no television. There was table hockey and ping-pong. Free massages, dental and medical services were offered as well as hairdressing for female athletes. A library was set up and movies played every night. A makeshift post office received over two hundred telegrams a day. Athletes had the use of lawn furniture, beach umbrellas, golf clubs, playing cards, dart boards and chess sets, all donated by Vancouver citizens. Newspapers from 23 countries as far away as Pakistan were flown in. The Dictaphone Corporation recorded athletes speaking and then sent these recordings home to their families. And the Village cafeterias served approximately 50,000 meals at a cost to the Society of $75,000 or three dollars a day per athlete.

Many of the 789 athletes, coaches and team officials who landed in Vancouver via plane, train, automobile and boat carrying luggage stickered from all corners of the Commonwealth also had remarkable stories stowed away. Some of these young men and women were already world beaters; others were barely the best in their own tiny villages. Some were well-to-do; others had scratched and clawed just to eat. Some had travelled the globe many times over; a handful had never before journeyed beyond the mountains guarding their corner of the world. Some had enjoyed all the modern

The arrival of the English team on July 24 attracted a crowd of over 3,500 to Vancouver International Airport.

As national teams arrived, daily flag-raising ceremonies took place at Empire Village on the UBC campus.

technological conveniences of a rapidly developing society; a few, such as the Kenyans in the midst of the Mau Mau conflict, had been fighting for basic freedoms and independence. Some still hunted their food with tribal spear, had never sat in a Chevy Bel Air or watched *I Love Lucy*, let alone seen a television set. A few tasted ice cream and saw a film projector for the first time in Vancouver. Some had far-off dreams, others were close to fulfilling them, and a few lived them as they spoke. Every single one had a unique story.

Seventeen-year-old broad jumper Sainiana Sorowale (pronounced Sigh-nee-anna Soro-wall-ee) was the first female athlete to leave her home island of Fiji for an athletic competition. Although she was the Fijian record holder for the broad jump, she had never been more than 150 miles away from the village where she grew up. The large Afro that she tended with a unique wooden comb made her a minor celebrity during the Games, and she was fascinated by the cars cruising Vancouver's streets and found them even more alluring when women were behind the wheel. Back home the few rustbucket antiques sputtering around on the dirt roads were driven exclusively by men. Television sets were nearly as enticing. None existed in her home village, 50 miles from Suva, the Fijian capital.

Male and female athletes were given separate accommodations at UBC. Here a flag raising ceremony takes place at the women's village at Mary Bollert Hall. Photo courtesy Vonna McDonald.

Dal Grauer or take a city tour to see Stanley Park and the Capilano Suspension Bridge. Others took part in the Brockton Point square dance festival, gained free admission to inter-city lacrosse games and Theatre Under the Stars performances of *Brigadoon* or took up the Royal Vancouver Yacht Club's offer of free boating and yachting. For many the highlight was a ride up Grouse Mountain's open-air chairlift. On one particularly memorable night ride New Zealand runner Lawrie King sang traditional Maori serenades as the twinkling lights of Vancouver's skyline glowed in the background. "In those eerily beautiful conditions it was a fascinating but overpowering sound," teammate Murray Halberg remembered.

A few athletes journeyed down to Peace Arch Provincial Park to hear American actor Paul Robeson sing classics from his many film roles including *Show Boat*. Blacklisted by the US government for his criticism of the treatment of black Americans and his sympathetic stance toward the Soviet Union, it was too risky for Robeson to cross the border, so Canadian concertgoers listened from the grass on the Canadian side while he sang from the back of a flatbed truck on the American side. Others took in the BECG curling bonspiel at the Pacific Curling Club. As the Games' official demonstration sport, it attracted over 3,500 spectators as Fred Tinling's Vancouver foursome out-swept stiff competition, including Matt Baldwin's Edmonton rink, the defending Brier champions. Dorothy Sawyer's Manitoba rink took the women's side. As a wind-up to all the events for athletes, a huge "Indian potlatch" was held at Brockton Oval featuring fireworks, traditional dancing by Pacific Coast peoples and a massive salmon barbeque.

Meanwhile, the BC Athletic Round Table Society, Eric Whitehead's newest project after leaving his daily writing job for the *Province*, offered a $20,000 Quiz, which required entrants who paid the one dollar entry fee to correctly predict the Games' final medal standings. First prize was a $15,000 North Vancouver dream home. Although no formal medal standings were kept by the BEG Federation, interested Vancouverites could consult medal tables in local newspapers or a massive scoreboard atop the Shell service station at Hastings and Renfrew. The Athletic Round Table had also provided all-expense-paid trips to the Games for young athletes from around BC. One from Trail who benefitted was 15-year-old Cesare Maniago, who later stopped pucks in the NHL for the Canadiens, North Stars and Canucks.

Of course, as with any event this large, there were hiccups. Vancouver businesses had looked forward to the financial windfall the Games could bring, but ultimately few saw any significant effect on their bottom line. Most hotels, restaurants, stores and taxi companies called the summer of 1954 the worst in memory for the tourist trade as people avoided the city in droves. They blamed the early BECG publicity that stated Vancouver would be booked solid for the summer. Fearing a lack of accommodation, many tourists seemed to have stayed away. This didn't stop businesses from buying BECG-themed advertisements in an attempt to snap up a piece of the pie. Newspaper ads that had nothing to do with the Games added the letters B.E.G. in every way possible, hoping to grab readers' attention. On the other hand, most Vancouver businesses refused to grant employees even a half day off to see Games events, fearing "efficiency" losses. And one employer told the *Province* paper on July 22 that, "First thing we know they will be asking leave to see any entertainment that comes along—such as *Brigadoon*." Stan Smith's response to the paper the next day was to decry the "deplorable situation. Surely a way could be found to enable the staff to get an afternoon off if there was any cooperation."

Crime rose in the city, beginning just days before the Games when vandals smashed a half-ton, 8ft plaster statue of a runner breasting the tape *a la* Percy Williams; it had been sculpted by a Vancouver Art School student, ready to be placed at Empire Stadium. Vancouver homes and businesses suffered a rash of burglaries while citizens were attending events, including 19 separate break-ins in one weekend alone. The most blatant occurred while Empire Village was a veritable ghost town during the Opening Ceremonies. Burglars broke into the camp commandant's office and carted off a 250lb safe containing athlete's passports, valuables and traveller's cheques worth more than $6,000. Police found the safe chopped open three blocks away; fortunately they were able to recover a portion of the stolen funds and the rest was covered by insurance.

Amid fears that a lack of parking would be a major problem, extraordinary measures were enacted to alleviate congestion. Still, some of the worst traffic jams ever seen in Vancouver ensued during BECG week, but none was bigger than that following the Opening Ceremonies. Spectators remained stuck in their cars for over 90 minutes after leaving the stadium, and police worked past midnight to clear the gridlock. Part of the problem lay with the fact spectators had difficulty finding their vehicles in the unlit parking lots.

❂

As the athletes arrived and filled Empire Village, word spread like wildfire among locals eager to pay a sightseeing visit. Where else could they find tall, dark Fijian athletes wearing silk blouses and sarongs eating at the same table as pale, crisp-blazered New Zealanders, a few strumming ukuleles to their hearts' content? Or gaze in wonder at the regal native *jinnah* and gold-embroidered magnificence of the *jutti* worn by Pakistani competitors between workouts on Varsity Stadium's grass? They might have seen female athletes from South Africa and Australia trading make-up tips and gossip and washing one another's hair, while the Aussies and Kiwis organized pick-up rugby and soccer scrimmages to entertain themselves, and athletes from Hong Kong and Gold Coast bantered and horse-played like long-lost brothers. Or if they wandered into one of the informal dance parties in the lounge that overflowed onto the lawns around the recreation hall, they might see Jamaican hurdler Keith Gardner jiving as a record player blared through open windows. For a few weeks that summer, Empire Village reigned as perhaps the most cosmopolitan and vibrant enclave in the Commonwealth. The spirit of the Games was exemplified around every corner and would live on in the hearts and memories of its youthful populace, who would leave these shores a little closer to brothers and sisters of a larger family.

On many days hundreds of cars lined up to enter the Village gates. The crowds became so massive the Society was forced to take precautionary security measures. They posted signs—"Home of BEG competitors, please respect their privacy"—and stationed two guards at the gates to limit entry. Neither had any effect. Hundreds of invited and uninvited guests milled through the lounges, recreation halls and dormitories at all hours of the day. Autograph hunting became the Games' unofficial pastime as packs circled athletes everywhere. Many competitors discarded

Athletes from several African nations enjoy a meal at Empire Village's cafeteria. Photo courtesy Vonna Mc-Donald.

their national warm-up suits and dressed as ordinary citizens in order to blend in. More people came out to watch the daily practice workouts at Varsity Stadium than attended city championship track meets. On July 25 an estimated 10,000 people visited Empire Village, while July 28 brought a record 20,000 visitors. One day English half-miler Brian Hewson saw a massive traffic jam at the Village gates, but it was actually a long string of Vancouverites lined up in their cars to tour foreign athletes around the city. Hewson picked a car with a pretty girl behind the wheel and over the ensuing days she drove him around several times. Organizers later estimated that volunteer drivers drove athletes more than 50,000 miles.

In the days leading up to the Games the importance of displaying Vancouver's "best side" while welcoming the world had become increasingly important. In the minds of the Society and city boosters—and communicated through the press—how the larger world perceived the city would be determined by the experience of the visiting foreign athletes and officials. On July 14 the *Vancouver Sun* had told its readers:

> Roll out the welcome mats and unfurl your flags and bunting—the sons of the Commonwealth with thousands of supporters and visitors are starting to arrive in Vancouver for the British Empire Games. Vancouver never had so splendid an opportunity to show brotherly hospitality... Our welcome must be wholehearted, unstinted and sincere... with both hands outstretched, brother to brother."

Sainiana Sorowale (left) was the first female athlete to leave her home island of Fiji to compete abroad. She became a minor celebrity in Vancouver. Photo courtesy of Vonna McDonald.

But while this had been easy enough to say or write, no one knew what the average Vancouverite would actually *do* because for many this would be their first glimpse of a black African man or woman. In addition, this overwhelmingly white Anglo-Saxon populace had a far-from-perfect history when it came to the treatment of its Asian and First Nations populations. This was the city of the *Komagata Maru* incident, the place where the head tax and the Chinese Exclusion Act had been felt most strongly, where memories remained fresh of the WWII internment of Canadians of Japanese descent at Hastings Park, just a stone's throw from Empire Stadium. And where just five years after the 1954 BECG, citizens of a North Vancouver neighbourhood would petition for the removal of the family of future Olympic sprinter Harry Jerome because their skin colour unsettled them.

But the citizens of Vancouver did welcome the foreign athletes into their homes for visits and meals with little urging from the Society. No doubt this was partly in response to a snide South African newspaper comment that was reported in the *Vancouver Sun* on June 8; it ridiculed Canadian claims of non-discrimination by saying, "I'll bet none of the Negro athletes will be invited to stay in a Canadian home."

Avoiding racial animosities was a concerning issue for Smith, who was quoted in the *News-Herald* of July 26 as saying, "All our visitors, no matter what their creed, colour or religion, will be treated alike." Newspapers reported that there would be no racial segregation in Empire Village, and Smith added, "In fact, we will encourage mixing of races." For the most part, Smith's declarations proved correct. Everyone did get along fine. Reports from the Village said that athletes from all nations were friendly and harmonious with only one exception: a coolness between white and black South African participants. South African swimming manager Alex Bulley provided a glimpse of that intolerance toward black athletes by white Afrikaaners through the lens of apartheid in a *News-Herald* interview on August 7: "They do not understand fully the responsibility of competition. They will not train. There may be some potential champions among them... but take them away from their element and you cannot properly control them." Other athletes reported that racial tension existed nowhere else in the Village. Sylvanus Williams, captain of the Nigerian team and later Nigerian sports minister, told the *Sun*, "Our relations were very amicable with everyone, even the South Africans." Even the Pakistani and Indian athletes—nations openly at war only six years earlier and who would be at war again within a decade—mingled happily and attended events together.

In fact, something new and significant was taking place as the crowds of athletes, officials, volunteers and spectators met and mixed. "The United Nations will have to go far to improve on the international goodwill seen everywhere in Empire Village," the *Sun* had reported as the first athletes began to arrive on July 19. "In the dining halls, lounges, recreation rooms and living quarters it is the same. New friends are being made, racial and national barriers are broken, and never-to-be-forgotten lessons in friendly international relations are being learned." On this point the 1954 Games would be measured an unqualified success, perhaps one of the earliest signs of Vancouver's future of pervading multiculturalism. The city's squabbles and disputes were still there, and more would come later, yet others sensed the confident cosmopolitan city growing up before their eyes.

✪

Sunday, August 1, also saw the arrival on BC soil of His Royal Highness Prince Philip, the Duke of Edinburgh—although not in Vancouver. This was his second extended visit to Canada but the first unaccompanied by Queen Elizabeth, and he attracted rabid crowds of swooning thousands everywhere he went. Countless newspaper columns were devoted to his comings and goings, everything from the colour of his ties to what he ate at meals. And even though not a single American athlete was participating in the Games, when it had been made public that Philip would attend, five American wire services had applied for press credentials. During Games week the one question on everyone's lips seemed to be: "Have you seen him yet?"

However, a few Society members still nursed lingering bitterness that he would only arrive in Vancouver halfway through the Games. The Society had long coveted Philip to officially open the Games, although a handful of other individuals had been considered, most notably Winston Churchill, who was halfway through his final term as UK prime minister. While attending the 1952 Olympics in Helsinki, Stan Smith had appealed to Churchill's well-known Empire-building sensibilities by asking for "a message which I can take back with me to Vancouver, conveying your good wishes for the success of this great Imperial project." A week later on August 15, 1952, a reply arrived from 10 Downing Street:

> I send my best wishes for the success of the British Empire Games which are to be held in Vancouver in 1954 and feel sure that they will provide yet another opportunity for cementing the links which bind together Her Majesty's subjects throughout the Commonwealth.

Stanley Smith presents a gift to Prince Philip during one of many Games receptions attended by His Royal Highness. Large swooning crowds followed his every move during his stay in Vancouver.

It was clear Churchill had other commitments that would prevent him from attending, but his reply so pleased Smith that the Games general chairman mailed a 5£ donation to assist the prime minister's appeal to rehabilitate Westminster Abbey.

The Society's efforts had then turned toward securing Prince Philip to open the Games. The monarchy had never attended the BECG in the past, but the one thing Smith and his Society cohorts had going for them were connections: Arthur Porritt and Sandy Duncan, BEG Federation president and honourary secretary respectively, were both on a first name basis with Philip. Porritt had served as the royal family's sergeant-surgeon—a fancy name for family doctor—and thus could speak one-on-one with Philip to obtain his verbal commitment. That at least was the idea until Ottawa in the form of Governor General Vincent Massey caught wind of Vancouver's quaint plan and bogged the Society's formal request down in protocol. The Society attempted to get around this through Mayor Hume, who attended Queen Elizabeth's coronation in early June 1953 and received unofficial confirmation from Philip himself at a garden party.

Remarkably, Buckingham Palace's first public confirmation that Philip would indeed attend the Games came by way of a *Vancouver Sun* cartoon. Len Norris, whose work ran daily for nearly forty years beginning in 1950, drew a cartoon when it was first announced the Duke may be coming to Vancouver.

Philip was so taken with Norris' work that he offered to purchase the original. Norris went one better and delivered the cartoon to Buckingham Palace in person as a gift. Philip's private secretary, Commander Michael Parker, was there to receive him, and

Norris cabled Parker's quote back home to Vancouver, which the *Sun* splashed on its front page on July 29, 1953: "The Duke of Edinburgh has told Governor General Vincent Massey about his visit to the British Empire Games in Vancouver and said he was greatly looking forward to being present."

The Society was happy with this until Philip's official itinerary was released, and it was learned that on the day of the Games' Opening Ceremonies, His Royal Highness would be in Chalk River, 120 miles north of Ottawa, visiting Canada's newest atomic energy development. Just two years removed from a serious nuclear meltdown, the facility needed the good press of a smiling Duke touring the atomic reactor in fine working order to quell any remaining fears about the new energy source. As a result of his new schedule, Philip would not actually attend any Games events until August 4, when they would be half over. The consolation prize was that he would be present to formally bring the Games to an end at the Closing Ceremonies—which was little solace to the Society. Smith took up his beef with Massey personally, but despite hollow promises that Philip's itinerary could change, it did not, leaving the Games out in the cold. Smith and company had then locked down Lord Alexander to open the Games, a wholly capable replacement.

It was only when *Vancouver Sun* cartoonist Len Norris presented his drawing in person at Buckingham Palace that organizers received public confirmation of Prince Philip's attendance at the Games. Cartoon courtesy of Steve Norris.

So perhaps it was not so surprising that when Philip's C-5 North Star touched down on the tarmac of Patricia Bay Airport in Victoria, there was only a crowd of somewhere between 500 and 1,500 persons looking on from behind a wire fence. As he descended the stairs acknowledging the crowd, no guns saluted him, few uniforms greeted him, and no band struck up a welcoming fanfare. After a day touring naval base HMCS *Naden* and Victoria's inner harbour aboard the minesweeper HMCS *Comox*, Philip paused for his only official Canadian tour portrait with BC Lieutenant-Governor Clarence Wallace at Government House. From there, he travelled overnight to Kemano and Kitimat on BC's rugged northern Pacific Coast to tour Alcan's massive $500 million (today equivalent to $3.3 billion) power plant and aluminum smelter, at the time the largest of its kind in the world.

Thus, although Prince Philip had arrived on the West Coast, for the next two days he was beyond the range of the BECG's radar.

CHAPTER 5
MONDAY, AUGUST 2, 1954

While Roger Bannister shrewdly trained in private out of the public eye, on Monday, August 2, the second full day of Games competition, John Landy was out in the open running at UBC's Varsity Stadium track, exactly where he'd been the day before and the day before that. With the possible exception of the marathoners, no one worked harder and longer. Ironically, the track was the one place where the suffocating crowds—equal parts press and public admirers—allowed him some peace.

When not on the track, he put himself out there, laughing and smiling, opening up to the hounding press, mingling with the crowds, rarely ever hiding, and as a result he was barely granted a moment's respite. Just getting from the Village to the track and back again, he ran the daily gauntlet of reporters, cameramen and incessant streams of autograph hunters. He rarely said no to Society officials who trotted him out for guest appearances to promote the Games. One day he presented the Seagram Trophy to Pat Fletcher for winning the PGA Tour's Canadian Open event at the Point Grey Golf and Country Club. Another day a crowd of several thousand came out to see him introduced at a warm-up meet in Aldergrove, and one evening the Helms Athletic Foundation presented him with the Los Angeles Coliseum Relays "Miracle Mile" Trophy for his world record run in Finland earlier in the spring. In quieter moments he might be found at Monty's restaurant at the south end of Richards Street, where he fell in love with their famous spare ribs. On many occasions he was accompanied by a Vancouver tennis player named Pamela Rose, reportedly a new love interest.

Despite the demands placed on him while he was trying to maintain some semblance of a training routine, in later years Landy remembered his Vancouver experience fondly. "I just ran on in the sunshine and took whatever came," he said matter-of-factly in a 2007 interview. "We didn't try to keep away from it, although the pressure did get a bit much at times."

As August 7, 1954, approached, widespread awareness of the Bannister-Landy showdown in the BECG Mile grew exponentially around the world, almost bordering on mania. Vancouver, at the epicentre of the fuss, had certainly never taken to any track and field event quite like this before. This was a town devoted to Canucks Western Hockey League games, senior men's lacrosse, Capilanos baseball, club soccer at Callister Park, senior men's basketball and regular boxing cards at the Forum. And with the birth of the Lions, football would soon emerge as a focus as well. But for the first time since the days of Percy Williams' 1928 double Olympic medal triumph, the Mile had thrust track into a totally new prominence.

If you had been in Vancouver that summer, it would have been impossible for you to have remained unaware. On crowded street corners, newspaper sellers argued over who would win. Countless bets were placed among the public. Mentioning "the Mile" in

Opposite: Australian swimmers Jon Henricks and Lorraine Crapp pose at Empire Pool. The two top swimmers in the Games won five gold medals between them. Photo courtesy of Jon Henricks.

John Landy relaxes in the sun with fellow athletes at Empire Village. Despite immense pressure, Landy rarely shied away from the attention, which earned him the public's admiration. Photo courtesy of Kaye Neale.

conversation, referring to it in print or speaking of it on the airwaves required no further explanation. Everyone knew of the only Mile that mattered, already frequently referred to as the "Miracle Mile" weeks before the race took place. News reporters hopped onto the sports beat. Political columnists suddenly had an opinion on race tactics. Even editorial cartoonists drew jokes about the Mile.

It seemed everyone suddenly had an opinion or wanted to talk about about it. And, indeed, the foremost question on many minds in late July and early August was who do you think will win? Or who are you pulling for?

Among the general public, most Canadians, particularly in BC, tended to lean toward Landy, the sentimental favourite. "Vancouver had really gone overboard for John Landy," recalled future BC Lieutenant-Governor Garde Gardom, who befriended him in 1954. "He was *extremely* personable, quiet, reserved and very low-key, a person that I'd say was *impossible* to dislike. He was admired. Bannister was aloof."

Vancouver was then—and still is—a town that loves backing the underdog and thirsts for a David to knock off Goliath. Thus, in a race with no clear favourite, Vancouverites' lingering Empire partialities dictated that Landy, the runner from one of the faraway colonies, was the underdog by default. In an unscientific polling among newsmen, it seemed that at least three-quarters also favoured Landy to win. "This time I run with the pack," said the *Sun*'s Dick Beddoes. "I go Landy." Big bandleader Dal Richards recalled that everyone in the 40-piece Arthur Delamont Band was pro-Landy because they felt he was the underdog. They could all readily identify with that status, having long shared a common footing with Australia in the Commonwealth, so while many thought Bannister might win, many more in Vancouver *wanted* Landy to win. They felt he deserved to.

JOHN LANDY, WELTERWEIGHT

When the stress became too intense, especially during the first few days before the initial media storm blew over, Landy tended to retreat to his room in the Village hut reserved for the Australian team, and his teammates sometimes switched the placard beside the door to read "Scotland" to throw the press off the scent. "Poor old John," recalled his teammate Geoff Warren, "he was under great pressure, and after a few days we noticed he was becoming a recluse. We said, 'Come on, John, we gotta go out somewhere,' but he fought us off. We finally convinced him to come along to a local family's neighbourhood party that some girls who gave us rides invited us to." The father of one of the girls asked each of the Australians about their events. When he seemed to recognize Landy from the papers, quick-witted Bryce "Macca" MacKay jumped in with "This here is Johnny Deckers. He's a boxer, our star welterweight." For a moment Landy hesitated, wondering what he should do. Finally he nodded in agreement. Laughing, Warren concluded the story with "Then seeing the unconvinced questioner, John threw a few shadow punches and did some boxing footwork. I could tell the father had suspicions but was too polite to question."

Beyond Bannister's understandably loyal English teammates, among the Games athletes Landy was also the overwhelming choice. "My money, emotionally, was behind John Landy," recalled Doug Clement, "and also when you look at the underlying tone of the Commonwealth Games of trying to beat the Mother Country. England was not a favourite from a social-political position, particularly for two of the colonies—Australia and Canada—that had a chance of actually beating them."

Few athletes ever found themselves under such bewildering public scrutiny—compared, analyzed, criticized and complimented. In *The Four Minute Mile*, Bannister recalled that "for some weeks before [the race], journalists had been comparing our chest measurements as if we were professional prize fighters and trying to find out what toothpaste we used." Arthur Daley of the *New York Times,* who previewed the Bannister-Landy match-up with an in-depth three-page article on August 1, noted "chances are that no single foot race has ever excited as much curiosity as this one. The prospect so titillates imaginations that it reaches far beyond the field of sports followers to embrace all newspaper readers."

❁

On Monday, August 2, just a stone's throw from the track where Landy trained each day, the second day of the six days of BECG swimming events began at Empire Pool. Paid attendance was lower than expected, although near-sellout crowds of over 6,000 on days four and five would make up for the poor showings on the first two days. And the final day broke the record for the largest swimming crowd in Canadian history.

Expectations were high for overall performance at pool events. Three world record holders in their prime—Australia's Jon Henricks and Lorraine Crapp and South Africa's Joan Harrison—were contestants in these Games and appeared poised to lead a rewriting of the BECG record books, aided by the new "fast" pool that competitors

Swimmers ready themselves for the start of a women's race at a packed Empire Pool. Crowds of around 6,000 spectators were common that week.

raved about. "It was better than anything we had seen," Henricks said in a 2009 interview. "That new pool in Vancouver with its signature diving platform was a joy." In fact, in the 13 swimming events only one BECG record survived the week: the men's 220yd breaststroke, a record that had stood since 1938. Perhaps it was no coincidence that it was the only men's event in which Australia failed to medal. The tanned, eight-member contingent from Down Under left behind more watery footprints on the basic, painted plywood victory podium than any other, power-stroking to 11 medals, including six gold. The Australians put on one of the most powerful team performances in any sport in these Games, and at the pool it became a running joke that with "Advance Australia Fair" playing almost daily during medal ceremonies, the tune should reach number one on local Top 40 charts by week's end. After it was all over, G.E. Mortimer of the *Victoria Daily Colonist* wrote:

> When you see a person with a haunted look in his eyes, whistling a strange tune, you know he has been to the Empire Games, poor fellow. The tune is the Australian victory song, "Advance Australia Fair"... a stirring piece of music, but when it comes at you many times in succession, as though from a jukebox that has sprung a cog, well, the tune loses its freshness.

Australia's medal haul was led by Henricks who, beginning with the first heat of the men's 110yd freestyle trials on Saturday, July 31, had toyed with his competition. Ripping through in 56.9 seconds—an eye-popping three full seconds faster than the existing BECG record—he was nearly out of the pool and dry before his closest competition caught up more than two seconds later. Clearly, he had recovered from a freak ankle injury sustained two weeks earlier when he had hurdled a concrete road barrier. Vancouver, his first international competition, ultimately became the coming-out party of this generation's fastest freestyler.

By swimming standards, Henricks, who hailed from Sydney, was a late-bloomer. At age 10 he had won a Cub Scout race, and because he hadn't done anything else of note athletically, he "had decided that was the sport for me." Sensing their son had talent, his parents built him a small training pool in their backyard. By 1952 he had emerged on the national radar as a middle and long distance specialist, but an ear infection forced him to miss that year's Olympics and led to his conversion to shorter distances. This suited his coaches—Harry Gallagher, who also guided the legendary swimmer Dawn Fraser, and Frank Cotton, professor of physiology at Sydney University—just fine. Cotton, who was known as the man who took Australian swimming into the science laboratory, had been experimenting on Hendricks to see how his body organs reacted to a variety of athletic stresses, and as a result of his tests, he and Gallagher agreed Henricks was better equipped for the sprints. Switching disciplines at age 17 with any chance for success at the international level is rare, but Gallagher and Cotton designed a revolutionary training regimen, and Henricks shocked the swimming world by breaking the Olympic 100m freestyle record at the 1953 Australian championships and followed that a year later by breaking the 110yd freestyle world record. (In 1955 he took down the 100m freestyle world record as well and would own the fastest time over both the imperial or metric short sprint distances for the next five years, an eternity in

Jon Henricks signs an autograph for a young fan. Between 1952 and 1957, the undisputed fastest man in water compiled an undefeated streak of over 100 sprint wins.

rules at that time, individual world records couldn't be set in a relay, but based purely on speed, there can be no denying it must rank as one of the greatest swims to ever occur in British Columbia.

Leaving Vancouver with more BECG gold medals and records than any other swimmer, Henricks' star was clearly rising fast. His peak arrived in 1956 at the Melbourne Olympics where he won the 100m freestyle and led the Aussies to gold in the 4x200m freestyle relay, both in world record times. Between 1952 and 1957 the undisputed fastest man in water compiled an undefeated streak of over 100 sprint wins. But although he loved the sport and trained obscenely hard to get to the top, Henricks wasn't blind to the ridiculousness of the commitment needed and occasionally poked fun at his own dedication. Once when asked about the secret to his success, Henricks replied:

> You see that goddamn pool there—well, if you want to get to the top of it, dive in and start swimming. You do that for three, four or five years, and every time you stop swimming your coach bawls you out... You get a crazy ear disease from these tropical waters, but you've still got to keep on swimming. You get your head shaved to make you look like a zombie so that you will cut down water resistance, and you shave your legs for the same reason. You get invitations to a party and you write back regretting you are unable to attend owing to a prior engagement. That's a lie, of course, the only

prior engagement is at the pool, going up and down, up and down, then up and down again. You finish going up and down and it's time to do some weightlifting—or maybe go to sleep while your coach goes out playing golf or fishing.

In the women's swimming competitions, a playful exuberance charged the atmosphere at the pool all week, reflecting the youth of many of the female competitors. They included both the Games' youngest competitor—Canada's Sara "Giggles" Barber, aged 13, from Brantford, Ontario—and the Games' youngest medalist—South Africa's Natalie "Toy" Myburgh, aged 14. Both appeared mere babes in arms compared to the "old maids" of the pool like Australia's Lorraine Crapp at 15, Canada's Virginia Grant at 16, and South Africa's Joan Harrison at an ancient 18. It was the three "older" women, however, who combined for arguably the best race seen in Vancouver—the final of the women's 110yd freestyle on Monday, August 2.

Making her international debut, Crapp, who was from Sydney, Australia, was already a world record holder three times over in the 440yd, 880yd and 400m freestyle events. She was not yet at

The top two finishers in the women's 110yd freestyle, Australia's Lorraine Crapp (right) and Canada's Virginia Grant (left), were actually among the "older" women's swimmers competing at ages 15 and 16 respectively.

her full potential, yet her resume was the envy of most everyone in the swimming world. "Ginny" Grant from Toronto was also making her international debut. As a young girl, she had learned to swim as a safety precaution after her parents bought a boat. At 10 she began swimming competitively with the Toronto Dolphinets and by 1954 held four Canadian records. Nicknamed "Crazy Legs" because of the two 42in propellers thrusting her forward, Grant, who was an even six feet in height, may have been the competition's tallest female swimmer. Modest Joan Harrison of South Africa came to Vancouver as world record-holder in the 110yd backstroke. By age 12, just two years after her first competitive race, she was already breaking national records. At the 1950 BEG she won the 440yd freestyle, beating the existing record by 13 seconds and the rest of the field by seven. Two years later in Helsinki, she won Olympic gold in the 100m backstroke by a hundredth of a second over Dutch pre-race favourite Geertje Wielema, the world's fastest backstroker at the time. The massive upset so surprised South Africa's swimming manager that he fainted on the pool deck when her victory was announced.

THE GREAT STEAK DEBATE

Two weeks before the Games began many of the participating teams had already moved into the Empire Village at UBC, and within a week the first complaint was heard. The trouble started on July 23 when newspapers in Sydney, Australia, reported that Aussie athletes weren't getting enough meat at Village meals. To avert the supposed shortage, concerned Australian businessmen rushed 50lbs of Aussie beefsteak to Vancouver. When Vancouver papers caught wind of it, they had a field day, and Aussie team officials scrambled to save face after appearing ungrateful for Canadian hospitality. They even agreed to share their steak with all Games competitors. And that appeared to turn down the heat on the Great Steak Debate.

However, three days later when coach Percy Norman's Canadian team members began to underperform in their training sessions, Norman latched onto the first explanation readily at hand. As they were dropping weight like a bad habit, some as much as ten pounds in the past couple of weeks, he blamed a lack of steak at breakfast and pulled all the Canadian swimmers out of the Village cafeteria. His swimmers, on the other hand, must have wondered if it was due to the stress of the near-daily swim-offs he had instituted for positions on the team. For the next few days both the *Sun* and *Province* stirred the pot in front-page stories, turning up the information from Mrs. Eileen Bacon, the head of meal preparation for the Village, that steaks had been available at the Village cafeteria all along for any athlete who wanted one at any time of day—for an extra fifty cents each. Coach Norman had just failed to submit his steak request to the Village kitchen staff. The irony of the entire situation was that by day Norman worked as a meat salesman for Jack Diamond's Pacific Meat Company. From a nutritional standpoint, Norman's calls for steak amounted to a whole lot of baloney even by the unsophisticated sports nutrition wisdom of the day. Under a delicious headline of "Bacon Meets Beef About Breakfast Food," that delightfully named lady was quoted as saying that breakfast steaks for athletes were just "a psychological item... They get the equivalent in proteins in their present food." As quickly as the furor had been fired up, it came to a sudden end. Norman's swimmers returned to the Village cafeteria and received steak for breakfast, the extra cost picked up by the Canadian Amateur Swimming Association. Yet even with all the steak in the world, Canada's swimmers weren't a major factor in Vancouver. In total, they grabbed four medals—all silver—Canada's poorest swimming performance ever in a Commonwealth Games.

The three heats for the women's 110yd freestyle held on Saturday, July 31, had winnowed the field to six finalists who all swam under the previous BECG record set only four years earlier, so anticipation was high when the starter's gun went off for the 110yd freestyle final two days later. At the blast, all six women uncoiled like springs, stretching for open water, and began slicing the surface with dolphin ease. Grant took the lead early and held it through to the wall. The only competitor using the Olympic turn, she whirled for home. Harrison and Crapp followed close behind, their economical strokes bearing down on a clearly tiring Grant. The Canadian crowd did their best to prod Grant on, but Crapp passed her with 20 feet remaining and touched the wall in a BECG record 1:05.8, half a second ahead of Grant. Harrison finished another two seconds back in third. Afterwards,

Crapp and Grant hugged and stood arm-in-arm in the water, smiling widely for the cameras. Officials then ushered Crapp to a recorder where she taped a message to be broadcast back home in Australia. "Hello Mummy and Daddy," she exclaimed excitedly. "Mr. Guthrie, I did what you said," referring to the fact she swam all-out for the entire race as her coach had instructed. But shortly afterwards as she stood on the medal podium, the enormity of her first individual international championship hit her. Tears streamed down her cheeks as she gazed proudly towards the Australian flag. The moment struck a nerve with all who witnessed it, even hardened pessimists like the *Sun*'s Dick Beddoes who wrote on August 3:

Lorraine Crapp stands atop the podium in gold medal position for the 440yd freestyle. Canada's Gladys Priestley (left) and Scotland's Margaret Girvan (right) took silver and bronze respectively.

> Considerable cannonball material and cheap sentimentality has been dredged up about the majesty of the BEG, but none of it erased cynicism as easily as Lorraine Crapp, a 15-year-old Sydney schoolgirl. Winner of the women's 110-yard free style swim yesterday, she stood on the victory podium in delightful simplicity, a young girl whose face had caught the sunrise. There was a trickle down each cheek as the band honoured her... The best things in life may not be free, but watching and sharing a heady moment with an unaffected youngster, you knew you could obtain some of them wholesale.

Crapp left Vancouver at the end of the week with three BECG medals—two individual golds (the second was for the 440yd freestyle on Friday, August 6) and a bronze for the 330yd medley relay on Tuesday, August 3. Of all the athletes in any sport to compete at the 1954 BECG, she may have had the most impressive post-Games resume. Two short years later on the eve of the Melbourne Olympics, *Sports Illustrated* singled her out as potentially the outstanding athlete of the Games, a woman who could have medaled in the 400m freestyle in the US *men's* championships and the only swimmer who struck fear into legendary Dawn Fraser. Ultimately, Crapp took away two golds and a silver from Melbourne and became such a sensation Aussie teenagers began mimicking her haircut, a close-cropped bob called the "Crapp cut." Over her career she would own or share 23 world records, which for a swimmer must be approaching the world record for world records.

Along with Gladys Priestley, Grant became Canada's most decorated swimmer at the 1954 Games, both winning an individual silver medal—Priestley in the 440yd freestyle—to match the silvers they won in the 4x110yd freestyle relay on the first day of the Games. In two years' time, Grant scored Canada's first-ever top-five individual women's swimming result at an Olympic Games. She retired from swimming in 1958 and worked for thirty years as an interior decorator in Toronto before opening a restaurant in Orangeville in 1998.

Of all the swimmers—male and female—at the Vancouver Games, Joan Harrison of South Africa was the busiest, competing in six races including heats. She also ended up as the Games' most decorated aquatic athlete—cruising to golds in the 110yd backstroke and 4x110yd freestyle relay, both in BECG record times, a silver in the 3x110yd medley relay and the aforesaid 110yd freestyle bronze. She retired from competitive swimming after Vancouver and soon married prominent Border rugby captain Charles Breetzke. She retained a graceful modesty throughout her life when it came to her swimming career; in 2002 David Denison, *East London Dispatch* sports editor, wrote that: "coaxing Joan Breetzke to talk about the teenaged Joan Harrison... requires a probing scalpel to unearth the jewels hidden behind demure fawn-like diffidence." She still lives close to the Quanza pool where she began training, but it now bears her name in honour of her remarkable swimming career.

With a few exceptions, Canada's swimmers at the Games were clearly overmatched, although Percy Norman, who had been appointed team coach, continually implored the press and public to have patience and not count his boys and girls out. However, there were a few bright spots for the Canadian team, among them the seven swimmers who had come from the tiny, isolated company town of Ocean Falls on Cousins Inlet on BC's central coast. Lenore Fisher, Allen and Ron Gilchrist, Allan Brew and Jim Portelance swam for Canada, while Derek Laverty competed for Northern Ireland, and John Phillips was the lone representative from British Guiana. All had been trained by George Gate, coach for the Ocean Falls Amateur Swimming Club and an assistant coach at the Games, who is the only swimming coach in Commonwealth Games history to coach athletes representing three different nations in the same Games. (This may also be a first for any Commonwealth sport, perhaps any international games, period.) Beginning in 1950, using Ocean Falls' 20-yard indoor pool, he elevated the club into perhaps the strongest in Canada. Between 1948 and 1974 his swimmers accounted for 26 percent of all male placements on Canadian international swim teams and won 35 pecent of all Canadian Olympic, Commonwealth, and Pan American swimming medals; during this period Ocean Falls swimmers won 59 international medals versus 112 for swimmers from the rest of the country.

Another of the Canadian team's bright spots was 15-year-old Helen Stewart of Vancouver, who survived the nerve-wracking daily swim-offs that Percy Norman introduced to force team members to earn their spots on Canada's 4x110yd freestyle relay team, a team that captured silver in the final held on the first day of the Games. In a 2007 interview Stewart recalled that those daily battles against her teammates were more distressing than competing in the Games, but they did serve as a critical stepping stone to the international level. Within two years, under the guidance of coach Howard Firby, she emerged as one of the best female freestylers on the planet. In the 100m freestyle

Opposite: After surviving gruelling daily swim-offs with teammates, Helen Stewart helped the Canadian 4x110yd freestyle relay team to win silver.

at the 1955 Pan American Games in Mexico she won Canada's first-ever Pan Am gold medal, defeating all the top American swimmers in the process, and then added two silver medals in the medley and freestyle relays. A year later she swam at the Olympics in Melbourne and shortly after that broke the 100yd freestyle world record in a special time trial at Vancouver's Crystal Pool. Her time of 57.6 seconds shaved half a second off the world best time that had stood for over two years. In 1958 Stewart married multi-sports star Ted Hunt to form one of British Columbia sports' all-time power couples. After retiring from swimming, she took up volleyball and represented Canada at the Pan Am Games in 1967 and 1971 in her second sport. She followed that with a career in teaching in Vancouver.

❁

On Monday, August 2, the second of the three nights of the BECG wrestling competition enthralled a crowd of nearly 1,400 at the Kerrisdale Arena. Wrestling in 1954 only vaguely resembled the amateur variety seen today at major events such as the Olympics. Strapping wrestlers—there were no women's events—stretched, snapped and swung one another around a massive cushion-topped pyramid-like platform. The only boundaries were the platform's steep edges. Abrasive horsehair mats left brutal rug burns on competitors, who wore primitive clothing and footwear. Stretchless singlets soaked up all perspiration and rapidly became damp and heavy. Their boots—usually leather, sometimes stiff canvas—had flat rubber soles and little tread. Protective headgear was rarely worn, although in training some wrestlers wore vintage leather aviation helmets to protect against cauliflower ears.

On this night South Africa's national anthem, "Die Stem v Suid Afrika" (The Voice of South Africa), was played several times during medal ceremonies for different weight classes, and by the end of the wrestling competitions on Wednesday, spectators could have whistled the tune flawlessly. Although only six South African wrestlers competed in Vancouver, all six claimed gold medals at their respective weights: Louis Baise (flyweight), Abraham Geldenhuys (featherweight), Godfrey "Blondie" Pienaar (lightweight), Nicolas Loubscher (welterweight), Hermanus Van Zyl (middleweight) and Jacob Theron (light heavyweight). To this day, the performance of the Springbok wrestling team in 1954, winning six out of the possible eight weight classes, merits serious consideration as the most dominant by any nation contesting any Commonwealth sport—ever. Much of the credit for the extra snap in the Springbok clinch goes to coach Andy Dell, who had seen four of his own Liesbeek Park Club wrestlers accepted for the national squad.

South Africa's gold medal in the lightweight category (67kg or 147½lbs) came at the expense of the most accomplished wrestler ever seen in the Commonwealth. When Australia's Dick Garrard left his fleet of Melbourne taxis behind and waltzed into Vancouver, he stood as the greatest wrestler Australia had produced (a designation that stands to this day) and the first athlete to participate in four BECGs. The average man simply isn't wrestling in his mid-forties and certainly not internationally against chiselled human torture racks half his age. But Garrard wasn't your average man. Over a period of 25 years he had survived 525 career mat battles and could count his losses on two hands with a thumb back in change. In that time he had never lost a match at home in Australia, and by the time he arrived in Vancouver, he had won three BECG lightweight gold medals—in 1934, 1938 and 1950—to go along with a 1948 Olympic silver medal. In Vancouver, the 43-year-old planned to add to his unprecedented medal haul.

Garrard's opening match went according to plan with an easy unanimous decision over Scotland's George McKenzie; at one point, Garrard tossed McKenzie off the wrestling platform and into the laps of spectators in the first row, grazing a surprised Pakistani judge. Next, Garrard faced the young Canadian Ruby Leibovitch, who had been barely a year old and confined to diapers when Garrard earned his first BECG gold medal. As Garrard stared down Leibovitch, the wild gleam in the older man's eye, the schoolboy curls that added inches to his height, his thick sinewy arms, and the woolly sweater of chest hair his singlet couldn't contain all contributed to his uniquely intimidating appearance. But for some reason none of this affected Leibovitch as it had so many others before him, and as a result, by the time they headed into the final round, their match stood even with Leibovitch anticipating the now-tired Garrard's uncharacteristically sluggish offensive forays. Still, most of the spectators conceded Garrard had been the aggressor, but the judges awarded Leibovitch a shocking split decision victory. The Australians immediately filed an angry protest, but the jury of appeal dismissed it without explanation. And just like that, Garrard's two-decade run of near-invincibility had vanished into the ether like steam off his perspiring forehead.

Australian wrestler Dick Garrard (right) shows his disappointment after losing just his second match in 20 years to South Africa's Godrey Pienaar (left).

Cruelly, Garrard's second match of the evening ended with a similar result. South Africa's Pienaar had already clinched the lightweight gold medal, but that didn't stop him taking a split decision off Garrard, who suddenly had suffered two defeats in mere hours where there had been none for two decades. Garrard's chin dropped to his chest in dejection as the decision was announced. If any consolation existed for this grand old man of grapple, he still won the bronze. To this day Garrard remains the most decorated wrestler in Commonwealth Games history. After retiring from international competition at age 46, he became an international judge and referee. He also served as chairman of the Olympic Wrestling Technical Committee, taking part in every Olympics (except for the 1980 boycott) in some capacity until 2000, and attended every Commonwealth Games as a wrestling official until 1998. Garrard's seventy-year association with the sport was recognized numerous times, most notably with the Order of the British Empire in 1976.

Perhaps the most interesting wrestling match-up of the Games occurred on the last evening of the sport, Wednesday, August 4. It involved the only two wrestlers contesting the heavyweight division: Canada's Keith Maltman, a 35-year-old "rookie" at the international level, and England's Ken Richmond, an experienced journeyman grappler, who had captured Olympic bronze in 1952.

Maltman, born in Berry Mills, New Brunswick, in 1918, had grown up on a modest farm on the fertile rolling grasslands of Minitonas, Manitoba, 320km northwest of Brandon. His family had struggled to put food on the table at the best of times, but when the Depression hit, they were only holding the farm together with little more than sweat and hope. So, at 13, Maltman quit school and set off to find work to earn money for his family. For the next decade, he lived a vagabond existence, sometimes living in bush cabins, chopping and delivering wood, trapping wild game, anything for

Canada's Keith Maltman (dark trunks) grapples with England's Ken Richmond (white singlet) in the heavyweight wrestling final.

food or a little money. Other times he rode the rails back and forth across the Prairies pursuing farm jobs—stooking, haying, doing handyman work. It was a tough, threadbare existence, yet also liberating as he learned what it took to make it on his own. In an interview in 2007 his daughter, Margaret Vallance, said that he had once told her he had learned that "Life is a chess game. Just like wrestling—you have to out-manoeuvre, you have to outwit, you have to out-strength, you have to out-calculate, you have to *out-do*."

WWII opened new doors of opportunity for Maltman. In 1941 he enlisted in the RCAF as an aircraft engine fitter and was stationed at Toronto's Manning Depot, and it was in the barracks there that he learned the basics of wrestling. He proved to be a natural and soon won the Manning Depot championship. Wrestling was in his blood for good after that, but in 1942 he was sent to Britain to work at a Rolls Royce plant near the City of York installing punchy Merlin engines into Allied aircraft. While riding out the day-to-day uncertainty that came with working in a facility strategically targeted by the Luftwaffe, he met a young English girl named Freda; their courtship bloomed quickly and they married in 1944. When the war ended a year later, Corporal Maltman was free to go home, and as part of his discharge he was given the choice of a piece of land or a paid university degree back in Canada. He chose education. After completing his high school diploma in Winnipeg, he was joined by Freda and their infant daughter, Margaret, and the three of them came west in a rickety flatbed Chevy truck loaded with all their worldly possessions. At UBC, Maltman studied physical education, but he also took up wrestling more seriously and became an unstoppable force. Improbably for someone entering his thirties, beginning in 1948 he won the UBC heavyweight championship four years in a row. In an intramural match he pinned Herb Capozzi, the best athlete on campus, with a reverse flip. (This is the same Capozzi who was later offered an NFL contract with the New York Giants, played in the CFL, and served as BC Lions general manager for a decade.) Not long after, Maltman defeated Canadian heavyweight champion Albert Ovenden to take the unofficial Canadian title.

After graduating from UBC, Maltman settled his family in Quesnel where he took a job as the Pro-Rec supervisor for the Northern BC Department of Education. But once work and family obligations were settled, he decided if he ever wanted to see how far his wrestling could go, this was the time. He was now 35 years old. Although he had a solid physical base to start from, an athlete *beginning* an extended period of elite performance at that age would today be considered an anomaly. In 1954 it was unheard of. He began a rigorous training regimen, lifting weights and running up and down local mountains with a training partner on his back. His children grew accustomed to hearing muffled clangs of iron filtering up through basement vents as their father pushed himself through yet another midnight workout after a long day at the office. Although he fought as a heavyweight his entire career, based on body size he was actually a middleweight wrestling up a weight class or two, but by working harder than others and using his wits, he overcame competitors who held natural size and strength advantages over him. "It was a psychological underdog thing," said his daughter Margaret. "It was easier for him to settle for second as a heavyweight than first as a 'secondweight.'" His commitment to training made an impression on everyone who saw him work. One day he told Margaret something that stayed with her: "When you see the rope, you don't slow down—you run through it."

Kerrisdale Arena played host to the BECG wrestling competition, with matches atop a unique pyramid-like platform. Photo by Brian Kent.

Constantly striving to overcome his humble beginnings, Maltman became a tough-as-rawhide product of his past. Paul Nemeth, head of the BC Amateur Wrestling Association and a key organizer for the 1954 BECG wrestling events, remembered that Maltman's fierce tactics weren't for the faint of heart. In a BC Sports Hall of Fame interview recorded in 1990, Nemeth recalled: "He used to soften up his opponent by pulling their head in, getting the fellow's forehead into his cheekbones, and just holding it in there. He was so strong they couldn't get loose." Typical was the time he faced a bigger, younger Ontario wrestler who thought beating an old guy would be a breeze. "Maltman got hold of this fellow and worked him over so badly," remembered Nemeth, "that the Ontario fellow was so upset and frustrated, he sat down at the edge of the mat and started crying, tears running down his face and his forehead scraped raw."

Yet few knew any of this when they saw Maltman in 1954. When he entered himself in the provincial wrestling tournament that year, to others he seemed to be throwing his weather-beaten hat into the ring at least a decade too late. But he simply went out and defeated all comers to take the provincial crown. Then he pulled the same trick in Montreal at the national tournament to earn a spot on the Canadian BECG team. However, a minor last-minute controversy threw into doubt the participation of all the Canadian wrestlers who had earned BECG team spots. Three days before the opening night of the BECG competition, Canadian wrestling officials forced each of the "champions" from the Montreal trials to contest a best-of-three "wrestle-off" with an alternate chosen by the officials; the winners would officially represent Canada at the Games. Nemeth considered it strange to choose a Games team so near the actual competition and expressed his concern publicly in local papers. "How can they turn around now and hold another trial?" he demanded. "We have voiced a protest so this won't happen in the future because we don't think the wrestlers should have to go through so much tension just before the Games." Fortunately, Maltman avoided defeat and injury while winning his wrestle-off. Only one alternate in the eight "wrestle-offs" actually scored an upset to grab a team spot, but the unusual timing and extra stress likely played a role in determining Canada's disappointing wrestling medal tally at the Games. Although this country had dominated the sport in four previous Games, in 1954 Canadians failed to win a single wrestling gold medal.

Facing Maltman on the mat on Wednesday, August 4, was Ken Richmond, who had one of the most peculiar backgrounds away from sport of any athlete competing in Vancouver. Richmond had grown up near London's Pinewood Studios, the heart of the J. Arthur Rank filmmaking empire, and hanging around the studio lot had led to small roles in the films *Henry V* (1944) and *Blithe Spirit* (1945), as well as numerous appearances as a nameless Roman soldier in biblical epics. In the late 1940s Richmond discovered wrestling, and every year from 1949 to 1954 he won the British heavyweight wrestling championship, while on the international stage he grabbed bronze medals in the heavyweight division of the 1950 BEG and 1952 Olympics. Yet, surprisingly for a rippling grappler of tremendous size and strength—6ft 2in, 265lb—Richmond abhorred violence, and the only time he used his bulging strength outside the wrestling arena was when a burglar broke into his house and he clamped a sleeper hold on him until police arrived. During World War II he had registered as a conscientious objector, which caused British authorities to jail him for several months. After the war, work was hard to come by in war-torn London, so Richmond paid the bills by washing windows and took a nine-month turn as a deck hand on an Antarctic whaling ship.

He returned to acting for J. Arthur Rank in the 1950s, appearing as the wrestler "Nikolas of Athens" in Jules Dassin's noir classic *Night and the City* (1950) as well as a small part in *Mad About Men* (1954). But in 1955 he won the role that until the 1990s made him perhaps the most recognized though unknown British athlete in the world. If you have seen any J. Arthur Rank film made after 1955, you have seen Richmond without even realizing it because that was when he became the iconic strongman who strikes the massive, reverberating gong at the beginning of the Rank films. He was paid a one-time fee of £100 for the role as the golden gongmaster. To the end of his life he kept silent about one of the great examples of movie-making deception: that enormous bronze gong was actually made of a combination of paper mache and plaster. He only mimed striking it. The audio of a Chinese tam tam was then dubbed over Richmond's gong footage to complete a spectacular piece of cinema illusion.

These two men—Maltman and Richmond—were poised to lock up on Wednesday, August 4, the final night of BECG wrestling, and observers naturally favoured Richmond, the established international competitor. On the other hand, Maltman, who had dozens of friends and family members in the stands, was the crowd favourite. From the beginning, their match proved a tight one. Richmond used his size and experience to manoeuvre the Canadian to the brink of prone positions, while Maltman relied on swift bursts of action and the guts of a burglar to stall the Englishman's advances. Maltman's strength occasionally provided a momentary position of power, teasing the unthinkable pin, but each time Richmond would muscle his way to safety with a spine-twisting lunge of his own. As the seconds ticked off and the final bell grew near, the crowd's appreciation of the Englishman's technical proficiency and the Canadian's sheer determination not to go down quietly grew from polite applause to ear-splitting howls. In the end, when the full 15 minutes had elapsed and both men were still standing, all agreed it a fitting conclusion: neither man deserved an early exit. With smiles of respect on their faces, the two warriors acknowledged one another and stood shoulder-to-shoulder waiting for the judges' decision, their palms locked in a grip one expected of childhood friends. Ultimately Richmond's arm was raised for the win, but Maltman's eyes betrayed no remorse: he'd left it all out there and couldn't possibly feel ashamed. "He gave me the toughest bout I've had," he told the *Vancouver Sun*.

Wrestler Fred Flannery of Australia had only one working eye, a distinct disadvantage when fending off the cobra-like reflexes of the wiry men staring him down. However, he discovered that his glass eye could provide odd psychological aid. In his match against Canadian Dave Clutchey, the two grapplers were tangled in a pretzled deadlock when Flannery's glass eye popped out and fell to the mat. Seeing the fugitive pupil rolling about unnerved the Canadian, who was quickly defeated. Flannery won a silver medal in the flyweight category.

The referee declares England's Ken Richmond (centre) the winner over Canada's Keith Maltman (left) in a spirited heavyweight wrestling final.

Richmond returned the compliment: "I really worked to take him."

They parted after that, their confrontation acting like a tiny knot that had very briefly bound two extraordinary life strands together. There were more extraordinary events for each in the future too. Richmond finished a respectable fourth at the 1956 Olympics, and later with wife Valentina, whom he met on a Rank movie set in the 1960s, he served on a religious mission to Malta; as the years passed he became more devout and took the gospel of Jehovah door-to-door. He also discovered a love for in-line skating and windsurfing, actually winning a windsurfing competition at the unlikely age of 67.

In a province that has produced some of the nation's best amateur wrestlers in recent decades, Keith Maltman remains an unsung forerunner to those who have followed in his footsteps. After Vancouver he continued wrestling competitively, winning a silver medal at the 1959 Pan American Games in Chicago and reigning as BC heavyweight champion from 1954 to 1964. He retired from wrestling at age 46 after finishing fourth at the 1964 national championships. He then worked as a regional recreation organizer in various parts of BC, including eight years as provincial coordinator of sport and physical fitness. He loved all sports but maintained a special connection to his beloved wrestling long after he'd left the world of crippling crossfaces and pinpoint pinfalls behind. That became especially clear a year before his death in 2005 when he was recovering from heart surgery in Kelowna General Hospital. He had survived a risky procedure that involved stopping his heart and starting it up again, but when he didn't wake up, the doctors feared he might have slipped into an irreversible coma, and they tried different techniques to coax him back to consciousness. When nothing worked, Maltman's youngest son, Tom, pushed past nurses in the room, bent down to his father's ear, and yelled as loudly as his lungs allowed: "Dad! You're on the mat! You're up! It's your turn! You're on the mat!" Suddenly Maltman's eyes opened and he woke up. When nothing else could, faint memories of pre-match tension that had been buried for decades snapped the old wrestler back to life. As it always had, wrestling still gripped his heart as tightly as the strongest half nelson.

CHAPTER 6
TUESDAY, AUGUST 3, 1954

Jim Peters had always been a worrier. Whether it was a drafty plane ride to the 1952 Olympics or a restless sleep the night before the Boston Marathon, leading up to a big race he inevitably found something to trouble him. So it was natural that in the days preceding the BECG marathon his anxiety spiked. He had legitimate concerns about the course's hills, the summer heat, the start time at the hottest part of the day, his damaged heel and the recent strong form demonstrated by his training partner, Stan Cox. Then there was the European marathon in Berne only three weeks into the future and that ominous premonition that had come to him in the Hainault Forest. But foremost was his anxiety about staying ahead of Cox. Nearly every entry in Peters' training journal after his arrival in Vancouver included some mention of his friend's progress. Sometimes he noted Cox's times and distances; other times he gauged his own current form against Cox's form. "He seemed to be running very well indeed and was definitely stronger than I," Peters said later. "I knew Stan was absolutely determined, perhaps as never before, to do his utmost to win the marathon, and consequently I began to fear him more than I had ever done." This admission represented a subtle, yet significant altering of Peters' frame of mind—from wanting to win to *not wanting to lose*.

To combat his apprehension, Peters did as he always did: he ran. Often he trained in bare feet on nearby grass fields or, to save his ailing heel, on the soft turf of the University Golf Club. Other times he donned his trusty plimsolls and ran on the road or the track. With no workday to worry about while he was in Vancouver, he set up a new three-run-a-day training schedule, ambitious even by his prodigious standards. A typical day included a slow five miles before breakfast, usually with Cox, six to eight miles speed work at the track before lunch, and six to ten miles in the evenings. His journal on August 1 noted that he had completed his 500th run and 5,000th mile since the current season's training began in September 1953. He planned to average 19 runs a week with estimated mileages in the neighbourhood of 130-140 miles and maintain this schedule until the 1956 Olympics. How he expected to fit this much road work into his already humming daily schedule short of quitting his job and finding a way to slow down time is anyone's guess, but the plan was there.

At the same time, many young Games athletes were gravitating toward him, eager to learn. On one of his morning runs he was joined by Barry Lush, a 25-year-old cattle farmer from St. George, Ontario. "He was a very quiet fellow, very hospitable," recalled Lush. "He didn't talk much but if you asked him a question, he'd give you an honest answer." The two men conversed throughout their run, which was long enough for the Canadian to share his training methods, which amounted to 15 miles in the evening after

Opposite: Canadian world champion weightlifter Doug Hepburn consumed enormous quantities of food to bulk up.

a long day on the farm. He often ran the hills of Highway 24 in army boots as far as the hospital on the edge of the town of Brantford and then back again, sometimes through deep snow. Though he had run the Boston Marathon, the Games were his first big international test. Peters was impressed and opened up to Lush about his hopes for the BECG marathon. "I really need this race," he admitted and explained that a victory in Vancouver, whatever the cost, would erase the disappointments he'd experienced in big events like the 1952 Olympics.

Most of the time, however, Peters ran with Cox, and to get a feel for the marathon course, they ran the route in 10-mile sections, each day continuing from the point where they left off the previous day. They were helped in this effort by Ken and Violet Eckley, a retired Burnaby couple, who drove the Englishmen to and from their training run start and end points and measured off each day's 10-mile segment on their car's odometer. While they ran, Peters and Cox finalized their race plans. Making notes on a course map that identified the changes in grade, they decided the best place to kill off their opposition was on the steep hills between Deer Lake and Burnaby Lake about eight miles in. (The two runners later signed the map and gave it to the Eckleys as a token of gratitude for their help.)

However, even without the aid of the Eckleys' car, by running as many miles as they did, Peters and Cox had become finely tuned to measuring pace and distance with surprising accuracy. Peters claimed he relied on an imaginary metronome ticking back and forth in his head to the cadence of his stride. After a couple incremental completions of the marathon route, both Peters and Cox agreed it felt too long, and they asked Ken Eckley to drive them over the entire course in one trip to measure the distance on the car's odometer. That drive and all their repeated test drives brought the same result: the odometer said 27 miles each time, and they hadn't even entered Empire Stadium where marathon runners would face a further 385yds around the track. Even taking into account the imprecision of the average car's odometer, the course appeared to measure more than a mile over the standard 26-mile 385yd marathon distance. Neither Peters nor Cox were the kind of men to complain about such things. They were resolute, hard-headed, blue collar Englishmen who put their heads down, gritted their teeth, and simply got on with it when things got tough. But on this occasion they felt organizers should at least be told of their concerns.

Despite the fact that an engineering professor from UBC had scientifically measured the designated route for the marathon, Alex Frew, the head marathon official and referee, joined the two runners in a car driven around the course. He was also shocked at the distance that popped up on the odometer. Next he had the car driven over the official city mile, which was used to check the accuracy of odometers in court cases involving speeding, and found the odometer's reading accurate to within 176yds. He then re-measured the course five times using a "footometer," which confirmed the discrepancy. Seeing the Englishmen had just cause for their complaint, he announced the course was indeed too long, but only by *250ft* and he adjusted its length accordingly. The English found such a miniscule change laughable and remained convinced the course measured at least half a mile too long. However, the distance was the same for every competitor who ran, so they let the matter drop.

English marathoners Jim Peters (left) and Stan Cox (right) befriended retired Burnaby couple Ken and Violet Eckley (centre), who drove them around the marathon route.

✲

When Games tickets had been first offered to the public in the spring of 1954, BEG Society officials were optimistic that sales would take care of themselves. "Here we had the greatest sports spectacle ever to come to Canada," Sam Rosen, director of ticket sales, told the *Vancouver Province* 20 years after the Games. "I figured it was just a matter of getting the tickets ready, opening the door and standing back. On April 1 we opened the door of the ticket office carefully, so as not to get hurt in the crush, and then stood back out of the way. That day two people came in. *Two people.* I nearly died. The Games were just four months away, and at this rate we might just fill a couple of phone booths."

However, lagging sales had been about to receive a shot in the arm. Word of Roger Bannister's historic four-minute mile at Oxford reached Vancouver in May, and phones at the Society's office began ringing off the hook. Locals clogged the switchboard hoping to find out what day of the Games Bannister would be running and whether they could reserve tickets right away. Weekly ticket sales nearly doubled from $5,000 to $9,000. Six weeks later news of Landy's world-record mile run eclipsing Bannister's run created an even bigger frenzy. The only thing louder than the lip-smacking of relieved Society officials was the ringing of Rosen's cash register. Sales spiked to $3,500 *a day* as applications for tickets flooded in from around the world. Soon only a few of the 35,000 tickets remained for the final day of track and field featuring the race already being billed as the "Mile of the Century."

English three-miler Chris Chataway won over most everyone he encountered with his likeable personality.

Considering very few prior sports crowds in Vancouver's history had ever exceeded 10,000 spectators, this represented a massive audience.

Unfortunately, sales of all other Games events remained slower than expected. Attendance numbers were never more disappointing than for Tuesday, August 3, the second day of track and field competition at Empire Stadium. Braving the wet, chilly weather, just over 8,000 spectators turned out, a number that breathed new life into the criticisms coming from New Zealand and Australia that Vancouverites were not as engaged in the Games as past host cities. But those who did turn out on that drizzly afternoon witnessed one of the Games' most electrifying races.

The Three Mile race boasted one of the strongest fields of any track event. The runners included England's newly crowned world record holder for the distance, Fred Green, a Birmingham electrical factory clerk and WWII paratroop instructor who had been credited with 42 jumps during the war. Coming from behind at the British AAA championships earlier that summer, Green had run the race of his life to topple the world mark in 13min 32.2sec. His training routine of over 110 miles a week, which mimicked the brutally tough regimen of the triple gold Olympic winner Emil Zatopec, clearly had him in razor-sharp fitness.

Other notables lined up for the race were Green's English teammates Peter Driver and Frank Sando, both medalists in the Six Miles that was run on the first day of the Games. Also racing was a bare-footed Kisii runner from Kiogoro, Kenya— Nyandika Maiyoro, and his teammate, Lazaro Chepkwony. The press felt neither posed any serious threat because at that time African runners were dismissed as either novelties or novices. Most reporters focussed on Maiyoro's lack of footwear and suggested that western training regimens were far too sophisticated and required too much discipline for African athletes. In reality, these two men were early harbingers of the shifting power bases in world distance running. Altitude and genetics would soon combine with access to modern training techniques to elevate African runners to the point where they would dominate virtually all long-distance racing.

And then there was Chris Chataway, perhaps the third most famous athlete at the Games behind Bannister and Landy—two men to whose fame he had directly contributed.

The 23-year-old Oxford graduate, now working as a brewer's assistant with London's Guinness Brewery, brought with him a most peculiar recent track record. In each of three races leading up to the 1954 Games, he had finished a close second to the man who walked away not only with the victory but also the world record. He had paced his friend Bannister to the first four-minute mile in May, raced Landy to the second in a new world record time in June and finished scant inches behind Green in his world record run in the three miles in July. But it was the last of these three that particularly stung because the officials had ruled that Chataway finished in identical world record time, yet in second place. "That was no consolation," he said in a 2007 interview, a hint of bitterness still evident from losing to a runner who had never previously won a major race and—as it turned out—never would again. Approaching the BECG, Chataway found himself in the midst of a remarkable series of historic races where often it wasn't just the final results that counted but who he was battling, a veritable hall of fame of some of the greatest competitors track and field has ever known. This was a far cry from where he had begun. As a young runner, he had been naturally gifted, but while he absolutely loved the thrill of competition, he abhorred hard training. As his friend Bannister said, "Chris could not run for long without getting bored by it. Running for him—as for all of us—was a sport, not a business, and he assumed that those who could run for hours must be completely insensitive.

The turning point for Chataway came after he met coach Franz Stampfl, whose charisma and enthusiasm inspired the necessary effort from him and elevated the talented runner to a new level. According to *The Perfect Mile* (2005) by Neal Bascomb, Chataway explained:

> He invested with magic this whole painful business of trying to run fast. He made you feel that this would be the most wonderful thing. It would put you along with Michelangelo, Leonardo da Vinci, if you could do it, and he was quite convinced you *could* do it.

But as famous as Chataway was when he arrived in Vancouver, perhaps more than any athlete he had something to prove because the press had tagged him as the best second-place runner in the world, perhaps of all time. At the same time, they had fallen in love with his everyman, bloke-next-door magnetism and his sly English wit. Once when news cameramen were posing Bannister and Landy for an awkward photo, Chataway cut the tension by bouncing in between the two and wrapping his arms around their shoulders. "I made them what they are today," he declared to laughter all around. "I hope they're satisfied." When the press corps were not asking his opinion on the upcoming Bannister-Landy Mile showdown, they wanted to know whether he loved beer and cigars as much as it was claimed. The *Sun*'s Beddoes noted that "if you read Peter Wilson of the *Daily Mirror,* you get the impression that before stepping on a track Chris swills down a pint of bitter and then hiccups delightfully in the last lap." Chataway shot down such depictions as "highly imaginative tripe," but on the topic of beer he bantered, "Well, I don't train *entirely* on it." After all, his employer's advertising slogan at the time was "Guinness is good for you!" This was pure Chataway in a snapshot—friendly, sharply intelligent, always with a ready quip at hand, amply comfortable in the spotlight though never giving the impression he craved it. A man you couldn't help but admire. "As fine a sportsman as there is competing here," the *Province*'s Ross Munro wrote. "He had all the qualities of the cavalier English amateur," concurred historian John Bryant in *The Quest to Break the 4 Minute Mile*, "respected and loved... the first to reach for a cigarette after the race, the first to lift a glass in celebration."

Yet lost in the buzz about the mile, training on suds, and Chataway's utterly likable personality was the Three Mile race and what he intended to do in it. Curiously, not one reporter queried him on this topic. "I did come to Vancouver with something to prove," he said in 2007. "It was very important to me to beat Freddie [Green] and to establish myself as Zatopek's leading contender." In fact, beneath the surface, the smiling Chataway was burning with a white-hot need to be a winner and shed the crown as king of the also-rans. With Green having already derailed Chataway's coming-out party once that summer, in Vancouver Chataway had a plan to prevent it happening again. He would shadow Green until the final lap and then on the back straight unleash as fierce a finishing burst as possible. He hoped the months of training with Stampfl would take care of the rest.

Prior to the race's start gusts of wind blew across the track at Empire Stadium. As the field gathered at the start line, Chataway later confessed to having felt "very keyed up," so keyed up, in fact, that he jumped early and caused a false start, a very rare occurrence for this distance. On the second try the field got away cleanly. Seven runners immediately pulled away from the rest of the pack, jostling for positions through the first few strides, but it was Scotland's Ian Binnie who took the early lead in front. Chataway calmly nestled himself near the back of a pack that included Green, Sando, Driver, Maiyoro and Australia's Geoff Warren. After Sando moved up to challenge Binnie, the two pushed the pace for over a mile, opening up a gap of over 10 yards on the rest. But Chataway continued to hang back in sixth place, waiting, conserving and never once showing any desire to fight with anyone ahead.

Binnie took the pack through the first mile in 4min 27sec, a brisk pace that was two seconds under world record time. Sando trailed two yards behind, his competitor number hanging by a single pin and flailing in the wind. On laps five through ten, the pace slowed, no runner wanting to risk wasting energy with a breakaway this early. At the head of the pack, Maiyoro reeled in Binnie and Sando and the lead began passing back and forth. Chataway lurked comfortably back in about fifth spot, his rusty mop of hair flapping freely as he patiently watched those ahead and waited for the ideal moment to strike.

On the second-to-last lap, the bare-footed Kenyan, Maiyoro, powered to the front and took the pack through the last-lap bell in an unofficial time of 12min 37sec. There would be no world records today, but the race now appeared up for grabs with six runners following closely behind the Kenyan. The bell snapped the pack out of its rhythmic trance. The pace quickened as the dash for the line—and gold—was on. Only legs, lungs and hearts mattered now. The crowd leaned closer to the track and the buzzing hum hovering over the stadium grew louder with each stride.

Binnie, Warren and Driver dropped back around the first corner. Maiyoro opened up his stride in the back straight, but he was clearly tiring—he had made his dash too early. With 300 yards to go, Green and Sando caught up and passed him. Chataway went with them. Entering the final corner, just as if he had flicked a switch, he sprang into his charging all-or-nothing stride, leaving Maiyoro in his wake, and then with an exceptional burst of acceleration he passed Sando, too. It happened so suddenly the startled CBC cameraman struggled to follow him, and TV viewers at home almost lost Chataway on their screens.

Green tried vainly to match his teammate's extraordinary speed, but Chataway ran like a man possessed. No one would catch him on this day. The gap between him and Green grew with each stride around the corner, first two yards, then five, soon ten. The crowd erupted, rising in unison as Chataway sprinted away. There was no question which man Vancouverites wanted to win this race. "No athlete was ever a more sentimental choice," confirmed the *Sun*'s Beddoes.

About 50 yards from the finish line, Chataway glanced back to see where his rivals were. No one was even close. His face broke into the widest of smiles, and he crossed the finish line with a look that said, "That wasn't so hard now, was it?" Then appearing still fresh and springy 10 yards after sprinting through the line, he turned back to greet his teammates Green and Sando with open arms. Soon they were swarmed by well-wishers. The crowd remained standing and applauding what had undoubtedly been the most thrilling finish of the Games thus far. Up in the stands Bannister stood and yelled "Bravo!" for his close friend. After months of training side by side and stressing over every last detail of their races, he knew better than anyone what this victory meant. Sixty years later Bannister still counted Chataway's victory as his strongest memory of the Vancouver Games after his own race and Jim Peters' marathon finish.

Chataway's winning time of 13min 35.2sec fell three seconds short of the world record, but it was a smashing 24.4sec faster than the old BECG mark. Timers also marvelled at his last-lap sprint: 56.8sec for the final lap and a scorching 26.7 for the last 220 yards. Green took the silver and Sando the bronze for an English sweep of the medals, while the top six runners all finished inside the old BECG record, and Binnie, the seventh, tied the mark.

Vancouver's press couldn't say enough about Chataway's stirring victory, many playing on his name, that he finally did indeed go "that-a-way" for the win. Beddoes wrote:

> It was the kind of race that leaves you all nervous with trembling. Watching that last kick to the wire, you strained to the tape with Chataway, pulling him home, cheering, whacking your neighbour up and down with your program. In the press box Austin Delaney said: "I'm near ashamed... I don't cheer at sporting events and here this red-haired johnny's got me hoarse."

The *Province*'s Bud Elsie wrote that "Chataway... deserved a gold medal for his personality anyway," while his colleague Ross Munro called his race "the most spine-tingling performance yet seen" at these Games. The newspaper also reported that the English track experts Joe Binks and Norris and Ross McWhirter had ranked this Three Mile as the greatest ever run. Chataway's own memory of his victory was

Following pages: English teammates Chris Chataway (left) and Fred Green (right) shake hands after the Three Mile race.

typically understated. In a 2007 interview he said it was "definitely one of the few that I remember best. Not one of the fastest and not against Zatopek or Kuts—the giants of our era—but an important championship beautifully staged."

In the immediate aftermath of the race, Chataway and Green propped each other up on Empire Stadium's infield as a dozen cameramen snapped photos. Later at the top of the bleachers Chataway puffed on a cigarette while he held court with *Vancouver Sun* and *Victoria Daily Times* reporters for nearly an hour.

"Were you trying for the world record?" one reporter asked.

"No, we weren't... I could have been faster in the middle of the race. Had Green and I planned it, I think we would have knocked three seconds off today's time. But as you've heard, I've been second a number of times. All I wanted to do here was win."

"How did it feel to win after so many seconds?"

"I prefer to finish first," he said with a sly smile.

After the interviews and medal ceremony, the reporters followed Chataway and Green as they clasped their medals and trotted off to the showers. "Give me a cig," called Green, his voice echoing down the concrete halls. "First in three weeks, y'know. And let's have a beer tonight. Let's live up a storm."

Christopher Chataway's remarkable roller-coaster year didn't end with the 1954 Games in Vancouver. Back on the track at the European championships in Switzerland, he faced the one man he had geared all his efforts into defeating in the 5000m: the great Emil Zatopek. Chataway made good this time, beating the unbeatable Czech, who had not lost at any distance in six years but whose career was admittedly on the wane. The only problem was that both Chataway and Zatopek were outpaced by a young, unknown Russian named Vladimir Kuts, who won by an embarrassing 100m margin and smashed the world record.

THE GUINNESS BOOK OF RECORDS

When Chataway returned to work at the Guinness Brewery barely a month after the Vancouver Games, he learned his boss, Sir Hugh Beaver, was contemplating creating a book of records to list the fastest, heaviest, tallest and a million other world bests. Legend has it that while hunting in Ireland, he had become embroiled in a debate with his shooting partners on whether the golden plover was Europe's fastest game bird, but no reference book existed to settle their dispute. Now he asked for Chataway's help in finding someone with the time and expertise to pull together such disparate information. Chataway suggested that his Oxford University friends, the twin brothers Norris and Ross McWhirter, who had been in Vancouver covering the Games, might be ideal for the job. At that time the McWhirters ran a London fact-finding agency that provided information to newspapers, yearbooks, encyclopedias and advertisers. One meeting between Beaver and the twins proved enough for *The Guinness Book of Records* to come to fruition. The first edition was published in 1955 and eventually sold 187,000 copies. To this day the book continues to be a remarkable bestseller and the gold standard for "record-keeping" with off-shoot television programs and chains of themed museums. Interestingly, Vancouver business tycoon Jimmy Pattison purchased the Guinness World Records empire in 2008 for a reported $93 million CDN—a further Vancouver connection to this remarkable institution.

Chataway receives congratulations from English team manager Leslie Truelove following the Three Miles.

Redemption for Chataway came just six weeks later in a televised London-vs-Moscow meet at White City Stadium. Forty thousand people attended the meet and across Europe another 10-15 million watched on an early Eurovision network live broadcast as brilliant spotlights followed the lead runners in the 5000m race around the track in the ghostly dark. Kuts set a tortuous tempo—at one point a full 10 seconds ahead of the world record pace—alternating between surging sprints and brief respites in a merciless assault to prevent his rival from launching his lethal last-lap kick. But Chataway stuck to him despite immense suffering, certain he could take no more and would be forced to quit. In the final 80m Kuts was astonished to see Chataway still clawing and straining with what little remained in him. Never had either man felt such pain. Five metres from the finish Chataway pulled into the lead and decimated the world record by five full seconds, winning in 13min 51.6sec, three-tenths of a second ahead of the Russian. This early Cold War battle made such an indelible impact on the British consciousness that Chataway was awarded the first-ever BBC Sports Personality of the Year, taking that honour ahead of his close friend Bannister, who had also collected a remarkable string of victories that year.

✿

The biggest surprise of that second day of track and field events at Empire Stadium proved to be the women's high jump. Going in, the gold and silver were all but conceded to the English contestants Sheila Lerwill and Dorothy (Odam) Tyler, elder stateswomen in the twilight of their illustrious careers. Lerwill had held the world record of 1.72m until just recently and during her reign had added a silver medal at the 1952 Olympics, Britain's top athletics performance of those Games. But she had taken the full 1953 season off while having her first child and living with her husband on a date plantation in the Middle East. In a 2002 interview she said that on returning to Britain, she had still craved "another bite of the cherry" and she made a comeback in time for the 1954 Games. Despite Lerwill's year-long lay-off, the venerable track observer Harold Abrahams (1924 Olympics 100m sprint winner and the inspiration for the film *Chariots of Fire*) told *World Sports* that she would be "the most likely English winner in any event."

Thirty-four-year-old London-born Tyler already had two gold BECG medals before she came to Vancouver. She had also won two Olympic silver medals, one from either side of World War II, the only athlete in the world who could claim such an accomplishment. While at the 1936 Olympics in Berlin, she had met Adolf Hitler and Josef Goebbels at a party thrown for female competitors. A few years later Tyler worked as an auxiliary lorry driver, steering the crews of the famous RAF 617 "Dam-busters" Squadron to their take-offs and doing her small part to take down those same Nazi madmen. Upon her arrival in Vancouver, she came down with a serious stomach bug and spent nearly a week in the hospital, though fortunately she recovered in time to compete.

Challenging Lerwill and Tyler were two young athletes: Northern Ireland's Thelma Hopkins and Alice Whitty of Vancouver. In her home village of Milverton in Somerset, Hopkins was known as the young girl with legs like springs. On one of her earliest attempts at the long jump she had sailed clear over the landing pit to the grass beyond. She began playing around at the high jump after her father strung up a rope in the backyard. When she was 13, her parents took her to see Franz Stampfl at Queen's University in Belfast, where he coached many top Northern Ireland athletes. After her first training session, they asked if their daughter had any potential.

"Well, we'll have you in the Helsinki [1952] Olympics," Stampfl reportedly replied.

At the time few would have believed this possible, but as he soon showed with Bannister, Chataway and Brasher, Stampfl possessed great skill in coaxing the very best out of athletes in a very short time. He immediately had Hopkins abandon the western roll and taught her the "straddle" so that she became part of the evolutionary bridge in high jump technique, pushing the antiquated "scissors" farther into the past, though it was still over a decade before Dick Fosbury's "flop" and Debbie Brill's "bend." As a result of Stampfl's training, at the 1952 Olympics 16-year-old Hopkins came out of nowhere to jump a personal best of 5ft 2¼in and finish a surprising fourth, missing a medal by five centimetres. "I was very disappointed I only got fourth," Hopkins said when interviewed in 2013. "When you're young, you're awfully confident, you know?"

The other upstart in the high jump had the support of the hometown crowd. Twenty-year-old Alice Whitty was a second-year UBC physical education student who was paying her way through school by working in the BC Telephone Company's accounting department. Her coach, Tauno Viiri, who had been one of the best in Finland before the war, had come to Vancouver through Lapland after a long stint in a POW camp. Under his guidance Whitty soon began distinguishing herself. She was already one of the first women in the world to utilize the straddle technique, having learned it from world record holder Les Steers in 1950, but she mastered it under Viiri. She was also one of the first women in BC to train year round, joining an informal group of male track athletes training at UBC. "I copied what they did," she said in a 2013 interview. "The exercises were brutal." But they certainly helped. Whitty had finished tenth at the 1952 Olympics and more recently had broken Ethel Catherwood's 1928 Canadian record, jumping 5ft 3¼in. Although overlooked by most experts, Whitty felt cautiously confident: "I was scared of Lerwill, but I was hoping to take it." But her cause wasn't helped when she awoke on the morning of the competition with a terrible case of laryngitis.

The BECG high jump field, which had begun with nine women, was soon whittled down to these four: Lerwill, Tyler, Hopkins and Whitty, a group that included three world record holders (two past and one future). By this point the bar had risen to 5ft 3in—the BECG record height since 1934. With the exception of Lerwill, the remaining women looked in fine form; Lerwill was limping slightly, the result of a minor ankle injury sustained when she had rolled on an early attempt. Except for Tyler and Lerwill, who always grew cold with each other when in competition, the four competitors seemed remarkably friendly with one another. The aging English stars also kept their distance from Hopkins, but were nice enough to "the little interloper." All of this suited Hopkins just fine. "They had a feud going sort of all the time in competition and I was left out of it, which was great," she recalled. "I could just concentrate on my jumping."

Tyler and Hopkins cleared 5ft 3in with ease. When a few moments later the stadium announcer mistakenly credited Lerwill with Tyler's successful jump, the two women shared an awkward laugh. Next Whitty surprised everyone with a soaring effort to also make the height. When Lerwill narrowly missed on her first two attempts, no one appeared concerned. She had, after all, survived this scenario countless times and had only just returned to jumping after a year away. Then in a truly shocking turn, on her third attempt she badly misjudged her takeoff and her hand knocked the bar to the ground. The first-place favourite was suddenly out.

Whitty recalled thinking, "Ohh! I'm in!" She was now assured at least a bronze.

With the bar at 5ft 4in, Hopkins made her coming-out party official, leaping that height with ease for a new BECG record. Both Whitty and Tyler failed on their three attempts. The hometown girl took the bronze owing to more missed attempts than Tyler, who added a silver to her two previous BECG gold medals (1938 and 1950), all of them won jumping the identical height of 5ft 3in. However, Hopkins, the unexpected victor in the competition, wanted more, and like Emmanuel Ifeajuna three days earlier, she appeared to have grown stronger as the competition went on. With all eyes on her alone now, she harnessed all her momentum into two calm jumps, leaping 5ft 5in and 5ft 6in in rapid succession, though nearly plunking face-first into the sawdust landing pit each time. These jumps seemed mirror images of one another, with only

Following pages: The women's high jump medalists (left to right): Alice Whitty, Dorothy Tyler and Thelma Hopkins.

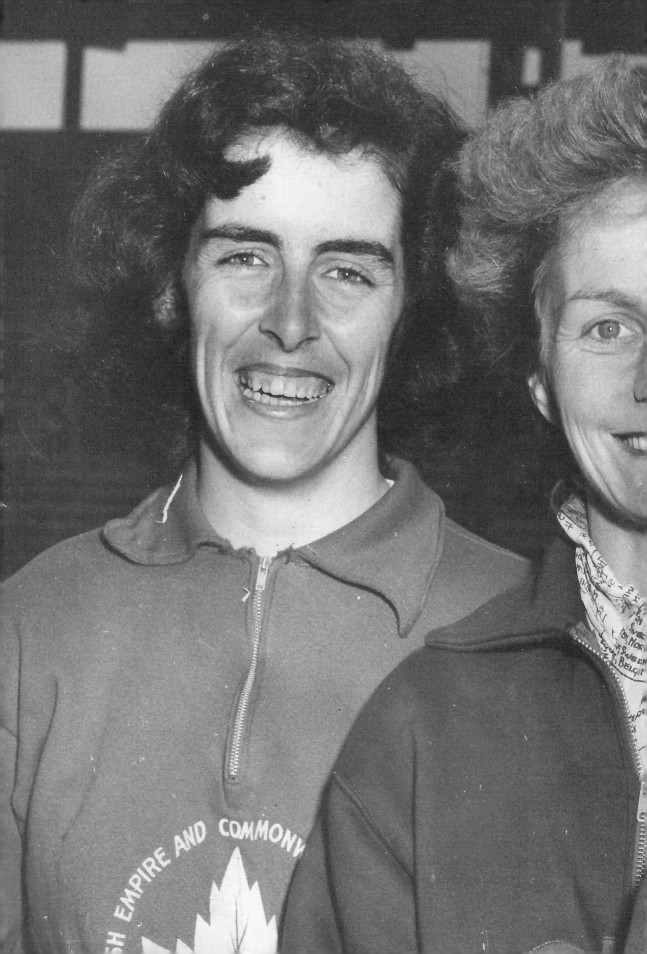

Northern Ireland's Thelma Hopkins clears 5ft 6in to win the women's high jump.

the bar's height changing. From there, Hopkins raised the bar to 5ft 8½in, enough to break the world record. It was heady stuff for an 18-year-old, but by the way she was jumping many in the crowd felt she just might do it. But after three game attempts, including one particularly close near-miss, her day finally ended. She had a gold medal, a new BECG record (1.68m), and the second-best jump in the world for the year. "I didn't really expect I'd win in Vancouver, but I hoped I would place," she said years later. "I expected to pay my dues a bit longer before I won anything, you know? So winning was a surprise in a way."

Still glowing from her victory a day after the high jump, Hopkins sent a telegram to her parents in Belfast. It comprised just two small, yet significant words: "I WON." It was all she could afford to send. Later in the Games she won a broad jump silver medal and competed in the 80m hurdles, completing one of the better all-round performances by any athlete. And although she had missed the world record in Vancouver, in May 1956 she leapt a world-best 1.74m in Belfast in front of family and friends. Later that year she took the Olympic silver medal in Melbourne. She also achieved the remarkable distinction of representing Ireland in three different sports. Besides track and field, she also played squash and field hockey at the highest levels. Her field hockey accomplishments, in particular, are notable: suiting up for Ireland in 42 internationals, scoring 90 goals in one season, and sniping eight in a single game—achievements that warranted induction into the Irish Hockey Hall of Fame. Interestingly, Canada played a major role in Hopkins' life after Vancouver as well. She and her then-husband moved from Belfast to Toronto in 1966 and with their three children settled in Edmonton two years later. There she remains, a diehard Oilers and Eskimos fan to this day.

Whitty's performance in Vancouver attracted the attention of legendary University of Oregon coach Bill Bowerman, who offered her an athletic scholarship, and in the fall of 1954 she became the first female member of Oregon's track team. She represented Canada at the 1956 Olympics, by which time she had pioneered another aspect of women's high jump as the first Canadian woman jumper to wear a heel spike, having been shown a rudimentary form of spike a year earlier by American jumper Ernie Shelton. Using a piece of an old saw blade Whitty's father had found while he was working at New Westminster's railway yards, Bowerman riveted the blade to the leather covering her heel. Today most elite high jumpers use some form of heel spike.

PICTURE PERFECT

Alice Whitty learned one final lesson from Dorothy Odam Tyler, the savvy veteran, at the 1954 Games in Vancouver. After the high jump competition, photographers requested the three medalists gather for a picture. "There I am with no lipstick on and my hair standing up on end," Whitty recalled. Then she turned to see Tyler briskly preparing. "She reached down into her bag, pulled out a scarf, stuffed it into her sweatshirt and applied her makeup. She's 34 and here I am 20 and, gosh, she's gonna look so good!"

❁

The third and final night of the BECG weightlifting competition was Tuesday, August 3, at the PNE's Exhibition Gardens, a large auditorium built in 1941 with seating for 2,300 spectators. Only a few hundred people had attended the first two evenings, but they had witnessed fine performances by some of the Commonwealth's strongest.

Among those competing was England's "Jumping" Jim Halliday, a 37-year-old engineer from Bolton, Lancashire, who had been nicknamed for his habit of leaping over the barbell after successful lifts. On the opening night in Vancouver he won the middleweight gold medal with a BECG record 800lb three-lift total and smashed the BECG clean-and-jerk mark by hoisting 325lbs. These were not his first victories: he had won a 1948 Olympic bronze medal and a 1950 BEG gold—all of which were remarkable feats as he was a survivor of four years in a Japanese prisoner-of-war camp during WWII.

Canada's first gold medal in the 1954 Games went to middle heavyweight Keevil Daly, who had been born in British Guiana (Guyana since 1966) in 1923 and only became a Canadian citizen in 1950. As a young man he had worked as a merchant seaman and during World War II had survived the torpedoing of the Canadian merchant ship SS *Lady Nelson*. He then joined the RCAF, and after graduating from Ryerson Polytechnical, had served as a radar technician at Ottawa's RCAF Uplands base. Daly's primary competition, Ken McDonald, a multiple BECG record holder from Australia, withdrew after tearing shoulder ligaments while hoisting a 265lb clean-and-press. This had thrown the door open for the 187lb Daly, the lightest man in the middle heavyweight division, who pressed 275lbs, snatched 275lbs, and jerked 330lbs for an 880lb total—all new BECG records.

Gerry Gratton, a 1950 BEG gold and 1952 Olympic silver medalist, had served as Canada's flag bearer at the Games' Opening Ceremonies on July 30. Having rewritten the Commonwealth's middleweight division record book at the 1950 Games, in Vancouver the waiter from Montreal moved up to the light heavyweight division. Here he set new BECG records in all three lifts and his three-lift total of 890lbs—another record—even bettered all of those a full weight class up.

As the lone representative from Barbados, George Nicholls had also served as his country's flag bearer. The Games in Vancouver must have felt like a relaxing holiday for him compared to his job back home in a sugar factory where every day he lifted approximately 800 sacks of sugar, each weighing 228lbs for a total of 91 tons, enough to fill 16 trucks. In Vancouver the 23-year-old broke the lightweight clean-and-press world record with a 255lb effort. However, knowing that a Russian claim of 259lbs was pending official approval, Nicholls attempted to better it by trying a fourth lift of 262lbs but was unsuccessful. It may have cost him the gold medal. Lacking zip after that attempt, he was edged out of the gold by Australia's Verdi Barberis whose three-lift total of 760lb bested his total by a slim 5lbs.

While these were all fine performances, in the minds of the hometown faithful they only served as the undercard for Tuesday, August 3, the third night of weightlifting, when Vancouver's own Doug Hepburn, the reigning world's strongest man, would contest his crown. That night a near-sellout audience of over 2,100 crowded into the PNE's Exhibition Gardens, and even the other weightlifters conceded that these people were all here to see the Kitsilano colossus flex. Looking on as Hepburn pressed with ridiculous ease a barbell loaded with weight that only a handful of men on the planet could have handled, Lionel Spence, a Jamaican bantamweight, remarked in admiration, "That man is six lions!"

Watching Hepburn lift, few would argue. Although he was only 5ft 8½in in height, at his peak he weighed a bulging 300lbs. He had more muscle mass than definition, but he was solid as granite. His shoulders, seemingly hewn from chunks of telephone poles, may have been the strongest in history, and Hepburn often said he could lift any bar-bending weight above his head if starting from chest height—his twin derrick shoulders would take care of the rest. His 24in biceps measured larger than the average man's thighs. His fists resembled meaty rotary telephones. A watch looked cartoonishly small on his wrist, and a *News-Herald* reporter quipped that gripping his hand was "like trying to wrap your fingers around the hind ankle of an elephant." His legs above the knees resembled two bulging tree trunks. Bob Hoffman, the domineering founder of

The barbell bends as Canada's Doug Hepburn hoists 370lbs for a BECG clean-and-press record.

York Barbell in Pennsylvania, once confided to him: "You realize you don't have the organs of a normal man." Hoffman was right. They didn't break the mold with Doug Hepburn; he was so much larger-than-life he wouldn't have fit the mold to begin with.

As there was a bit of the showman in him, in some ways Hepburn seemed a throwback to the days of the travelling circus strongman. He sported neatly coiffed hair and a finely trimmed moustache, and he relished performing feats of strength for a gasping audience, whether ripping licence plates apart with his bare hands, holding a 110lb anvil in the crucifix position, or lifting two full forward lines of hockey players on his back. And yet he was also nothing like the stereotypical dim-witted, muscle-bound oaf that graced so many gyms. He was intelligent, sensitive and reflective. He wrote poetry and spoke eloquently. The *Georgia Straight*'s Kerry Banks once wrote that "talking with him is like engaging in a game of metaphysical pinball." At the same time there always seemed to be a touch of melancholy colouring Hepburn's character. His smile, on the rare occasions he showed it, always seemed sad at the corners.

There was good reason for that sadness. Doug Hepburn was the strongest man in the world not just for the bar-bending loads he could lift, but also for the physical, emotional and spiritual burdens he had overcome to reach the top of his sport. In fact, it was a minor miracle he was even there competing. He had been born with a clubbed right foot and a severe alternating squint that caused his eyes to lock up. An operation later corrected his eyes, but doctors botched the procedure on his foot, leaving him with a fused ankle, virtually no calf muscle and a right leg that was an inch shorter than his left. He walked with a limp his entire life. His father was a violent alcoholic, and after his parents divorced, his single mother bounced from one low-paying job to another. Rebelling against the conformity of school where he was ridiculed by his classmates, he turned inward and became a loner. But then he discovered that he could gain acceptance in sports, and despite his physical impairments, he excelled at almost every sport he tried. When a friend introduced him to weightlifting, at first he only saw it as a means to impress girls. But it soon became much more—his calling—and he began devoting all his time and energy to becoming the ultimate strongman. Part of this involved eating enormous amounts of food to gain as much body mass as he could as quickly as possible. While the average active 25-year-old male's daily food intake amounts to approximately 3,000 calories, Hepburn was inhaling over 8,000. "I ate three times a day, and three times a day I had to fight to keep from throwing up," he told a reporter for the *Vancouver Province Magazine* in 1967. "A couple of times I did. One day I gained seven pounds."

Hepburn experimented with every conceivable type of exercise to find the most effective workout. He tried training at night, during the day, using many short workouts, then a few long workouts, varying the number of workouts per week, then per month. As his knowledge and experience piled up, he found what worked better, then best, although he still searched for further refinements. Eventually, he devised a program that involved lifting the heaviest weights possible for a single repetition, while performing these "heavy singles" eight to ten times in a row. This simple, revolutionary variation on common techniques afforded him startling gains in size and strength, and it is one of the reasons strength aficionados still cite him as one of the "grandfathers" of modern powerlifting techniques.

However, Hepburn's lifting gains came at the expense of everything else in his life. He quit school and soon his mother and step-father threw him out on his own. Working as a lifeguard to support himself, he began entering local weightlifting competitions and blew the competition out of the water. But the press paid him scant attention, and acceptance on the Canadian weightlifting scene was even harder to come by. When he began breaking national records, officials in eastern Canada refused to accept his performances on the grounds they appeared *too good*. On one occasion the record forms sent to the AAU were returned with a note saying: "Impossible. This man could not possibly have lifted 300lbs. The best here in the east does only 220. You have made a mistake." Hepburn later surpassed the world clean-and-press record by hoisting 341lbs, while also completing a 400lb strict bench press and a full squat of 504lb. But the AAU refused to recognize any of these marks because the lifts were performed on a Sunday. Frustration mounting, Hepburn looked abroad. He travelled to New York and amazed the American lifting fraternity there by setting a 330lb world clean-and-press record. At the US Open Championships he defeated all comers, including a young Paul Anderson, who would win gold at the 1956 Olympics and is considered by many the strongest natural man ever; Hepburn was the only man to ever defeat him in competition. These head-turning accomplishments failed to earn a single line of print in any Vancouver newspaper. Even worse, Canadian officials passed on him for selection to the 1952 Canadian Olympic team. In protest Hepburn gave a lifting exhibition at Kitsilano Pool to display how ridiculous the selection politics were. There he unofficially set one world and two Canadian records—which the AAU predictably refused to accept—and his 971lb three-lift total fell just shy of the Olympic gold medalist's sum.

Disappointed but undeterred, Hepburn shifted his focus to the 1953 world championships in Stockholm, Sweden. He was in peak form, evidenced by a 502lb bench press, the first man in history to break the 500lb barrier. Yet in their infinite wisdom, the AAU decided to send no Canadian lifters to Stockholm, not even the Vancouver world record holder, so Hepburn passed the hat during his lifting exhibitions to cover his $1,377 plane ticket for the opportunity to prove himself overseas. In Stockholm a severely sprained ankle almost derailed his chances, but he persevered and ultimately out-lifted all the heavyweights, including the American Olympic gold medalist, John Davis. With the barbell lying at Hepburn's feet after his winning lift, he flashed a broad smile and raised a thick arm in a long wave of acknowledgement to the roaring crowd. All the years of despair and frustration had been worth it for just this one moment. Suddenly he was the toast of the strength and bodybuilding world, and finally his hometown took notice. No longer able to pass him off as a curiosity, on August 31, 1953, the *Sun* ran a headline that read: "Hepburn's Mighty Heart Earns Plaudits of World."

For Vancouver's first individual world champion since the days of boxer Jimmy McLarnin and sprinter Percy Williams, Hepburn's triumphant homecoming proved not all he had dreamed it would be. A handful of prominent officials, including Mayor Hume, greeted his plane upon arrival, and he was toured around the city in the mayor's limo waving to residents, but then it was over. That night as he trudged to an all-too-familiar flea-bitten East Hastings hotel, Hepburn experienced one of his darkest moments. "Can you imagine how I felt that first night home?" he told a *Vancouver Province Magazine* reporter in 1967. "Here I was, the strongest man in the world, sleeping in a flophouse." The plunge from the spirit-soaring highs of Stockholm to the rock-bottom emptiness of East Hastings had taken less than a day.

Eventually more recognition did come Hepburn's way, and in early 1954 *Canadian Press* named him the top Canadian athlete of 1953 and he was honoured with induction into the Canadian Olympic Hall of Fame. In the meantime he had returned to the daily struggle of trying to make ends meet while maintaining his foothold as the world's strongest man—two pursuits that often ran at cross purposes. Finally, when no assistance materialized at home, he decided to drop weightlifting altogether and set off for southern California and a career in professional wrestling. When the press reported his departure just months before the city was due to host the 1954 BECG, Mayor Hume's fear of no Vancouver-based athletes capturing a Games gold medal seemed an all-too-likely scenario. Suddenly the city needed him to prevent an impending embarrassment. Phoning Hepburn in Los Angeles, Hume threw him the lifeline he needed to stay amateur and forget about pro wrestling. "Win us the gold medal and we will give you your gym!" the mayor promised. He also offered to pay Hepburn $300 monthly so he could focus on nothing but training.

Hepburn countered with "A hundred and fifty would do—just enough to eat, pay rent and train," and the deal was sealed. To get around the stringent amateur code, Hume paid Hepburn out of his own pocket but listed him on the city payroll as his "personal bodyguard." Of course, Hepburn never worked a day at the job.

At the Games one might have expected Hepburn to bask in the spotlight, yet the delayed homecoming for the local lad-turned-world champion often felt more bitter than sweet. He always struggled to come to terms with his own fame, both craving and loathing it; one day he felt underappreciated, the next he wanted to be left alone. His Games experience proved much the same. He experienced a scattering of happy moments and he made friends among the Canadian team, yet even as one of the Games' biggest attractions, he never truly fit in. "Am I a misfit?" he asked a *Province* reporter in May 1981. "I don't think so, but then I can't think of any organization or niche that I fit into."

Hepburn felt alone even among the large crowds he himself created. Many athletes recalled gathering around his table in the Village cafeteria to witness his enormous appetite up close. On an average day he consumed over seven quarts of milk, six boiled eggs, five pieces of toast, two bowls of pudding, six bananas, six oranges, six cans of tomato juice, two large cans of spaghetti, a bowl of soup, two hamburgers and four large steaks. In between plates he demonstrated his strength by performing one-arm handstands.

On the opening day of track and field at Empire Stadium, Hepburn was unexpectedly called down to the infield for a special presentation: he was to receive the Lou Marsh Award as outstanding athlete of the year from Lord Alexander. But Hepburn became lost on his way down, unable to find the correct tunnel, and to the amusement of the crowd Alexander took the opportunity to stretch out on the edge of the sawdust-filled pole vault pit until Hepburn finally emerged. Although Alexander was unperturbed by the delay, the press took Hepburn to task. "Lord Alexander Waits— Hepburn In No Hurry" read a *News-Herald* headline, while the *Sun* ran a large photo of a bored Alexander sitting and examining his hands. While the incident was inconsequential and simply the result of Hepburn losing his way, the local papers devoted more space to it than to anything he accomplished in the weightlifting competition the following week. And their stories influenced many readers. The same morning they appeared, Hepburn was out for a walk when a small Englishman stopped him, poked his cane into Hepburn's chest and sniped, "Look here, Hepburn! The next time Lord Alexander waits to meet with you, you nip down there smartly!"

Yet this unpleasantness was not Hepburn's biggest worry. Early one morning a few weeks before the BECG weightlifting competition began, he had decided that a solid workout might clear his head after leaving a team dinner. Upset by the drunken antics of team officials, he had begun his workout with a series of heavy snatches when without warning his front foot slipped and twisted with a sickening jerk, tearing his right thigh muscle nearly through just above the knee. The injury threw a gorilla-sized wrench into his pre-Games preparations and training: push the leg too hard and too soon and his part in the Games—perhaps his whole career—was over.

Before each competitor could participate in the BECG weightlifting competition, he had to complete a series of minimum qualifying lifts. Most times they served as little more than a formality, but with an untested leg, Hepburn feared these qualifiers would put him out of the running. First came a 300lb clean-and-press—normally child's play for Hepburn—and without putting undue strain on his thigh, he let his shoulders absorb the weight and raised it skyward. One down. Next came a 270lb snatch, and there was no way to avoid the pain this time. As he bent his knee, the searing pain was such a shock that he let the barbell drop to the floor. His second attempt failed as well. Those watching him were puzzled, and Hepburn was obviously shaken. It now came down to one final attempt. Make it and move on. Miss it and the BECG competition—and his dream of that promised gym—were over before even beginning. He knew his thigh could not take any further strain, so now he planned to hoist the 270lbs on arm and shoulder strength alone. Locking his knees straight and setting his jaw, he snapped the barbell skyward from the floor as rapidly as possible. The bar flashed overhead and he held it there until the judges, jaws agape, motioned that the lift was "good." Even Hepburn appeared surprised at his own strength. "For that brief moment I was certain that I could have snatched any weight that was placed before me," he recalled many years later. He muscled a 300lb clean-and-jerk with similar effort, arms and shoulders steeled against any possibility of failure. Having survived this crisis, his mindset entering the competition underwent a complete about-face. "What had first appeared as a physical setback had turned out to be a spiritual and emotional godsend," he explained. He was still hurt, but at least now he had found his focus.

Only three men were contesting the heavyweight division in the Vancouver Games: Hepburn, fellow Canadian Dave Baillie and New Zealand's Harold Cleghorn, the 41-year-old defending BECG heavyweight champion. While Cleghorn appeared determined, the two Canadians were clearly in another class. Hepburn's world press record measured a full 100lbs clear of Cleghorn's 1950 Games record, and while few could approach Hepburn in physical bulk, Baillie only gave up 10lbs to Vancouver's finest. With blonde crewcut and horn-rimmed glasses pushed up against pudgy cheeks, Baillie looked more like the college jock caught somewhere between the weight room and the library. Appearances aside, his sixth-place 1952 Olympic finish meant he could not be taken lightly as a competitor. He also had pedigree. Right after World War I his father had played football for the McGill Redmen, and both of his brothers now played in the Canadian Football League. On Baillie's best day he could not approach Hepburn, but with the reigning world champion obviously hobbling, he could get close enough to make the big man work.

For the introductions to the crowd on Tuesday evening Hepburn was the last to emerge from behind the curtain, and he was wearing cloth bandages around his right calf and left knee. But when he walked down the narrow runway to the raised lifting platform, the building shook down to its foundations as the crowd gave him an extended standing ovation. Hepburn was stunned and touched. He'd had his grievances with the city in the past—warranted or not—but in that one breathless moment he forgot about them and vowed to win the gold medal for these people, for *his* city.

First up was Hepburn's specialty, the clean-and-press. Cleghorn finished with a best lift of 305lbs—20lbs over his own BECG record—before the Canadians even started lifting. Baillie rang up a best lift of 340lbs. Then Hepburn went to work. He slammed the bar to shoulder height before comfortably pressing 370lbs above his head with barely a waver. He had hardly extended himself yet had still broken the BECG record by 85lbs. It was not a world record, but you would not have known that by the roar of the crowd.

Doug Hepburn overcame an injured quadriceps to become the only Vancouver athlete to win an individual gold medal.

The snatch proved much closer. Cleghorn again bettered his own BECG record with a best hoist of 275lbs, but the snatch was Baillie's best lift and he matched Hepburn weight-for-weight. On Baillie's final attempt, he snatched an even 300lbs and walked off the platform with a satisfied smile. Hepburn limped on, glanced at the poundages chalked on the blackboard and set his jaw for the job at hand. As he bent over the bar, he knew he needed to match Baillie here. The crowd grew silent as Hepburn adjusted his grip. Gritting his teeth against the sharp twinge from his thigh, he rapidly yanked the bar above his head, then paused in a low crouch before powering upwards until he was standing erect. He held the weight there until the three lights flashed "good." The crowd exploded as he dropped the weight to the platform. In the dressing room between lifts, he sipped honey and coffee spiked with brandy for energy, and to keep loose, he discussed religion and philosophy with other lifters.

The final lift, the clean-and-jerk, proved the closest of the three. For the third time gritty Cleghorn beat his own BECG record, finishing with a best jerk of 350lbs and a three-lift total of 930lbs—a 30lb improvement over his 1950 record. Baillie finished with a 360lb jerk, giving him a three-lift total of an even half-ton—1000lbs. Hepburn matched him at 360lbs then chose to attempt 370 for his final lift. He had wrapped up the gold medal by this point but wanted to show he ranked as the class of the Commonwealth even with an injured leg. As he limped down the narrow runway to the waiting barbell, he turned back to reporters and said with a cocky smile, "I'll toy with it." As he approached

The two Canadian heavyweights, Hepburn and Dave Baillie (right), proved the class of the weightlifting competition.

the bar, rubbing talcum on his palms, the crowd waited silently. With a sudden burst, he hoisted the bar to his shoulders, paused, and drove with his legs to power the bar over-head. It was effortless and breathtaking and unbelievable all at once.

The cheers cascaded down from the rafters, the overflow crowd showering him with an extended standing ovation, and he lingered on the platform soaking it up. "The big guy came home Tuesday night," wrote the *Sun*'s Jack Richards the next day. "Home to the roaring acclaim that is rightfully his." Fighting a severe muscle tear he had set four new BECG records. His 1040lb three-lift total ranked as one of the highest in history. Better yet, as the only Vancouver athlete to win an individual gold medal at these Games, he hoped that the gym Hume had promised him was now his. But even in Hepburn's moment of celebration up on the podium, when he should have felt on top of the world, a look of sadness crept across his face. He could not have known it that night in August 1954, but the dull clatter of iron hitting the platform effectively signalled the end of his international weightlifting career. He would never experience a moment quite like it again. But perhaps he felt a warning of what was to come. Many years later he would comment to Tom Thurston, author of *Strongman: The Doug Hepburn Story* (2003), "What a strange obsession to be tied to. Why, of all the pursuits under God's heaven, did I choose to spend my time defying gravity? Or did it choose me?"

❖

Late that same evening, Tuesday, August 3, as the weightlifting events came to a close at Exhibition Gardens, Prince Philip's plane finally touched down at Vancouver International Airport. Waiting was a crowd of over three thousand jammed a dozen deep along every inch of the chain-link fence set up by airport officials, who had finally grown wise after the earlier debacles. As Philip shook hands with the line of welcoming officials, behind the fencing women shrieked, children waved and men hollered, though some did stand silently observing the scene in pride and curiosity. The bright light of flashbulbs on the cameras of two dozen photographers lit up the night as Philip's every move was captured for posterity, while a horde of reporters scribbled furiously in their notebooks. With the handshaking complete, Philip was directed to a salmon-coloured Chrysler convertible, and turning to Lieutenant-Governor Clarence Wallace, he remarked with a smile, "Do you think we'll get through this mob?" He was unaware how famous those words were about to become.

As the police escort and motorcycle brigade pulled away to lead the royal car along a well-rehearsed route to the Hotel Vancouver, Philip requested the convertible's roof be lowered so the crowd could see him. His driver, RCMP Sergeant Jim Duffin, stopped the car and struggled to pull the canvas top back. Unaware of the delay behind them, the lead car continued out through the gate, leaving it wide open. Seeing this, the crowd flooded in, and within seconds Philip's car was surrounded on all sides by a 20-deep human wall. Men, women and children pushed against the Chrysler's fenders and doors, each trying to get as close as possible to the royal visitor. One young boy leaned in and levelled his Brownie camera less than two feet from Philip's nose, nearly dropping the camera into the car as the amused Duke smiled for him. Duffin tried nudging the vehicle forward against the crowd to no avail. Another police officer fought through the mob and climbed on the Chrysler's front bumper to plead with the crowd to move back. Knowing the potential for imminent disaster, one ashen-faced officer said later, "My heart was in my throat." Thankfully, after two minutes that seemed to stretch on forever, a line of RCMP officers navigated the gauntlet, linking arms to create a human chain, and pushed the crowd back to slowly free the car. That didn't stop the *Province* from skewering Duffin for the fiasco on its front page the following day: "Car Takes Wrong Turn, Duke Almost Engulfed."

Vindication came at a reception on Philip's last night in Vancouver when he presented wallets to each of the three officers who had been his drivers during his Vancouver stay, including the unfortunate Duffin. And having taken the wheel of the car himself several times during his time here, Philip cracked "I don't know if you really deserve this. I've been driving you more than you have been driving me!"

Opposite: A clean-shaven Hepburn salutes the crowd at the 1953 world weightlifting championships in Sweden after his winning lift.

CHAPTER 7
WEDNESDAY, AUGUST 4, 1954

Early in Games week Roger Bannister began easing off his daily workouts in preparation for the Mile, but he kept busy with many non-strenuous distractions. Twice a day he went on long walks around UBC's campus, sometimes with Chataway, his Village roommate. Occasionally, they explored the greater Vancouver area in their Austin Healey. Other times Bannister was spotted taking in various BECG events such as the fencing in the gymnasium of Lord Byng High School or picnicking on the banks of the Vedder Canal while watching the rowing trials or even attending the swimming events at Empire Pool the day before the Mile. In a CBC *Breakaway* interview in 1983 he recalled:

> It was a happy time in Vancouver, but a time of tremendous stress because I knew my running career was coming to an end. The race took on tremendous significance as an event I could either win or lose and leave my athletic career either successful or rather negative. That's why it was a great strain. But as it happened, I liked Vancouver.

However, by mid-week of the Games his preparations hit a snag. He woke up one morning coughing. His chest felt tight and his airways were congested. At the most inopportune moment he had caught a bug. The press and public remained unaware of his problem until Chataway, speaking to the assembled media after his Three Mile victory, let slip that Bannister was currently suffering from a "nasty cold." The condition of one of the Games' two prize milers suddenly sparked headlines everywhere. For the next several days it was no exaggeration that when Bannister sneezed it made worldwide news.

Coming down with a chest cold was hardly unique as highly fit athletes sometimes have lowered immunity to infections, but in this extremely pressurized environment where even the most mundane Bannister or Landy tidbits made front-page news, this item naturally blew up into a big story. "'Miracle Miler' Sick With Cold" blared one alarmed headline, while the accompanying article noted "his face was lighter than its normal pale pallor and his lips were cracked. He also wheezed slightly through a stuffy nose." One reporter asked Bannister to be photographed soaking his feet and drinking hot lemonade, to which he protested, "I neither soak my feet nor drink lemonade. However, you may take a picture of me smiling to signify that I'm all right." By August 4 his cold seemed to have "moderated" and the next day's *Victoria Daily Times* headline read: "Bannister Blows Nose, Claims Just Sniffles," possibly the most bizarre headline of the entire Games. A day later worries heightened once more when he confessed on a national radio broadcast that he felt "stuffed up." A *News-Herald* photo, showing him sneezing into a handkerchief, hardly alleviated concern. "Colds take their course," Bannister told a *Vancouver Sun* reporter, "and I haven't yet seen a doctor who could correct one. I'm a doctor and I know."

Opposite: Young Canadian diver Irene MacDonald emerged as a rising star at these Games.

However, the big question remained whether the most famous cold in the Commonwealth would run its course in time for the Mile. Bannister continually downplayed any effect it might have on his performance, wanting no alibi if he ran poorly. Yet even casual track followers understood that merely a tiny reduction in his optimum fitness could make the difference in such a closely contested race as this one. That thought also preyed on Bannister's mind as he read news of Landy's perfect health and latest training exploits, and he later recalled that: "I felt most depressed and dosed myself with all the medicines I could find." But ultimately Bannister remained determined to run with one lung if he had to.

Peters and Cox completed their training on Wednesday, August 4, three days before the BECG marathon, and as they headed out on one of their final runs, Lord Alexander, who was visiting the English team's Empire Village quarters, introduced himself to them. Learning they were marathoners, he recalled how he had stood at the finish line of the 1908 Olympic marathon in London. There he had watched the nearly unconscious runner Dorando Pietri helped by officials to the finish line of the race, although he was later disqualified because of the help he had received. Peters, of course, thought little of this exchange at the time, but Alexander's story planted another ominous seed that would later sprout.

✿

The schedulers for events at Empire Pool had interspersed men's and women's tower and springboard diving among the swimming events, starting on the afternoon of Tuesday, August 3, when the first sections of the men's and women's springboard diving events took place. The pool's churned waters calmed and spectators turned their gaze up to the gleaming diving tower. This specially built signature Games piece, which was painted canary yellow with a unique spiral staircase leading to the 5m and 10m cantilever platforms, was the first of its kind in Canada.

It was from one of the springboards in the shadow of that tower that Irene MacDonald introduced herself to Vancouver, her future home. The first time many saw the petite 20-year-old from Hamilton dive, it was an image inscribed forever in memory. With a deft hop off the board, she began her delicate, twisting plunge, hanging momentarily in graceful suspension like an angelic Christmas ornament. Slicing into the pool she sent out perfect rings, "just like a pebble dropping into the water" according to legendary *Province* photographer Bill Cunningham. "She really stood out on the springboard," agreed long-time CBC broadcaster Ted Reynolds in a 2007 interview. He had been just a greenhorn reporter for Victoria radio station CJVI at the time of the Games, but he remembered her as "remarkable."

Anyone who knew MacDonald's underdog story would have agreed. In fact, her dive from board to pool served as good metaphor for her unlikely rise—but *in reverse*. From the depths of a tumultuous childhood as an orphan, she had used diving to propel her to the heights, getting her *past* her past. Twisting through the air to the water below, she was transformed from the meek, almost fearful girl shivering under a towel on the pool deck. "When she was up there, she was an entirely different person than at any other time," Reynolds said. "She was in her own world."

Before discovering diving in her early teens, MacDonald had grown up in a Hamilton orphanage, a sad, tiny girl weighed down by low self-esteem and not knowing her parents. Bad acne and crooked teeth didn't help. She seemed to be drifting aimlessly until one day she accompanied another girl from the orphanage to a city pool. The other girl's coach suggested that since MacDonald was there, she might as well get into the pool too. She fell in love at first splash and proved a natural. Her strong, compact frame and tight centre of gravity allowed her to spin and twist like few others. She won the first of her 15 national titles in 1951 and somehow accomplished this while fighting a healthy fear of heights. Many years passed before she tried diving from the five-metre tower competitively, and even then she did it very reluctantly. And the 10-metre? Not a chance. "To put it bluntly, I was chicken to go up on the tower," MacDonald said in a BC Sports Hall of Fame interview in 1980. "I didn't really like it. I did it, but I didn't do it with the confidence and boldness that I did springboard diving. It was scary. I'd be hanging onto the rail."

As a young diver, this fear hindered her development, but fear in sports is a double-edged sword. If harnessed properly, it can be a powerful weapon. "I think that's what made her such a good competitor," offered Reynolds. "She was always a little bit afraid so when she broke through that and realized that she was as good if not better than anybody else, I think she decided then that it was her sport."

After winning the national diving title again in 1952, MacDonald earned selection to the Canadian Olympic team going to Helsinki. But only one plane carried the entire team in those days and she found herself a victim of selection politics. "They discovered they were missing two seats on the plane, so they took off a track girl and myself," MacDonald said in that 1980 interview. Luckily, her talent had blasted her so high so fast she had not fully comprehended what the Olympics were. "It wasn't a disappointment that I didn't go. But it also made me realize I would probably go to the next one."

Before the next Olympics rolled around, however, there was the 1954 BECG in Vancouver. MacDonald threw herself into training, displaying a daily determination that belied her timid personality. She focussed on form and technique, each slicing pool entry expanding her confidence and beating back the fear. By the time she reached Vancouver, she ranked as perhaps the most polished diving prospect this country had ever produced, and her form caught the trained eye of Dr. George Athans, who had seen all the best North American divers over the previous two decades. Athans had won 10 national championships, captured four BEG diving medals, including the 1950 springboard gold, and represented Canada at the 1936 and 1948 Olympics. Now retired to focus on his medical practice in Kelowna, he still coached young divers on the side. For the rest of his life he remembered the first moment he watched MacDonald on Empire Pool's springboard. "She bounced off the board like a bouncing ball and she made no splash when she went into the water," he later recalled. "She had more promise than anybody I had ever seen before." In the weeks leading up to the Games, Athans took MacDonald under his wing and worked to improve her repertoire of dives. Before long he had her brimming with confidence and boldly predicted to *Vancouver Province* reporters the day before the event that she would bring Canada a springboard gold despite this being her first big international meet.

But the women's springboard proved a tale of two extremes for young Irene Mac-Donald. On Tuesday, August 3, the first day of this two-day event, she was a vision, an exercise in perfection from the first chink of the diving board to the last. Every jump had spring, every twist stayed tight, every rotation spun crisply, every entry knifed flawlessly. She looked like the newest sensation in world diving; Athans looked like a genius; Canada looked to have sewn up an unexpected diving gold medal. Her own memories of that first day remained vivid, and years later she could still rattle off her first five dives: "running forward one-and-a-half somersault pike, standing back one-and-a-half header straight, running reverse one-and-a-half straight, standing inward one-and-a-half somersault tuck, and a running full twisting one-and-a-half straight."

"She was remarkable," marvelled Reynolds. "I'd never seen anybody make entries into the water like she made. She made it look *not easy*, but she made it look as though she knew *exactly* what she wanted to do and she did it." But it wasn't just how Mac-Donald did it on this day. It was by *how much* she did it. In a sport where medals and fates are decided by fractions of points, the shy rookie from Hamilton, who feared the heights from which she gracefully leapt, had stacked up a four-point lead after five dives. And chasing her were three of the Commonwealth's best international divers of the day. England's Ann Long would compete in three Olympics and claim three career BECG medals. Barbara McAulay of Australia, a Sydney piano teacher on the side, would win the women's tower competition on Friday, the last day of pool events. England's Charmian Welsh would collect both women's BECG diving gold medals in 1958.

But for MacDonald something changed overnight. Maybe it was inexperience or nerves or the unexpected pressure that got the better of her. Whatever it was, MacDonald seemed a different person on the second day of the springboard event, Wednesday, August 4. She looked stiff and jittery, like a person trapped in something over her head. Her best dives were only average. Anxious errors crept in everywhere. Dives that she had hit spot-on the day before she now missed badly. Long and McAulay chipped away at her sizable first-day buffer until they finished with gold and silver medal point totals of 128.26 and 127.74 respectively. On her final dive, MacDonald had one last chance to redeem herself. She spent a short eternity standing on the board attempting to summon what little composure remained to her. It wasn't enough. She finished a close third at 126.19 points, enough to continue Canada's streak of winning at least one BECG medal in women's springboard extending back to 1930.

Despite the poor finish, MacDonald appeared happy. "I really didn't expect to come this far," she admitted to reporters. Few knew how far she had come. And in her BC Sports Hall of Fame interview in 1980 she sounded refreshingly honest about the experience:

> The whole thing to me was a big adventure. I didn't think of winning when I went there. Getting a bronze was a bonus... I'll never forget it. I mean, it was my first one and you always remember [your first]. But I think the notoriety I had [in Vancouver] was the fact I blew my last dive. My biggest problem as a

Opposite: Irene MacDonald overcame an orphan childhood and fear of heights to become one of Canada's greatest divers.

competitor was being too emotional. It used to be a real letdown when it was all over or I'd be embarrassed if I missed a dive. One thing I learned is not to take it so seriously, but it took me a long time to really get over it. I think you do develop a thicker skin as you go along, but to me that was my biggest problem, being so thin-skinned.

For MacDonald, 1954 was something to build on. There were bigger things to come for her yet.

✺

On Thursday, August 5, another of Athans' protégés took on the men's 10m tower. Bill Patrick of Calgary, a former gymnast who began diving late, snuck up on the competition like a balmy Chinook to take one of Canada's more unexpected gold medals of the Games. After six of ten dives, the defending BECG tower champion Peter Heatly, a 30-year-old civil engineer from Edinburgh, held a slim lead of less than a point over the upstart Calgarian who was making his international debut. Patrick should have been well in front, but on his sixth dive he lost his balance and flubbed it. He then botched another handstand dive to fall even farther behind Heatly and Australian Kevin Newell.

But like any decent Stampede cowboy, Patrick hung on through the bucks and jives with two stellar final dives to slip in for gold by a whisker, edging Newell 142.70 points to 142.06. Afterwards he was congratulated by Calgary mayor Donald McKay, conspicuous for his white Stetson and loud encouragement. The man who had publicly criticized Vancouverites for not enough "hootin' and hollerin' in these here Games," galloped down to the pool deck, boot heels clinking on the metal stairs, and threw a meaty arm around young Patrick. "It's a great day for Calgary," McKay whooped, "a great day indeed!"

An annoyed Heatly, who took bronze less than a point back, sought redemption for uncharacteristically missing three dives. "First time in my life I've ever done that," he fumed to reporters. The following day he attacked the final section of the men's springboard with a vengeance, building an early lead with fine form and holding off all challengers to win gold with a final points total of 146.76. The silver

Canada's Bill Patrick took gold in the men's 10m tower diving in his international debut. Photo courtesy of Kay Neale.

Scottish diver Peter Heatly receives congratulations from his wife, Roberta (right), and an unidentified competitor after claiming gold in men's 3m springboard.

went to Tony Turner of England, the bronze to Jack Stewart of New Zealand. Another of those he defeated was England's Frank Mercer, who had good reason for finishing back of the pack. When he arrived in Vancouver, he had been feeling poorly, and doctors discovered he had contracted mumps and immediately placed him in quarantine. He spent the next 10 days in hospital, climbing from his bed and practising handstands when nurses weren't looking. He was released just the day before the springboard competition.

Heatly's 1954 BECG gold and bronze were added to the gold and silver he had earned in Auckland four years earlier, and no one was happier about this than his diving coach and wife, Roberta Heatly. "I keep watch and try to help him correct little failings," she told a reporter. Four years later in Cardiff, Heatly recaptured the 10m tower gold medal, and after a decade of dominating Commonwealth diving, he retired. He then served as a Scottish team official before rising to chairman of the Commonwealth Games Federation itself, serving in that capacity from 1982 to 1990. Twice he was instrumental in bringing the Games to his home city of Edinburgh, first in 1970 and then 1986.

Prince Philip's first full day at the Games, Wednesday, August 4, proved far less chaotic than his arrival in the city had been. RCMP officers escorted the two official cars carrying him and his entourage via a meandering route to the BECG rowing events held on the Vedder Canal near Chilliwack. Hundreds of flag-waving citizens lined the roadside, many surprised to see the royal visitor waving to them from behind the wheel for a portion of the drive. By this time the frenzy that Philip had produced in an otherwise laid-back populace was proving, at times, comical, and *Sun* cartoonist Len Norris perfectly captured the atmosphere, which seemed to transcend even the Games themselves.

Above: Fraser Valley Rowing Committee chair Cecil Hacker (right) and Prince Philip at the Vedder Canal.

Below: Cartoonist Len Norris perfectly captured the excitement caused by Prince Philip's arrival. Cartoon courtesy of Steve Norris.

✱

Once the Fraser Valley Rowing Committee (FVRC) had taken over the project on the Vedder Canal, everything had proceeded smoothly with preparations for the Games. However, in early July, just weeks before Commonwealth oarsmen were scheduled to take up residence in the nearby military barracks, the waters of the Vedder began rising rapidly, owing to a heavy melt of accumulated alpine snow. At its highest point, the water level reached 13ft, more than double the ideal depth. The potential for flooding remained small—it was still 4ft from the crisis level of 1948 when the dikes were breached—but residents living along the river remained nervous.

As water began lapping over the bottom three rows of spectator seating for the rowing events, the committee decided that construction plans had to be greatly altered on the fly. They scrapped plans for boathouse and crew quarters to be erected on pilings pounded into the edge of the canal bed in favour of floating facilities built on hundreds of empty oil drums. And then Mother Nature served up another cruel twist. As quickly as the Vedder's waters had risen, they began to drop. First a couple of feet, then a few more, until by the third week of July the water had settled at a depth of 8ft, but now the new floating facilities were sitting high above the water and stuck in the mud. Roofs sagged and floors rolled like waves on the mucky contours of the canal berm, while the pontoon-supported walkways twisted helter-skelter like an accordion. Slimy reeds poked through the shallower areas, while the current had increased to five knots.

To ensure the turbid waters remained above the minimum 6ft and to slow the current, the chair of the Rowing Events Engineering Committee, Fred Sinclair, gave the go-ahead for a $21,500 temporary dam at the Vedder's north end. If anyone could determine the best way to tame the unpredictable canal, it was this 83-year-old retired railway engineer since he had designed and built the Vedder Canal in the first place. Sinclair had moved to BC at the turn of the century and become interested in the enormous agricultural potential of the 35,000 acres of fertile soil lying under the shallow waters of Sumas Lake. After designing a plan to drain the lake via a diked canal that diverted the Vedder River into the mighty Fraser, he had raised the necessary capital himself and convinced the BC government to appoint him head of the canal's construction. When the $3.7 million project was completed in 1923, it made some of the most fertile farmland in Canada available.

Now, sporting a fedora and bowtie and carrying a long wooden ruler to measure the water depth, Sinclair cut a curious figure as he marched along the canal banks. "I don't know anything about this rowing, but I sure know the water," he told reporters. He believed the temporary dam would alleviate any concerns over water depth and current, but with only 12 working days left before the BECG rowing events kicked off, they had to move fast. The plan was to pile-drive timbers into the canal bed and allow the high volume of fast-moving water to spill over the top. It sounded good in theory, but the high run-off proved too strong, making the pile-driving difficult, and after several days of double-shifts to rush the dam to completion, Sinclair halted all work and abandoned the project. The ill-fated dam soon washed away with a loss of $13,103 even after salvaging materials. It proved to be one of the Games' biggest financial boondoggles, and even worse, the water conditions did the rowers no favours. After fighting the current, which was estimated to slow training times for every crew by over a minute, a few of the rowers assessed the waters as "sluggish," and some complained of an elevation gain of 4ft from start to finish.

Colonel Tommy Taylor, who had fought so determinedly to have Burnaby Lake anointed as the rowing site, saw the Vedder's rising and falling floodwaters as the perfect time to recommence the smear campaign against the Vedder. Newspaper articles with the hallmarks of his earlier press offerings appeared, including one erroneously reporting that conditions at the Vedder would mean the cancellation of all rowing events. Taylor even gave boat tours to visiting Commonwealth oarsmen and their coaches on Burnaby Lake. Afterwards, he persuaded English rowing coach Arthur Sulley to tell the press that Burnaby Lake "present[ed] possibilities that should not be missed," while Canadian coach Frank Read called the lake "potentially the finest rowing course in the world."

Cecil Hacker, head of the FVRC and publisher of the *Chilliwack Progress*, responded with a deluge of media praise for the Vedder to protect the $40,000 investment made by various Fraser Valley rowing backers, prevent the erosion of a large crowd turnout and entice visitors to spend their hard-earned coin while they were in the Valley communities for the rowing events. Fighting for the pride of his rowing committee and that of the Valley in general, Hacker ran an article headlined "Vedder Course Wins Highest Accolades" and quoted Australian rowing manager Ray Thursfield as describing the Vedder as "one of the world's finest courses... good enough for the world Olympic Games any day." The *Vancouver Sun* joined the fray with an article headlined "Aussies Declare Vedder World's Best For Rowing." And on July 24, with rowing events only 10 days off, George Marshall, a VRC member who had captained the Cambridge eight to victory over Oxford in the 1953 Boat Race on the Thames, praised the Vedder in the *Province* as a "First Class Choice For Rowing":

> I have not seen a finer natural regatta course... The surrounding fertile Fraser Valley plains and the grand hills of British Columbia, apparently rising sheer out of either end of the canal, give as spectacular a setting as anyone could wish for, and it is my guess that the actual course is just about the oarsman's dream.

Thankfully, the rowing course battle halted for the duration of the Games and events on the Vedder went off without a hitch. The good people of Chilliwack and Abbotsford bent over backwards to make the experience for everyone the best it could possibly be. Even when a torrential downpour soaked the rowing competition's opening day, Tuesday, August 3, the 2,000 hardy souls who had braved the rain to watch the heats for the single sculls and coxed fours simply armed themselves with makeshift tents, newspaper ponchos, even grain sack rain jackets.

Under drier skies the next day more than 10,000 people lined the Vedder's banks to see the finals in all of the rowing competitions. Among the rowers that afternoon was Australia's Mervyn Wood, a fingerprint expert with the Sydney police force, who in the course of one frenzied hour on the Vedder won two gold BECG medals to stand as the most successful rower of the 1954 Games. He won the first when he and his partner Murray Riley, a fellow police officer, easily captured the double sculls event in a time of 7:54.5, which was over 10 seconds clear of the second-place Kiwis and 34 seconds ahead

Rowing organizers battled the Vedder Canal's unpredictable waters, which rose and fell by several feet in the weeks before the regatta.

of the third-place Canadian team. Wood's second gold came as a member of the Aussie's coxed fours that took their race with a time of 7:58.3 with New Zealand second and England third.

At 37, Mervyn Wood was also the oldest man in the regatta, old enough that he had been part of Australia's eights crew at the 1936 Olympics. Post-WWII, while working for the New South Wales Criminal Investigation Branch, he had bought oars and a second-hand shell named *Audrey* and developed into one of the world's great scullers. He would eventually accumulate three Olympic and five Commonwealth medals as well as two Diamond Sculls titles at Henley, a Philadelphia Cup as 1948's best amateur sculler and 12 national titles. He remains the only athlete to serve as Australia's Olympic flag bearer twice. After retiring from sculling, Wood focussed on his police work and rose to become Sydney's commissioner in 1977. Shockingly, it was Riley, his 1954 BECG gold-medal doubles partner, who contributed to the abrupt end of Wood's police career just two years later. Riley had left the police force in the early 1960s to become an international drug smuggler and kingpin of the Sydney drug trade. After Wood's link to his former rowing partner began generating intense media scrutiny, he was forced into retirement.

Colonel Victor Spencer (left) stands with Frank Read (second from left) and the UBC-VRC rowing eights crew.

The heavy eights event typically highlighted any regatta, but owing to high shipping costs for the delicate, cumbersome 62ft rowing shells, only two nations had entered eights crews in the 1954 Games, and they appeared to be a serious mismatch. Canada, represented by a bunch of green UBC students rowing out of the Vancouver Rowing Club, faced England's proven international crew from the famed Thames Rowing Club. On paper at least, Britannia appeared destined to rule the Vedder's waves. Each English crew member was on average five years older and nearly 10lbs heavier than the Canadians—it was literally men versus boys. Hardly surprising then that most of the pundits conceded BECG gold to the English on experience and past results alone. Earlier in the summer at the Henley Regatta, the Thames oarsmen had narrowly lost to the USSR's reigning world champion eight by half a boat-length, and the English could claim six recent high finishes or victories in significant competitions at home or in Europe. Other than an impressive victory at the Canadian BECG trials, the UBC boys had nothing to match this.

A crowd of 10,000 lined the Vedder's banks during the second day of BECG rowing events.

They were a bunch of working class students from backwoods BC towns, the boys from nowhere. Their most experienced member had been rowing just a few years, the majority a few scant months. As Dick Beddoes said in his *Sun* column on August 5, "Two of their number had never rowed anything more seaworthy than a manure spreader."

By comparison, the men from the Thames Rowing Club oozed establishment and experience. The crew featured several Olympians educated at august institutions like Oxford, some had nearly two decades of rowing experience, and they claimed membership in the largest rowing club in the world, a club boasting several hundred members, an establishment date of 1860, and an active president in the Duke of Gloucester. Their coach, Arthur Sulley, was a Derby man, an Olympic silver medalist who managed James Smith and Co. (Derby Limited), one of Britain's top manufacturers of military uniforms. Their manager, Guy "Gully" Nickalls, was a two-time Olympic silver medalist educated at Eton and Oxford, a man whose family tree boasted several oarsmen highly placed in the English rowing fraternity.

came was yelling at his rowers through an oversized megaphone as he stood in a trailing 18ft runabout powered by an outboard motor. Yet his willpower fuelled his crew's boats through unrelenting motivation and persuasion. On the one hand, he saw himself as a father figure to his young rowers, steering them towards lives as productive members of society. He felt it his duty to teach and guide them, race results being less important than the learning gained on the journey. On the other hand, there was the harder side to Read, the strict disciplinarian with the legendary temper. His rowers called him "Simon Legree" behind his back, after the fictional slave owner. He saw himself as "the man with the big black whip." He demanded complete compliance from anyone who wanted to be a part of his crew. Anything less was unacceptable. And he saw exhaustion as the point when an oarsman *really* began to work: "Rowing is rowing when you are tired, so get tired and then learn how to row." To this he added one qualifier: "Any crew can look good while paddling, but they must be good under pressure, so put the pressure on."

Perhaps no coach drove his athletes harder, and team members inevitably cite Read as the most significant reason for their ultimate success. "No question he's the biggest," underscored crew member Phil Kueber in a 2007 interview, "the *only* reason. He had it in his mind's eye that he was going to do something with us and he did. I mean, he didn't have a bunch of athletes. We were a bunch of misfits." But Read also had an effect on their lives in general. "Read took the raw materials of the crew—that small-town outdoor ethic, the lack of fear, the ton of brains, the athleticism—he took all that and aimed it in one direction," said team manager Don Laishley in a 2007 interview. "Not only was he the driving force behind the crew, but his influence on us as individuals was absolutely enormous. I think half of us could have been mediocre stumblebums. There was no question that Read had more influence on me as a young man moving into adulthood than any other person."

But no mysterious formula existed for Read's success. In fact, when he became well-known all over the world as a sort of rowing Svengali, he still remained very clear about how to find success in rowing: "I have no secrets re moving a boat. So-called different styles have and still do win boat races; there is no one way or style that is the entire answer; it is the men in the boat first, last and always!" And therein lay his secret. His proficiency with raw human material proved exceptional. He tuned individuals to just the right winning frequency.

The pieces of Read's 1954 eights crew began falling into place in early 1950 when stroke Glen Smith of Grand Forks, the cerebral and hard-working "old man of the sea" as teammates dubbed him, first turned out for the crew. Abbotsford's Mike Harris, the team's brightest student, arrived in the fall of 1952, as did the gangly 115lb cox, Ray Sierpina, a 16-year-old prodigy from Richmond. The tiny town of Ganges on Saltspring Island produced two crew members: team captain Tom Toynbee and 17-year-old Doug McDonald. The fall of 1953 brought team manager Don Laishley and spare Phil Kueber from Nelson and Duncan respectively. Prince George's Herman Zloklikovits (later Kovits), the best pure athlete on the 1954 crew, joined up with Kamloops' Bob Wilson, nicknamed "Death" for his skin tone and resemblance to actor Jack Palance. As the calendar flipped to 1954, the ultra-laid-back 17-year-old Laurie West from Vancouver worked himself onto the team. "Bulldog" Ken Drummond from tiny Burton—underwater since the 1968 construction of the Keenleyside Dam—earned a call-up from the

Barking through a tin megaphone, coach Frank Read knew how to get the most out of his rowing crews.

junior varsity squad just months before the Games. Displaced by huge distances from their families, homes and ways of life, all these young men were brought together by rowing to become family, a band of brothers.

It is said Read never cut a single athlete in all the years he coached, but Harris laughed when he explained that Read's gruelling dry land training regimen took care of weeding out the pool of prospects. "You didn't have to be one of the *best* eight, just one of the *last* eight." Read's infamous liking for a form of rudimentary calisthenics known as "McDonald's abominable abdominal exercises" whipped those who stayed the course into shape. On one occasion the team put themselves through a US Navy fitness test where a perfect score was 300 sit-ups. A couple of the boys stopped after two hours and over 2,500 crunches—not from fatigue but from scraping the skin of their buttocks raw.

Read's nightly training grind on Burrard Inlet was no easier. Rowing 16km from the VRC dock in Coal Harbour to the Second Narrows Bridge and back every evening by the light of a lantern hanging on the end of a barge, the crew grew to expect the unexpected because it was such a rapidly changing obstacle course. Driftwood floated menacingly everywhere. Tugboats and freighters sent waves cutting across the shells, occasionally swamping the fragile vessels or worse. One day the tide was up, the next down; one day the current ran with them, the next against. "We never knew when we launched our shells whether we would get them back in one piece or in pieces," said Read.

In spring the crew switched to two-a-day workouts, averaging two-and-a-half hours on the water daily and covering about 26km. Whenever the weather cooperated, they rowed all the way to Port Moody and back. Every workout ended with a 2,000m timed sprint beginning at the CPR docks and finishing at the VRC. The route became so familiar that landmarks worked themselves into the calls delivered by cox Sierpina and helped the crew gauge distances. The important marker was *Taconite*, the Boeing family's 125ft yacht that was always moored at the end of the VRC marina. The crew would commence their final sprint at the *Taconite*'s stern, usually thirty strokes or three extra hard "Big Tens." Everywhere they competed, Coal Harbour's landmarks came with them, so that even in competitions on other waterways, the crew would designate a tree or barn as the *Taconite*.

Once classes at UBC ended in April, the boys moved into the VRC clubhouse for the summer, even though rats infested the lower reaches of the aging building. They slept in bunks set up in a corner of the main dining hall with blankets hung on clotheslines to give them some privacy while Friday night dances roared around them. Most still managed to sleep soundly as they were so exhausted from their workouts. A wispy English woman named Mrs. Longmeyer—nicknamed "The Prowl"—cooked for them. Together this band of brothers discovered rock and roll with the release of "Rock Around The Clock" by Bill Haley and The Comets, and they walked over to Granville Street to see the movie *Blackboard Jungle*. They grew to appreciate the beauty and splendour of Stanley Park, which was right on their doorstep, and they kept the clubhouse windows open on summer nights to allow the sweet singing of the pretty girls in Theatre Under the Stars productions to drift in on the breeze from Malkin Bowl. "We were encouraged to be together, to do things together," said McDonald in a 2007 interview. "That was the key to our boat. Once our blades were in the water, everybody was trying to do *exactly* the same thing at *exactly* the same time. That was how the boat would virtually fly."

But this Cinderella team did have some help getting to the grand ball. Whenever they needed something—funding, equipment, clothing, food, time off from summer and weekend jobs—if Read could not provide it himself, he found benefactors who could. He convinced Colonel Victor Spencer, owner of Spencer's Department Stores and the Douglas Lake Cattle Company, to pay for the $2,500 sleek 62ft Pocock racing shell that bore his name. Tong Louie, president of the H.Y. Louie Company, donated fruits and vegetables, while horse racing magnate Jack Diamond provided steaks. Charles "Chunky" Woodward, later president of Woodward's Department Stores, supplied the deep freezers for the crew's food. Timothy Eaton provided clothing. Future Lieutenant-Governor Frank Ross, architect Ned Pratt, Vancouver Stock Exchange head Sedley Campbell "Bimbo" Sweeny and the owner of Vancouver's Harley-Davidson dealership, Fred Deeley, all helped out in a pinch. But perhaps the team's most important supporter was Seattle boat builder George Pocock, who built their racing shell and rescued them in their most dire moment.

Two weeks after receiving their new *Victor Spencer II* racing shell and only days before departing for St. Catharines, Ontario, and the Canadian BECG trials, the crew was sweating through one final workout at dusk. Approaching the VRC boathouse, they struck a submerged log, and a burbling trickle of water began seeping from fresh cracks that ran nearly the entire length of the delicate cedar craft. To the crew it seemed the end of the world. In bowman Wilson's meticulously kept rowing scrapbook the page for that date bears the simple title: "Tragedy." But in response to a phone call, Pocock raced up to Vancouver that night and using space-age glues from his friends at Boeing and age-old boat-building tricks, this master boat builder fixed the damaged craft in record time. Those who witnessed him work equated it to Michelangelo touching up the David. While humming Perry Como's 1954 Billboard chart-topping tune "Wanted," Pocock skillfully re-carved the damaged bow's soft wood with his jackknife, shaving away thin ringlets of cedar until the surface was smooth and unsullied once more. "It didn't leak *at all*," recalled Drummond. "After George fixed it, it was good as new."

Read and the UBC-VRC crew—now formally known as the UBC Thunderbirds—couldn't help feeling confident as they set off for the BECG trials. They knew, however, that since the initiation of formal Games selection rowing trials, no West Coast team had ever accomplished anything of note at the St. Catharines Henley Rowing Centre, and to supporters of the BC team who were listening to the play-by-play delivered by CBC Radio's Ward Cornell, it initially appeared this year would be no different. While the UBC crew was stroking away from the field, Cornell in his far-off observation tower totally ignored them, espousing instead the histories and virtues of the eastern crews that were falling behind, particularly the Hamilton Leanders, whom he especially fancied. Read's boys captured the race in one of the most dominant displays in Canadian rowing history, made all the more impressive by being so unexpected. "Oh, we didn't have a clue whether we were going to be first or last," Wilson said when interviewed later. "Shocked the hell out of everybody." Eastern newspapers conservatively listed the Thunderbird margin of victory at four boat lengths; some western papers listed the gap at over five. The *St. Catharines Standard* needed more than half the width of its sports page to print the panoramic photo showing all five crews at the finish—the four eastern crews clustered on the far right, the elegant Thunderbirds alone on the far left edge, with acres of open water and two full column widths between them. "When we crossed the finish line, it looked like the tail end of one race and the beginning of another!" McDonald said, chortling. Congratulatory telegrams poured into Read's hotel room, one of them from the Fraser Valley Rowing Committee, who must have been particularly delighted at the prospect of having a local crew representing Canada:

CONGRATULATIONS ON TERRIFIC VICTORY. MAY THE VEDDER BE EVEN BETTER. — THE VEDDER GANG

The eights showdown was the first event on the second afternoon of the Games regatta, on Wednesday, August 4. The air felt heavy and hot. Newspapers that had been held up by onlookers as cover from the rain the previous day were now folded into fans and waved furiously. By protocol, the event could not start until Prince Philip took his place in the royal stand, its bare plywood dressed up with billowing tri-coloured bunting. However, he and his entourage had been delayed and everyone, including the English and Canadian eights crews, waited anxiously, sitting in their respective racing

With Prince Philip running late, the start of the eights race was delayed while both crews waiting nervously.

shells at the start line, which was positioned at the canal's north end. For the UBC boys, wearing their scarlet shorts and fancy white Canadian singlets for the first time, these seemed the longest moments of their lives.

"We were out at the start, twiddling and waiting," recalled Wilson. "It seemed like an eternity. You're all pent up, full of nerves, nervous adrenalin. We must have been out there for half an hour." And Harris agreed. "We sat there looking at the other team, and they kind of looked at us. They looked much more calm. It didn't help our nerves at all."

A few focussed on Coach Read's epic speech to them after their final workout the previous day, and this helped a little. "Work together and help each other and keep all phases of this adventure in its proper perspective," he had told them. "Use this wonderful sport of rowing to discover yourself, to understand others and to learn to live your daily life with full appreciation for others." Then he paused and changed his tone. "Now the big black whip comes out: hit that water with the legs driving... hit it with everything you've got... but hit it together... work as a crew." His voice had lowered. "Now tomorrow I want you to take it out at a high rate. If you hafta go at that rate the whole way, can you do it?"

"Yes! Of course!" they had replied.

Read had nodded. They were ready.

Prince Philip's Cadillac convertible finally rolled into view around 2:30 and was greeted by excited applause. It took another 10 minutes for Cecil Hacker to escort the prince and his party across the temporary Bailey bridge to the royal stand. At precisely 2:44, the starting gun blasted and the crews were off. Announcers in a motorboat that followed the shells kept spectators informed on all portions of the race, but even without their help, many in the stands could see things had gone sideways for the Canadian boys right from the gun, and a concerned murmur ricocheted through the crowd. Read, standing on a floating dock at the finish line with Laishley and Kueber, looked

Canada's underdog eights crew slices the finish line two boat-lengths ahead of the favoured English

through his binoculars and saw an enormous crest of white water splash up off the oars on the bow side. "Oh miiigaaawwdd…" he moaned. They were all out of sequence. He shifted his view to the English, who were stroking away as smooth as silk in the eastern lane. It couldn't get any worse.

The Canadian boat was in chaos. A disastrous chain reaction had begun with the first stroke off the line as Kovits, sitting in the number three position, washed out, sending a huge wall of water into McDonald's oar in front of him and causing McDonald to catch a massive "crab," as rowers call it when one's oar fails to clear the water's surface. It knocked the oar clean out of McDonald's hands, and he knew if he grabbed hold and fought it, he would be pitched into the water. Instinctively, he lay back and let the boat's momentum pass the oar over him, coming to rest parallel to the side of the shell. But all of this action had wreaked havoc with the rest of the crew's rhythm because they didn't know what was happening, and that caused additional minor crabs. Some recalled feeling the boat lurch to one side, while others felt a shuddered halting. Fortunately, Smith and Sierpina somehow managed to restart the stroke rhythm and the crew quickly fell back into sequence. McDonald, still lying back without his oar, waited for the appropriate moment, then swung the handle back and into line with the rest of the crew. Miraculously for a crew so green, they had reorganized and were rowing again—although they were now a full boat-length behind the English. The race should have been over right there. The experienced English should have sped off, pulling away from the valiant Canadians rowing out the string and trying not to look like complete fools—just as the speculative *Progress* article had predicted. But then something remarkable happened. The UBC boys didn't pack it in. Maybe the man with the big black whip and the countless miles logged out of Coal Harbour had hardened them so they would not—could not—buckle. Right about then the *Victor Spencer* began to fly as it never had in training.

"Goin' to 38!" yelled Sierpina, sitting in the boat's stern and crowing out the stroke rhythm like an enraged rooster. His arms flapped in a wide arc, slapping the shell's sides so hard reverberations were felt down its entire length. Their jitters faded into the brisk rhythm, each rower focussing on putting everything he had into the stroke at hand. At 100m the English were no longer pulling ahead, but the Canadians weren't gaining any ground either. "Goin' to 40! Big Ten! Big Ten!" yelled Sierpina, the tin megaphone strapped to his head vibrating like a tuning fork. "No mistakes now, boys, let's catch those limey bastards!"

It may have been the earliest call for a "Big Ten" push ever in a race, but desperate times call for desperate measures. They had to make up ground *now*. The English continued to plod along at a 36-beat rate and by the 250m mark, the Canadians had nearly caught them. By 400m they had pulled a metre into the lead. There would be a race today after all. The spooked English now chose to fight fire with fire and upped their rate to 40 to match the Canadians. At the 500m mark, both teams were virtually even, the lead swinging back and forth as each shell's bow nosed ahead. But here the superior fitness of Read's boys began to turn the tide. Somehow they maintained their 40-stroke pace—even upping it occasionally to 42 or a sapping 44—while the English faltered ever so slightly. At the halfway mark the Canadians had edged ahead by half a boat length, and the 10,000 spectators on the banks rose to their feet and began to roar as the boats came closer. Cries of "Come on, Canada!" drowned out the loudspeaker.

They say that in an eights race, most victories are *won* in the first 500m or *lost* in the third 500m. In this case Read's boys had miraculously fought back to give themselves a chance in the first quarter, but the English failed to step up from 1000m on. Maybe they could not believe a bunch of green kids could maintain this grinding effort and must inevitably tire. Whatever the reason, the English shifted back to a steady 36-beat, wanting none of the brute tempo of this wicked game, while the Canadians continued to plow ahead at 40. They were undoubtedly tiring. Their oars entered the water less smoothly and sloppy splashes became common. At times they looked jerky and raw, and maybe their inexperience showed more now than at any other point, but they also painted a picture of blunt, thrusting speed at its most unrefined, something the English had no answer for. By the three-quarter mark, the Canadians had built a full two-length lead, but every stroke felt like murder. Their shoulders ached, their thighs burned. Every breath seared their lungs. Smith and Sierpina allowed no relief. Read had instructed them to take it out hard—and they had—so now their cox and stroke simply wouldn't allow them to take it down. But they didn't have much left and there was still a long way to go, and the English, finally sensing it was now or never, upped their rate once more.

As they always did, the Canadians had chosen landmarks along the Vedder that matched up with familiar points on their training runs. They had placed the *Taconite* marker at the end of the plank seating, which had worked fine when the seating was empty, but when 10,000-plus people overflowed past its farthest extent on race day, it made the marker nearly impossible to discern. Rather than risk leaving their final push too late, Sierpina did the only sensible thing in the circumstances: as soon as the masses on the banks became thick enough, he began calling, "Taconite! Taconite!" and then another and another. Already exhausted, their stroke rate jumped to at least a frantic

44, maybe higher—a sustained sprint almost unheard of in rowing at the time. With tired arms, legs and lungs, on they reached for muddy water and heaved. Again and again. *Chung, chung, chung, chung.* The *Spencer* fairly flew those last few metres. The roar of the crowd seemed deafening, even drowning out Sierpina. "Taconite! Taconite! One last time! Don't let those limey bastards catch us now!"

There was little need to worry. The English were over two lengths in arrears. One final stroke and the *Spencer* sliced the line in a time of 6min 59.0sec as an official on the dock fired a shotgun blast skyward. The English followed nearly 12 seconds behind. The Canadians slumped forward or fell back exhausted but elated. Flashbulbs snapped as they slapped one another's backs and struggled to catch their breath. It was done: Canada's first gold medal in eights rowing in any international Games. Some called it the most unexpected victory of the 1954 Games. Others said it was the greatest upset in BECG history. No one denied either claim.

On the dock Laishley let loose a massive roar of relief, while Read beamed and chuckled to himself in a rare display of emotion. "They did it," he marvelled, shaking his head. He turned around to see Colonel Tommy Taylor dashing up a nearby float with tears in his eyes, celebrating the victory with any and all, apparently having shelved all thought of Burnaby Lake—at least for today.

An army boat loaded up the jubilant crew and ferried them to the victory stand. There, Major Jack Davies presented both teams with their medals before Canada's national anthem was played and many proud Canadians sang their hearts out. Afterwards, Sierpina received the customary cox dunking, tossed into the chilly Vedder by his celebrating teammates. Read and the crew then gathered back at the boathouse where they put the *Spencer* on its rack to dry before he pulled them in tight for a few quiet words of congratulation. A passing cameraman saw the chance for a good shot and gently interrupted. They turned arm-in-arm, all sparkling youthful eyes and gleaming teeth. Sierpina crouched in front flashing the "V for Victory" symbol with his fingers. The widest smile of all belonged to the man in the middle with his binoculars still hanging from his neck. Frank Read never looked so proud in all his life.

Reporters from the Vancouver papers crowded around Read and the crew clamouring to know how they did it. "We had England worried out here all week," Read told them. "They knew we were fit but also knew we were green. That's why I ordered them to get out in front and drive, drive all the way. They could have done a 52 a minute if they had to." Standing back and taking in all the animated celebratory chaos unfolding around him, Smith provided a *Sun* reporter with the quote that summed up all they had been through: "Brother, wasn't that a hairy one!" Wasn't it, though.

Outside of the Mile and Marathon, no other BECG event garnered the amount of press suddenly accorded the eights event on the Vedder. "UBC's Rowing Crew Scores Stunning Upset Win in BEG" trumpeted the *Sun*'s page one headline the next day, while the sports section carried a headline of "'Twas a Mighty Win, Indeed!" *Province* articles announced that "Canadian Rowers Sink Mighty England" and "Green Canadian Crew Scores Upset of BEG," while an editorial claimed: "They Did the Impossible." The following week's *Chilliwack Progress* stated "what they did today was comparable to an unknown beating Bannister or Landy in the miracle mile."

Canada's rowing eights show a mixture of exhaustion and elation just seconds after their unlikely victory.

The UBC-VRC crew on the podium, receiving Canada's first gold medal in eights rowing in any international Games.

Newspapers across the country carried similar coverage, and these unknowns were suddenly celebrities, their names known from BC to Newfoundland.

Praise came in from all sides for their effort. "The Canadians were very, very fit," a member of the vanquished English crew told a *Province* reporter. "And they have a lot of guts. In fact, old man, they are the gutsiest chaps I know." The English manager, Nickalls, hailed them as "the greatest young rowing crew" he had ever come across, while English coach Sulley, speaking to the *Victoria Daily Times*, went even further: "Never have I seen such superbly conditioned young animals. Their great drive and ability to hit a steady forty never gave us a chance to row our kind of race."

"They were magnificent," exulted Nelles Stacey, chair of the BECG rowing committee, to the *Province*. "Read's a coach who not only is competent from a rowing standpoint but who understands every man in his crew. He talks their language and he makes every one of them 'feel' rowing the way he does." Earlier, the BEG Federation secretary, Sandy Duncan, had been overheard in the royal stand incredulously asking aloud to anyone within earshot: "How can a green crew of college men beat England's best eight?" A newsman put Duncan's comment before Stacey, who without hesitation

The crew with Frank Read celebrating what some called the greatest upset victory in BECG history.

provided a reply that was carried across the country: "Frank Read and the damndest spirit you ever saw."

Although they had been just a bunch of beginners and hackers in the fall of 1953, by the following summer Read's crew had thrust themselves into the world's top 15 rowing crews, a polished well-oiled machine. Another year and the number of crews ranking higher worldwide could be counted on one hand with fingers left over. For a country that had known only fleeting rowing triumph previously, the story of this Cinderella Crew must stand as one of the great Canadian underdog stories. Few stories contain such unbelievable characters and plot, the stuff of which legends are made.

CHAPTER 8
THURSDAY, AUGUST 5, 1954

Of the eight athletes competing at the 1954 BECG who already held world records, one name stood above the rest: Marjorie Jackson-Nelson. The Australian sprinter had achieved a level of dominance few athletes in any sport in any era could match. Beyond breaking and re-breaking several world records, she was also a double Olympic medalist in 1952 and had won four BECG gold medals in 1950. In five years of international competition against the best female sprinters on the planet, she had *never* been beaten in competition, not even in a heat. In a discipline where a single broken stride or a slow start can be the difference between victory and defeat, even the greatest have "off days," but not the "Lithgow Flash." Once asked to explain how she ran, she said simply, "I just ran to win." By 1954 she was considered the greatest female sprinter the world had ever known, and to this day she must still be counted among the 10 best woman athletes to have ever laced on track spikes.

Jackson-Nelson's performance in the 220yds in Vancouver on Thursday afternoon, August 5, would only enhance that legacy, but by then, it had already been an eventful Games for her. First, the 22-year-old had weathered pangs of homesickness during the first prolonged separation from her new husband, Australian cyclist Peter Nelson, whom she had met at the Helsinki Olympics. Then she survived a minor furor with a Games official who publicly threatened to disqualify her if she used an illegal "rolling start" during races. This prompted one Sydney journalist to call for "Australia's immediate secession from the Commonwealth" if the overzealous official followed through. Jackson-Nelson had also been forced to vehemently deny a report in the *Adelaide News*, probably initiated by a former teammate and co-worker, that she was pregnant. This furor was soon topped by the *Province*'s Bud Elsie who broke a story about her that made headlines around the world: Marjorie Jackson-Nelson, the fastest woman in history, was retiring from athletics for good following the Games in Vancouver. The timing seemed odd as she was at the height of her sprinting powers and the Olympics in her home nation was just two years away, but she had won every major title and world record available to her, and she told Elsie she wanted "to go domestic and cook and sew and keep house" for her husband. "I can hardly wait to get back to him," she emphasized. Asked if she might change her mind, she remained firm: "[There] isn't a chance in the world." And suddenly the 1954 Games morphed into a farewell tour for her, although she looked as hungry and driven as ever, the opposite of an athlete with nothing left to prove. In her first appearance on Empire Stadium's cinder track earlier in the week, she had done what she did best—sprint and win—easily claiming the 100yds in a BECG record 10.7sec, which sadly could not be officially ratified owing to a stronger than allowable tailwind.

Opposite: Australia's Marjorie Jackson-Nelson blasts out of the starting blocks. Photo by Brian Kent.

So as the crowd of 18,497—the largest since the Opening Ceremonies—filed through the turnstiles of Empire Stadium on Thursday, August 5, everyone was anticipating more fireworks from Jackson-Nelson in her final hurrah in the 220. She didn't disappoint. She had drawn the far outside lane, usually a disadvantage, but she thrust to the lead with one stride after a bullet-type start. She looked smooth, accelerating almost effortlessly, and then like a rocket hitting the next burn stage, *boom*, she was gone. Around the corner her lead grew with each stride, and down the straight she flew like a whirlwind before splitting the finish line string in 24.0sec. The run equalled her own world record set in February, and it would prove to be the only world record performance achieved by any athlete at the 1954 Games. Her Australian teammate Winsome Cripps scrambled to the line in 24.5sec, ahead of England's Shirley Hampton by half a second.

After pushing herself to these enviable limits, Jackson-Nelson walked gingerly on the infield grass, occasionally gasping for a breath, as the Australian women's team manager ran up to her with a bouquet of yellow gladiolas and carnations bound with green ribbon, Australia's national colours. But Jackson-Nelson looked drawn and out of sorts, the emotion of her final individual race clearly getting to her. Dozens of athletes and officials wended their way through the milling crowds of competitors to offer her a word of congratulations or a simple thank-you. Officials passed her a world record application form, and having laid the form on the top step of the victory podium where she would soon stand to receive yet another gold medal, she inscribed her signature.

Following the medal ceremony, the press surrounded her, keen for a word from the departing Lithgow Flash. "This was definitely my last big race as an individual," she told the growing throng. "I will make my final farewell to athletics in the women's relay. I hope to end my career with another gold medal. It is definitely the life of a married woman for me from now on."

But would she miss running, they asked.

"Oh, I'm pleased in a way this is the end," she admitted. "It is real hard work to stay on top. I think it's a suitable ending to four years of competition."

Considering where this once-in-a-generation-or-two phenomenon had started, hers had been a remarkable rise. She was born in 1931 and raised in the small town of Lithgow, nestled on the western slopes of the Blue Mountains, 150km west of Sydney. When she was young, the Jackson family had used an outhouse, they didn't own a refrigerator, and the blocks of ice to keep their perishables cool were delivered by horse and cart. But her father had recognized her natural speed at school sports competitions, and one day he brought home a second-hand pair of men's track spikes. They were about two sizes too big, and Jackson-Nelson recalled that she "used to stuff them with newspaper to run in them." As she won more races and became more serious about running, her father had spikes specially made for her and crafted her wooden starting blocks himself. Not long after that, Jim Monaghan, a former professional runner who worked with her father at the Lithgow munitions factory, took over her training. Although supremely fast, her unrefined running style appeared awkward, with her elbows held rigidly at right angles and jerking up and down. But her clunky arm movement belied astonishing natural speed, and by the time she was 16, she appeared to be a solid prospect for Australia's

Opposite: The women's 220yd medalists, left to right: Australia's Winsome Cripps, silver; Jackson-Nelson, gold; and England's Shirley Hampton, bronze. Photo courtesy of Vonna McDonald.

1948 Olympic team. Unfortunately, inexperience did her in at the New South Wales championships when she incorrectly anticipated a false start and remained crouched in the starting blocks as the other runners dashed down the track. One year later Fanny Blankers-Koen of the Netherlands, who had won four gold medals in spectacular fashion in the 1948 Olympics, toured Australia, having been assured no "country girls" could touch her magnificent speed. Young Jackson-Nelson defeated the Olympic champion three times within eight days, and the legend of the Lithgow Flash was born.

After sweeping up four gold medals at the 1950 BEG and becoming a certifiable Australian sporting icon, Jackson-Nelson shifted her sights to the 1952 Olympics in Helsinki. However, as she would be running on a cinder track there, Lithgow's town council raised the money to build her a proper cinder track on which to train. "They didn't have any money left to put lights up," Jackson-Nelson told George Negus on his current affairs show on Australian television in 2004, "so I trained in the fog and the sleet and the snow by the lights of one motor car. Sometimes you couldn't even see your hand in front of you for the fog... I'd feel with my feet and hope I was in the middle of the track and then just keep running till I banged into the car because you only saw the light about the last five metres! Looking back, I don't know how I didn't break a leg."

Jackson-Nelson did go to Helsinki and became one of the Games' stars, winning the 100m and 200m, both in world record time, to claim Australia's first Olympic gold medals since 1896. Her margin of victory in the 100—over 3m or 0.38sec—remains the largest margin of any Olympic 100m final in history, women's or men's. Her victories prompted a tidal wave of headlines back home and even an original song called "Our Marjorie." The town fathers of Lithgow "went a little mad with pride," encouraging all citizens to celebrate this native daughter with "a full minute of sheer noise"—sirens, whistles, bells, drums and horns were all sounded at precisely 3pm the following day. Twenty thousand people in Lithgow welcomed her home amid flags, bunting and a 250lb cake. The only blot on her Olympic performance came in the 4x100m relay. She had anchored the Australian women to a new world record in the heats, so a third gold medal appeared all but assured, but disaster struck in the final. On the last baton exchange Jackson-Nelson had begun accelerating when her arm collided with teammate Winsome Cripps' knee, sending the baton flying into the air. Jackson-Nelson caught it on a single bounce, but by then it was too late. The "sure gold" was gone, and the Australians finished a distant fifth. The Aussie press had criticized the relay collapse harshly, which for Jackson-Nelson gave added importance to the BECG 4x110yd relay in Vancouver, a chance to make amends for the one black mark on her otherwise spotless international resume.

Only Australia, Canada and England contested the women's 4x110yd relay, which meant it would take a single final to settle the medals. Each nation was fielding a strong team, but significant doubt surrounded Australia's foursome because the number two sprinter, Marlene Mathews, had been injured, forcing the less-experienced Gwen Wallace to take her place alongside regulars Jackson-Nelson, Winsome Cripps and Nancy Fogarty. A *Sydney Morning Herald* article on July 16 reassured readers that the risky "European technique" the team had used in 1952 had been abandoned in favour of the lead runner keeping a cupped palm firmly planted against her hip while the trailing runner gently placed the baton in that hand. But as the team prepared, they were still dogged by a fear of repeating their Olympic failure because, although safer, the new technique was also decidedly slower. Whether the Aussie women had enough pure speed to make up for sluggish exchanges no one dared say lest they jinx the team's chances.

The thousands in Empire Stadium hushed expectantly, waiting for the crack of the starting gun. Although they got away cleanly, a poor start by Wallace put Australia behind from the get-go. By the time she handed off to Fogarty, they were in a 5yd hole, which grew to eight down the back straight as Fogarty lost ground behind the English and Canadians. The safe hand-offs and shuffled lineup were taking their toll, though Cripps chipped away at the English lead around the corner, fighting back a yard or two. Estimates vary greatly as to the deficit Jackson-Nelson faced with only the final 110yd straight between her and the finish line—and the finish of her sprinting career. Whether it was 10ft or 10yds—it seems likely it was between 3 and 5yds—never in any race in her career had she found herself running from so far behind.

Taking the baton cleanly from Cripps, Jackson-Nelson accelerated swiftly and soon reached full flight. She tore down the straight in hot pursuit of Canada's Gerry Bemister and England's Anne Pashley, each of whom had finished a mere two-tenths behind her in races earlier in the week. In an interview in 2013 she recalled that with each stride bringing her closer to the finish line, each footfall closing in on the leading runners, little snapshots flashed through her mind. She thought of the day in Sydney when she had sprinted away from Blankers-Koen down lanes of long grass, of running in the thick fog in Lithgow on the track built for her by her own neighbours, of streaking to gold in Helsinki and seeing the Australian flag silhouetted against the slate Norwegian sky. As she passed Bemister and drew even with Pashley, she thought of Cripps and how much this gold medal would mean to her after the Helsinki disaster. Blurred flashes of those who had helped her along the way came next—notably her parents and Coach Monaghan. But mostly as she neared the powdered white finish line laid across the cinder track, she thought of Peter and the life that awaited them. And when she crossed that line in a final glorious burst of speed, she did so—unbelievably—in the lead. Three feet in the lead.

Many in the stands stood in stunned disbelief before breaking into rapturous applause. The Australians had been timed in a new Games record of 46.8sec. The English finished a single tenth behind with the Canadians nearly a second farther back. Unofficially Jackson-Nelson's 110yd anchor leg was timed in an incredible 10.0sec flat, a time few of the world's top *male* sprinters could have matched. Speaking to members of the press afterwards, she said she felt the sprint was the fastest she had ever run. "That race gave me more satisfaction than any other in my career," she said, beaming.

On the victory podium receiving their gold medals, the faces of the Australian women simply shone. Any lingering remnants of Helsinki were laid to rest for good. For Jackson-Nelson, it was mission accomplished. She could go out on top and head home to begin a quiet life with the man of her dreams.

Marjorie Jackson-Nelson edges England's Anne Pashley at the finish line of the women's 4x110yd relay. Photo courtesy of Vonna McDonald.

✪

On Thursday, August 5, not long after Jackson-Nelson had ignited Empire Stadium with her world record-tying 220yd victory, spectators were treated to the opening chapter of one of the most stirring BC-centric stories of the 1954 Games. The hero of that story, Terry Tobacco from the town of Cumberland on Vancouver Island, wasn't even supposed to be in Vancouver for the 1954 BECG. His coach, Bruce Humber, had projected him as a prospect for the 1956 Olympics, but that spring the 18-year-old grade 11 student had almost single-handedly won the team trophy at the Vancouver Island track and field championships, triumphing in two events and placing in a third. Before that meet, Tobacco had only run in church picnic and Victoria Day races, usually in basketball shoes and without starting blocks. In fact, he was unsure whether basketball or track was his primary game, which was hardly surprising in Cumberland, a little hoop-mad mining community that was a regular stop for the Harlem Globetrotters.

At 6ft 3in and 165lb, the young man was an impressive physical specimen. The first thing anyone noticed were his long, thick legs like the trunks of the trees he felled while working in logging camps with his father. "I used to haul all of the power saw equipment, gasoline, food and bedding every time we moved camp, earning two dollars a trip," he recalled in a 2007 interview. "I was probably carrying 60 or 70lbs four times a day when I was just a kid. I know that had a lot to do with my development, especially in my upper legs. I was always strong there."

Leading up to the 1954 BECG, Humber convinced Tobacco to try his luck at the track trials. Then curiously he entered his young pupil in the 440yd (or 400m) race, a distance Tobacco had only run once before. It was a massive gamble because this distance is track's no man's land—too long to sprint all-out like the 100m but too short to slow the pace and conserve for a finishing burst like the Mile. Some say those who triumph in the 440 are not the ones who run the fastest, but those who slow down the least. Humber felt that, with Tobacco's long, cinder-gobbling stride and his raw athleticism, maybe he would sneak into the top six and the selection officials might have a decision on their hands. But this was no high school track meet. Lining up beside him in the trials were seasoned, well-trained athletes, many on track scholarships at American universities. But that day Tobacco ran like a man among schoolboys, when, of course, the opposite was true. With a late surge, the unpolished high schooler powered to second place behind Joe Foreman of Toronto, a Notre Dame University student, who held him off by a single tenth of a second in 48.6sec, the fastest quarter-mile ever run on Canadian soil. This was only the second time Tobacco had covered the distance in competition, and a *Vancouver Sun* reporter overheard one of his teammates joking, "No more Sunday school and picnic races for you, kid!"

Canadian officials decided to take a flyer on him, selecting him as the youngest male member of the Canadian BECG track team. They were probably thinking, *Why not? Can't hurt the kid to get some experience for bigger things up the road.* But while in their minds Tobacco may have been an inexperienced afterthought, at least he was going to the Games, and in his mind all he had to do was run. "I had nothing to lose and everything to gain," he remembered. "I wasn't awed by all the talent because I wasn't expected to do anything, and yet it was quite evident I had a lot of ability."

Sporting the fancy white-and-red Canadian team singlet and shorts in place of the faded old t-shirt he had worn at the trials, Tobacco showed poise and confidence beyond his years in the heats while he laid waste to some of the Commonwealth's best quarter-milers. With the crowd bellowing support for one of their own, he won heat three easily with a BC Open and Native record of 48.3sec, the second fastest time of the 28 competitors from 14 nations. The only runner faster was the stylish 21-year-old Australian Kevan Gosper who came from the coastal steel town of Newcastle in New South Wales. Gosper had easily won heat one in a BECG record time of 47.1sec, shattering the existing mark by 0.8sec and nearly taking out the world mark, too. He called it "one of the most relaxed races I've ever run." Gosper was finally delivering on his potential after several years of injuries. Earlier that year he had medaled for Michigan State University at the Big Ten Conference championship, a feat that earned him the opportunity to represent Australia in Vancouver. To save on travel costs to the West Coast, Gosper and Australian high jumper Doug Stuart had picked up a brand new 1954 Ford Crestline Skyliner in Dearborn, Michigan, and delivered it to a dealership in Seattle. On the way they only stopped in small towns with running ovals for breaks so they could get in a couple hours of solid training.

The semi-finals of the 440yds were held on the same afternoon as the heats, and Tobacco caused the stadium crowd to erupt in applause again. Running blind in the far outside lane with the field staggered behind him, he kept his head and ran his own race, crossing the finish in second place in 48.4sec, qualifying to advance to the final. Gosper took first quite comfortably, seven-tenths off his earlier record and looking as near to unbeatable as anyone could be. But it was Tobacco everyone was talking about that day. In a single afternoon the high

Canadian high schooler Terry Tobacco built his running strength hauling logging equipment between camps on Vancouver Island.

The first sports event Hall of Fame broadcaster Jim Robson ever watched on television was Terry Tobacco running at the 1954 BECG.

schooler had become Canadian track's most legitimate gold medal hopeful. The *Sun* called him the "greatest track prospect in Canada," while his high school coach, Humber, who was serving as a Games track judge, told the *Victoria Daily Times* that his prize pupil was "a potential future world beater." His long, loping stride brought immediate comparison to Bannister—heady praise for any runner. One writer later said Tobacco ran "with floating grace," and sports reporters began coining nicknames for him; two with a shot of sticking were "The Cumberland Rocket" and "The Cumberland Comet." About the only one not saying much about his performance was Tobacco himself. Asked by the *Victoria Daily Times* how he felt after the two races, he said simply, "I'm fine," as if outrunning all but one of the Commonwealth's best quarter-milers was an everyday thing.

However, you only had to walk into the Three Sisters Café in Port Alberni, not far from Tobacco's hometown on Vancouver Island, to get some sense of how big his performance was for Canadians. Mounted up in the corner was a 21in black-and-white Sylvania television set with a white bubble halo bar. When sports were shown on this TV, "all the jocks in town came there to watch," Jim Robson recalled many years later. Robson, who would log tens of thousands of hours in front of radio microphones and television cameras in a five-decade hall of fame career, was just 19 that summer when he sat in a booth at the Three Sisters to watch local boy Tobacco tear up the track—the first sports event he had ever seen on television. Meanwhile, Tobacco having passed every test placed before him to this point and looking infinitely better each run, now had to cool his heels for two whole days for the 440yd final and the squeeze of real pressure and escalating tensions.

✪

While Empire Stadium had buzzed all afternoon with track events on Thursday, August 5, across town the final evening of cycling events was beginning at Empire Bowl, more popularly known as China Creek Park, the only event venue that had avoided pre-Games controversies. Yet as smooth as the building of it was, ironically during the Games no other venue hosted more discord.

Trouble had begun on the first night, Monday, August 2, during the heats for the 1000m Match Sprint. England's Cyril Peacock, who would become world champion later that summer at a meet in Germany, sped away to an easy 10m victory—or so it seemed. However, in an effort to limit collisions near the finish line, organizers had imposed a rule forbidding riders to cut in on one another, so despite Peacock being so far in front that direct interference appeared impossible, officials disqualified him for cutting into the lane of Vancouver cyclist Johnny Millman. "Not so!" cried the English cyclist, arms raised in protest. When English officials appealed, the decision was reversed, but after Peacock was disqualified for the same infraction in the quarter-finals, the entire English camp erupted. Peacock threatened to walk out in protest, while English cycling manager Alfred Haine fumed that he had never heard of this ruling in previous Games. The Australian cycling manager, Bill Young, who had a hot-tempered history of starting disagreements rather than attempting to solve them, tried to reason with Haine. "Now look, Alf, it's all for the Games," Young soothed. "Let's take these decisions quietly and keep peace in the Commonwealth." (Considering Young's later behaviour, this ranked as the most outrageous comment of the entire Games!)

As the jury of appeal deliberated, a cluster of angry riders, coaches and officials gathered on the infield, and their heated shouts could be heard right across the oval. It was at this point that Young's best rider, Lionel Cox, 1952 Olympic gold and silver medalist, was disqualified for the same infraction as Peacock. Young, seeing the English were making headway with their fuss, approached the jury waving a 10-dollar bill and demanding a hearing. When told an appeal only cost two dollars, he effectively told them to keep the change. "At least try to be dinkum [fair] about this!" he hollered. After a few tense moments the appeals were sorted out, and the 1000m sprints resumed peacefully with both Peacock and Cox advancing to the final. But one last glitch waited to mar the evening. The event program had incorrectly indicated the finals would be held on the same night, so when the loudspeaker announced they would actually be held the next evening, the crowd made a grumbling rush for the exits. Meanwhile, a *Vancouver Province* reporter was near enough to Young to hear him deliver one final parting shot: sweeping a hand to indicate the entire cycling oval, he said in disgust, "You can sum this up in one word—inefficiency."

It was hardly the smooth introduction to international cycling the organizers were hoping for, but the following night—one of the strangest in Commonwealth Games history—proved even worse. In the first match of the best-two-out-of-three 1000m Match Sprint final, Cox cut in on Peacock, nearly clipping the Englishman's wheel. In self-defence Peacock shoved Cox away but swerved high on the curve to maintain control, which allowed the Australian to speed away to an easy 15m victory. Cox was declared the winner, which the English naturally protested. The jury of appeal called in Haine and Young, coaches of the riders in question, and suggested the race be re-run but couldn't get the coaches to agree. Then, without adequate explanation, the jury reversed its decision, disqualifying Cox and awarding the race to Peacock. The crowd, recognizing the apparent injustice in this arbitrary reversal began chanting, "We want Cox! We want Cox!" At that same moment Young dashed across the infield, lunged at the announcer's table and began pounding on it with clenched fists. He then demanded use of the loudspeaker microphone, which the cowering officials meekly handed over. "I thought that Canadians were good sports," he thundered, his words echoing menacingly around the oval. "Apparently I was wrong. After the raw deal Australia got last night and tonight, we are withdrawing!" He dropped the microphone with a thud and began marching toward the dressing room, motioning his riders to follow. The crowd, which had sat in stunned silence, booed the departing Aussies.

The officials then realized they would still have to conduct races to decide the medalists, and Peacock pedalled onto the track and waited patiently for Cox to emerge from the dressing room. Several awkward moments followed as officials pleaded with the Australians over the PA to return to the track. Finally they had no choice but to start the race without Cox. Peacock casually circled the track alone as the crowd cheered loudly, now firmly in the English corner. He crossed the finish line uncontested to win the gold medal. "It is unsatisfactory to win by default," he griped afterwards. The bronze medal matches between South Africa's Tom Shardelow and Australia's Dickie Ploog were similarly affected when Ploog failed to show. For the first—and only—time in Commonwealth Games history a silver medal was not awarded in the final of a title event that didn't involve a tie. As a result, the medal podium appeared strangely unbalanced as Peacock perched on the top step with only bronze medalist Shardelow to his left. The two cyclists

at the heart of the spat that caused the withdrawal of the Australians even refused to be photographed together. When pressed by a *Province* reporter, Cox snapped, "I'm choosey who I have my picture taken with"—although later the two men became good friends.

In the aftermath Australian officialdom released stiff public statements condemning Young's walkout. Harry Alderson, Australian BEG Federation chairman, cabled from Sydney: "I think a little more diplomacy could have been used." C.J. Gray, council chairman of the Victorian Amateur Cycling Union of Australia, called for Young to apologize publicly: "He let Australia down. He insulted Australian sportsmanship and Canada." The Australian press tended to agree. James Eve, general manager of the Australian team, told the *Vancouver Province* that Young "erred in withdrawing the team" and assured everyone that team members would return to China Creek peacefully. "For further events of the cycling program, the Australian team will be obliged to contest the races in accordance with the rules and regulations governing them." Video evidence further condemned Young's action. The day after the walkout, reporters were shown the Peacock-Cox clash in slow motion, and the conclusion drawn by all was that Cox had most definitely fouled Peacock and therefore his disqualification appeared undoubtedly warranted. Ultimately it was only Young's riders who had suffered.

Young and the humbled Aussies returned to the track the following evening, Wednesday, August 4, egg planted firmly on their faces. Any trace of hostility from the previous evening had largely vanished, but on this night officials found themselves scrambling to resolve yet another problem. The 1000m Time Trial had provided spectators with repeated thrills as six riders bettered the existing BECG record of 1min 13.4sec held by the great Australian wheelman Russell Mockridge. At one point it looked like young Dick Ploog, sitting in first with a time of 1min 12.5sec, would receive golden retribution for his loss of a medal in the previous night's walkout. However, on one of the final rides of the night the aptly named Jim Swift from South Africa scorched the track's yellow cedar planking with an identical time to tie Ploog. Officials were left with an unprecedented decision, and to avoid the acrimony a race-off might bring, they awarded gold medals to *both* Ploog and Swift—the first time in BECG history a first-place dead heat ever occurred in any sport's final race. For the second time in as many nights, no silver medal was awarded in a cycling event at China Creek. That medal ended up in the possession of Games chairman Stanley Smith, who later donated it to the BC Sports Hall of Fame where it is displayed today.

For spectators, the first three nights of cycling had offered unpredictable and entertaining action with perhaps the only disappointment being the poor performance of the Canadian contingent. Not a single Canadian rider could claim to have been in legitimate medal contention. But on Thursday, August 5, the fourth and final night of cycling at China Creek, Vancouver's Lorne "Ace" Atkinson finally gave the home crowd something to cheer about.

Ace was an easy man to pull for. The only thing bigger than his smile was his huge heart. From his childhood, the life of this 33-year-old, lifelong Kitsilano resident had revolved around cycling. His father had raced bicycles at carnivals while growing up in Scotland and later coached a few of Canada's best cyclists. He passed on his two-wheeled passion to his son. Ace's earliest memories date to watching Depression-era six-day cycling races on a steeply banked wooden track placed over the ice in Vancouver's Denman Arena. He began refining his own cycling skills as a delivery boy, distributing *Liberty*

Canada's 1954 BECG cycling team. Lorne Atkinson (7th from left) never saw eye-to-eye with coach George Graves (far left).

Previous pages: New Zealand's Colin Dickinson (right) lunges past England's Peter Brotherton (left) at the finish line of their 1000m match sprint heat.

magazine all over Vancouver, and he was soon winning races regularly. *Vancouver Sun* headlines the day after he won a Stanley Park race in 1937 trumpeted: "City Ace Triumphs in Province Cup." A nickname was born right there and only grew with BC and Canadian championship victories throughout the 1940s. "That stuck," he said, laughing, in a 2007 interview. Forever after there would only be one "Ace" in Vancouver.

After serving in the Canadian navy in eastern Canada in WWII, Ace returned to Vancouver and used his naval pay as the down payment on a West Broadway bicycle sales and repair shop. In the decades that followed, Ace Cycles would become a Vancouver landmark. The same year that he bought the shop he met pretty Evelyn Speer while she was performing in a musical ride at a Brockton Oval sports day. During the performance her tire went flat, and Ace offered to repair it, beginning a six-year courtship that led to marriage in 1952. After more BC and Canadian championship victories, he represented Canada at the 1948 Olympics in London then the 1950 BEG in Auckland where he finished fifth in the 10-mile track event, though he was still inside the previous BECG record for the distance. It was the kind of satisfying result you could hang your leather racing cap on, so having won a cabinet full of gleaming hardware, at the age of 29 Ace called it a career.

After that, Kitsilano residents regularly saw this little buzz saw of a man aboard his trademark yellow-and-black CCM, ripping along the streets, cutting corners and slicing through traffic. His retirement, however, lasted just two years. He was pushed back into serious competition when Vancouver was awarded the 1954 Games and China Creek was floated as the potential cycling venue. As a young boy he had lived just two blocks away and played on the bridges over the creek. At first, he considering coaching at the

Games, something he was already doing with local riders, and having doubled as Canada's cycling coach at the 1950 BEG, he certainly appeared the front-runner for the job again. Then news arrived that George Graves, a Montreal policeman who had cycled for Canada at the 1938 BEG, was to be coach in 1954. Ace's next decision was simple: "If I can't coach, I'm gonna ride!" He leapt into preparations in earnest, training with two young high school riders he was then coaching, Claire Bonner and Brian Henderson, both of whom ultimately competed at the 1954 BECG. Then, as he explained in a 2007 interview, he began building a new racing bicycle for himself from scratch on his lunch breaks, using the best features of several models to piece together his own customized masterpiece. He painted the frame a subdued flat black and carved elaborate steel lugs to bring a touch of elegance to a machine designed for brute speed.

In the spring of 1953, after a winter of pounding out chilling early morning training rides in rain and sleet, Ace jumped the fence into the China Creek construction site on weekends and rode the unfinished track. Dodging scraps of wood and loose nails, he and another young protégé, Johnny Millman, rode the 5ft band of track surface circling the oval, while beyond it, thick structural girders lay exposed like the ribcage of some great beast. This was China Creek's unofficial christening, fittingly performed by two Vancouver cyclists who would compete on it during the Games the following summer. These were heady days for a veteran cyclist grown used to picking cinders from his teeth and elbows, a man with permanent blue tattoos, painful reminders of crashes on the poorly suited tracks he had been racing on for years. By the time the oval was completed in December 1953, many were touting China Creek Park as the best cycling velodrome in North America.

To earn a place on the Canadian BECG team, Ace endured the most tumultuous month of his career, and at any of a half-dozen points the wheels really should have fallen off his comeback bid. It began at the Canadian championships at China Creek in early July when he collided with a lapped rider and went down. As he skidded along the cedar track, creating a pile-up with other competitors, he suffered a severely strained ligament in his right thigh, rendering it virtually immobile. He could barely walk, let alone ride. With his strongest races coming up the following day, he sought heat treatment, but a student doctor only succeeded in barbequing his flesh with a heat lamp. That night the searing pain proved so overwhelming he couldn't sleep. The next day, unable to manoeuvre his stiff leg onto his bike, he laid the bike flat at his feet, leaned against a fence and pulled the frame upwards. Friends tried to persuade him to withdraw for his own safety. "Look," he barked back, his eyes burning, "I have been training for two years for this. I'm gonna ride." He rode that day like a man possessed—some said brilliantly—working the 45-degree banked corners like a magician, doing everything to stay in contention. By the end of the day, despite missing races and being handicapped by his injury, he had racked up three second-place finishes to rank a solid fourth in the individual points standings. Many marvelled at his courage, unable to walk but riding like the wind. It may stand as one of the greatest single-day Canadian cycling performances by a man who didn't win a single race.

The Canadian BECG trials took place two days later. Ace's leg had barely begun to heal, but he fought the pain once more. After surviving the difficult early races with decent results, he felt one more solid finish would assure him a place on the Canadian team, so he entered the 100km Road Race. Here disaster struck again. Sharing the lead on the fifth lap of the West Point Grey road course, a black dog bolted across the road without warning directly into the path of the lead group. Every rider swerved crazily to avoid the animal, but one competitor clipped its hind legs and hit the pavement at over 25mph, causing a messy pile-up. Ace, who was directly behind the fallen rider, actually jumped his bicycle clear but lost all control on landing and tumbled headfirst into a ditch. He smashed his elbow sharply into a sewer grate and feared his lifeless arm could be broken. Amid the bent wheels and tangled bike frame, medical attendants staunched the blood gushing from his elbow before rushing him by ambulance to hospital. Miraculously, there were no broken bones, just severe lacerations and a frayed "funny bone" nerve, and for good measure he had also re-injured the still-tender ligament in his leg. At a formal dinner that night, when coach George Graves announced the 15-member Canadian BECG team, the biggest applause of the evening was saved for Ace, the plucky veteran who had pulled himself out of bed and painfully limped just to be there. Despite his injuries, in the days that followed he stayed remarkably upbeat as he slowly built himself back into racing form. "You run into these things," he said, recalling his misadventures in the 2007 interview. "It's not all peaches, but it works out."

But there would be one more cruel twist of fate for Ace. During the trials, the burly, blustering Graves had already raised the ire of many by throwing his weight around a little too forcefully in official decision-making. Then it was announced that, rather than stepping up training in the final weeks before the Games, he had chosen to take off on a 10-day holiday to California, justifying his ill-timed vacation by saying the Canadian team was "the most power-packed ever to represent Canada." But this was hardly the time for Canadian cyclists to rest on their laurels; the last BECG medal won by a Canadian cyclist had come 20 years earlier and Canada's record at the Olympics was even worse. When Ace magnanimously offered to oversee the team's training in Grave's absence, a few in the press, including the *Sun*'s Dick Beddoes under a headline of "Put a Foot in the Graves," suggested Ace's temporary appointment be permanent. To add insult to injury, when Graves returned from his fun in the California sun, he announced the Canadian riders for each event and bypassed Ace entirely, relegating Canada's most accomplished international cyclist in the postwar period to a mere spectator at the Games in his own hometown. For the fiercely competitive and proud Atkinson, it was too much to bear. "I'm not wasting my time here if I'm not riding," he snarled. After all he had been through that month, the man who never backed away from a pedal-to-pedal battle, who put his head down and ground out one more exhausting finish when his legs had nothing left, who would rather lose than give in and quit, did just that. He quit. Packed it in and quit the team cold, becoming the first and only athlete from any nation competing in Vancouver to willingly quit his team and leave the Village.

He hoped his departure might send a message that he was far too young to be written off so unceremoniously and far too old to put up with such bush tactics, political or not. Popular opinion seemed to reside in his corner, particularly after Beddoes broke the exclusive story in the *Sun*. But Graves and members of the Canadian team lashed back a day later. "Feelings don't enter the matter," said Graves, while an unidentified teammate was quoted in the *Province* in far less diplomatic terms: "When he quit, he proved he was out for himself, not for the team."

It was the reaction of Ace's teammates—*his* riders, the Vancouver boys he had coached for years, who were only at this level of proficiency in some cases because of what he had taught them—that stabbed the deepest. "Some of these guys I'd done so much for, they didn't come to my help," he recalled in the 2007 interview. "Sometimes everybody's for themselves, and guys I had helped so much..." His voice trailed off at the painful memory. But a man who had given as much as Ace could not help but have a few allies—often in high places—who would step up in a time of need. Cycling committee chair Dave Mathews was just such a friend. Mathews went above Graves to Bob Osborne, the Canadian team's assistant general manager, who then brought in the Canadian team's general manager, Hy Herschorn. "He'll ride," Herschorn ordered firmly. "What the hell does Graves know?" The only stipulations Herschorn demanded were that Ace must mend fences with Graves and then report back immediately to Empire Village and re-join the team, which he did. However, Graves remained noncommittal about entering Ace in any events: "My plan," he said, "is to keep you in reserve, but I have until half an hour before the program starts to make changes."

Ace humbly supported his Canadian teammates, but as the week progressed, he watched as inexperience and bad luck felled one after another. His wife, Evelyn, and Dave Mathews offered him sympathetic words, but he resigned himself to the probability that he would not be given one final chance to compete. On the other hand, he could sleep soundly knowing he had done all he could in spite of the injuries, foul luck, and selection politics of the past month. And then on Wednesday, August 4, Graves notified him he would be riding the following night in the Ten Mile Massed Start in place of one of his original selections. Ace Atkinson would race one last time.

On Thursday evening a mostly Canadian crowd of 4,300 paid spectators filed into China Creek, while another 1,500 watched from outside the fences. Everyone seemed to be hoping for some sort of Canadian result worth celebrating, but if Ace wanted to make something happen, he would have to do it against the deepest cycling field of the Games. All around him were the medalists from earlier races: South Africa's Shardelow and Swift, Englishmen Keith Harrison and Norman Sheil, Australia's Ploog, plus a raft of other solid internationals all wanting to leave their mark on these Games as badly as Ace did. Team tactics weren't working in his favour either. Graves picked him to shoulder the workload from the front, sacrificing his own performance to set up teammates Fred Markus and Pat Murphy, who would be conserving back in his draft for a late run at the podium.

At the crack of the starting gun, 24 steel chains strained under the accelerated thrust of piston-like thighs. Averaging nearly 30mph for 64 laps—completing a 250m circuit of the track every 20sec or so—the pack traded positions and elbows in a dizzying display of tactics, speed and endurance. After a few nervous laps, Ace decided he could not

Opposite: A customized masterpiece, Atkinson's racing bicycle used the best features of several models. Elaborate steel lugs added a touch of elegance.

Previous pages: "Ace" Atkinson (top row, second from left) was a master at working China Creek's steep corners.

only contend, but he also had an outside shot at winning. It came down to knowing the quirks of the track's corners. "When the guy in front of me moved out in the straightaway to improve his position," he explained a half century later, "I knew you couldn't get around him because as soon as you got to the steep corners, you didn't have enough speed to pass. So when somebody moved out, I moved inside and let *them* move out. So they kept moving out and I kept moving up."

The race proceeded according to Graves' plan until the latter stages when 17-year-old Markus, the youngest competitor in the field, quietly disappeared from the pack. Ace had known the youngster simply was not experienced enough to deal with "the knee and elbow stuff" under such intense conditions. It was one thing to be fast out in the open, but when scrapping in the middle of the crowded pack, it was how you dealt with the rough going that determined how you placed.

With nine laps to go and Murphy riding shotgun and waiting for the right moment, Ace allowed his teammate to shoot off and break for the lead. Murphy quickly opened up a 30yd cushion and looked to be in the clear, but without the benefit of the extra drafting Markus would have provided, he began to tire. With two laps to go, he scraped a pedal on the bank of the track, momentarily jamming it and allowing the chase group to catch up and pass him. He never recovered and finished well back.

THE LUNG-TESTER

Over dinner one evening at the Village cafeteria, Ace Atkinson pulled out his "lung tester" for some harmless fun, and weightlifter Doug Hepburn, who was familiar with the gadget, joined him to find a victim. The tester was made out of an evaporated milk can, and blowing into the small copper pipe welded to the side would spin a tiny metal fan welded to the top. How hard one blew also determined the amount of black soot that sifted through a nearly invisible slit just above the mouthpiece onto the unsuspecting victim's upper lip. Those with strong lungs ended up resembling Charlie Chaplin or worse.

On this particular evening Ace and Hepburn chose one of the largest men competing in any sport in Vancouver, Dave Baillie, the 290-lb weightlifter from Noranda, Quebec. It didn't take much to get the competitive Baillie raring to prove the strength of his cavernous lungs, and when they passed him the lung tester, he boasted, "I'll blow the wheel right off that thing!"

Baillie sucked in a massive breath of air and blew for all he was worth. The entire cafeteria went silent as he exhaled and sent a huge sooty cloud hovering over nearby tables. Even years later when Ace recalled the scene, he could hardly contain himself. "Six people around him had to trade in their dinners for another because there was so much soot!" While some grumbled about ruined meals and others rolled in the aisles laughing hysterically, the duped Baillie sat momentarily stunned, thick black soot covering his face from below the nose right back to his ears, before he took off in mad pursuit of the perpetrators.

With Markus and Murphy out of the running, Ace's cards had suddenly come up diamonds and well—*aces*. Once an afterthought, he was now Canada's final medal hope. Free of the restrictive team tactics, he began riding his own race, darting through the field and snapping up openings between riders. One by one, he picked off those in front of him, using the steep transitions between corner and straight to make up ground. When the others moved out, he moved in. When they moved down, he moved up. The crowd began to propel him along with their enthusiasm.

When a track marshal rang the last-lap bell, Ace was sitting in sixth place, but he was now in a dogfight with the toughest customers in the competition: the two South Africans, Tom Shardelow, who had won two Olympic silvers in 1952, and Jim Swift, who had one 1952 Olympic silver and would win a bronze in 1956. But they were about to learn things happen at speed on such unforgiving boards, even to the best riders. The pair crept up on Ace a bit too enthusiastically, rubbed his rear tire, and both tumbled in a heap to the track. Outright mayhem ensued, the pack frantically parting like a flock of birds, knocking elbows and clinking handlebars. Ace felt the rub and heard the collision behind him, yet somehow stayed upright. With little time to worry about a bent rear wheel, in the wild chaos he pedalled furiously in pursuit of the nearest riders. On the final corner, he drafted off England's Eric Thompson, who would win the 100km Road Race in two days' time, and shot down to the straight. He lunged desperately for the finish line, head down, chin nearly touching his knees, arms locked stock-straight from the handlebars, straining with every fibre to drive that home-built bike to the sweet side of that line. Miraculously, he sneaked by two more riders to slip into a photo-finish fourth. If it hadn't been for that slight rub from the South Africans, it might have been even higher. The crowd showered him with applause.

As Ace gently wound down the pedal strokes and gulped air, he flashed an elated smile at his wife, Evelyn, who was dutifully recording results on the infield. He had wanted to go out in style and, against all odds, he had done it, electrifying the hometown crowd. "If I'd ridden my race, I could have got second," he recalled later. "But the thing was, none of the national champions beat me. The top three and me were non-champions that got the best positions. Oh yeah, I *was* happy."

He had good reason to be. Ace Atkinson's ride proved to be the best performance by any Canadian cyclist in the Games. A man who had experienced nearly every conceivable calamity in the past month had fashioned the highest finish by a Canadian cyclist in BECG competition in 20 years, and his record remained unmatched until 1970. For a 36-year period, the small Kitsilano man from just around the corner, whose steely resolve and immense love of the bicycle allowed him to overcome so much, held the benchmark for Canadian cycling in the Commonwealth.

Australia's Lindsay Cocks took gold in the Ten Mile Massed Start with a BECG record time of 21min 59.5sec, battering the old mark by nearly 90sec. But a tragic epilogue awaited the Melbourne car salesman. A year later, after the world cycling championships in Milan, Italy, Cyril Peacock offered Cocks a ride to Paris, but in the French village of Sainte-Magnance they were involved in a horrific head-on collision. Cocks died of his injuries a day later; Peacock suffered chest injuries but survived.

❂

The Mile semi-finals at Empire Stadium on the late afternoon of Thursday, August 5, would provide the world with the first in-race glimpse of the two greatest milers in history and perhaps offer some clues to who might take the BECG Mile crown two days later. The 16 athletes running in the two semi-final heats made their preparations for the race in the future BC Lions' locker room underneath the west side bleachers. Intended for the hulking football players who would move in the following week, the room had unadorned light-bulbs hanging from long wires overhead while lockers and benches, freshly painted in in-stitutional evergreen, lined the room. In this setting Bannister and Landy were, of course, garnering the lion's share of attention, overshadowing the other 14 milers—unknowns, regional heroes and rising stars in their own right but dragged into this incredible focus of history, timing and showdown.

Today it's difficult to appreciate the significance that the mile held in the sport-ing world of 1954. The later switch to metric measurements and a shift in popularity to other distances has rendered it a relic of a bygone age. But for years leading up to the 1954 Games, the mile was top of mind where track was concerned. But why the mania surrounding it?

Boiled down to its most basic, the mile stood at the attractive convergence of clean, round numbers in both time and distance. Running one mile in four evenly paced 60sec laps would give the magical number of four minutes, the perfect distance in the perfect time. Even those unversed in athletics minutiae could easily grasp what was being accom-plished with none of the ungainliness of other distances. "If you'd said you're only run-ning 1760yds in 240sec, people would have yawned," said Norris McWhirter in 2004. "The magic was this phrase: *four minute mile.*"

Four minutes happened to fall near the ideal length of the average human atten-tion span, about the same time as the average song on the radio, a poem read from a book, or the top story on a television news broadcast. In terms of aesthetics, the mile was long enough to require strategy and elicit compelling drama—John Landy tellingly called it "a perfect drama in four acts"—while still short enough to demand thrilling, breakneck speed from its competitors and not lose the spectator's attention as longer, plodding distances are apt to.

And then there was its historical allure. For decades the myth of the sub-four-min-ute mile had been built up as some sort of impenetrable physical and psychological barri-er that became more concrete with each successive attempt that fell mere seconds short. "Like an unconquerable mountain, the closer it was approached the more daunting it seemed," wrote historian John Bryant in *The Quest to Break the 4 Minute Mile*. Count-less legendary runners had been unable to successfully scale its heights despite inching the world record ever closer. Revered athletes such as Walter George, Paavo Nurmi, Jack Lovelock, Glenn Cunningham, Sydney Wooderson, Gunder Haegg and Arne Andersson each became links in a great chain of milers stretching back to the 19th century. "Wheth-er as athletes we liked it or not, the four minute mile had become rather like an Ever-est—a challenge to the human spirit," wrote Roger Bannister in *The Four Minute Mile*.

As the Games proceeded, the enormity of the Mile had clearly elevated Vancouver, a regional sports town at best, to worldwide prominence. The CBC planned to broadcast the Mile live across the country by transcontinental hook-up via a network of US television stations as Canada did not yet have a cross-country cable or radio relay. NBC planned to do the same, thus marking the first international sports event ever to be seen live coast-to-coast on both Canadian and American television. Britain would wait for footage to arrive by air, but to speed things up, the Royal Air Force had sent a bomber to fly back kinescope film of the race, with a technician on board to develop the film during the flight. BBC Radio and the Australian Broadcast Network would carry radio descriptions of the race, while CBS, ABC and the Mutual Network would broadcast the race across the US.

In print, Mile stories often transcended their "sports designation" and appeared top of the fold on front pages of newspapers around the world, even in countries not participating in the Games. Prominent American publications, such as *Life Magazine*, sent reporters. A new magazine, *Sports Illustrated*, set to debut just a week after the Games ended, planned a feature story. Over 350 out-of-town journalists and photographers from over 20 countries had applied for press credentials. "[The race] had another dimension," Landy explained in a 2007 interview. "The Commonwealth Games could be held without anyone in the United States knowing, but in the case of the 1954 Games the fact I was matched with Roger Bannister created intense interest in American sporting terms."

All agreed that the match-up was a promoter's dream, almost too good to be true. First, you had Landy, the runner, the freshly minted mile world record holder, 12 times under 4min 6sec for the mile, winner in three of the nine fastest mile races of all time and unbeaten over the distance for the past 18 months. Opposing him was the only man alive with the ability at that moment to match his speed: Bannister, the racer, four times under 4min 6sec for the mile, the first man in history to break the four-minute barrier, and perhaps most dangerously for someone of large ambition, a man who suddenly had something to prove. As Landy characterized the match-up to Len Johnson in *The Landy Era*: "There was a wonderful symmetry... there was an inevitability to it." Many accounts, however, gloss over the rest of the field, as if the world's two four-minute milers were about to run against a bunch of talentless stiffs, which, of course, was far from the truth. Few knew the widely diverse and less celebrated backgrounds the other men brought to this race.

Readying for the race in one corner of that football locker room beneath the stands was John Disley, a 25-year-old Welsh schoolteacher. He had corralled a bronze medal in the 3000m steeplechase at the 1952 Olympics and carted off Britain's Outstanding Athlete of the Year award. Though an avid climber, in 1953 he had turned down an invitation to join Colonel John Hunt's British expedition that successfully ascended Everest, choosing to focus on training for the 1954 Games. Besides competing in Vancouver, Disley also successfully sold the BEG Federation on the idea of holding the 1958 BECG in Cardiff.

Across the room stood the towering Australian Don Macmillan, who had rewritten the Aussie track record book before Landy emerged on the scene. A two-time Olympian, Macmillan had been attending teacher's college in London when he was recruited by Bannister for his early record-breaking attempts.

Chris Brasher, who had paced the first two laps of Bannister's historic four minute mile at Oxford's Iffley Road track, prepared nearby. The spectacled Cambridge runner, born in Guyana, had built his track career more on guts and grit than the pure running talent of many of his contemporaries. After Vancouver he worked himself into a two-time

Olympian and ultimately won a wholly unexpected 3000m steeplechase gold at the 1956 Olympics, Britain's first Olympic gold medal in track and field since 1936. Much later Brasher would reveal that disappointment with his Vancouver performance had served as potent fuel for his greatest triumph.

Then there were two very solid Englishmen who had run at Oxford. The first was 23-year-old David Law, fittingly a London lawyer. One of Britain's top university runners, the sandy-haired litigator had won the 1953 World Student Games 1500m and excelled in cross-country. The other Oxford Blue was Ian Boyd, a dark-haired 20-year-old who was completing an honours degree in physics. In the midst of an excellent university running career, Boyd's best-ever result had happened just days before the Mile semis in the BECG 880yds, where he nabbed a bronze medal by running over a second faster than he ever had before. The Mile semi-final was his third race in six days, and his young legs were feeling the faintest pangs of fatigue.

At 26, North Vancouver's Bill Parnell, the defending BECG Mile champion, was the "old man" in the room. Four years earlier he had rocked Auckland's Eden Park to life with an electrifying last-gasp kick to snag gold to go along with an earlier bronze in the half-mile. Now, as a two-time Olympian and one of the host nation's few "name athletes," he had been asked to do a lot away from the track during the Games in Vancouver—handshakes, photos, presentations, dinners and speeches—when all he really wanted to do was train to prepare to defend his Mile crown. And now fresh worries were compounding things: he was struggling with a new teaching job, and the birth of his first child had been only three weeks earlier. The weight of that Auckland gold medal was suffocating and the pressure wasn't letting up; due to the stress he had lost 10 pounds in less than a week. Everyone kept asking him, "Are you ready, Bill?" His body felt all right but his mind was unsure.

Nearby, two New Zealanders, 21-year-old Murray Halberg and 20-year-old Bill Baillie, traded chatter back and forth. These young rough-and-tumble pups were the amiable icebreakers in the locker room and about as different as two mates could get. Halberg was the better known, having emerged earlier in the year as the fourth-fastest miler on the planet. After running 4min 4.4sec to set New Zealand's national record, he had received invitations to run all over the world and was expected to push Bannister and Landy in the Vancouver race. But many were surprised by his appearance. "A man who looks and runs less like a champion miler would be hard to imagine," Canada's 1952 Olympic track coach Bruce Humber told the *Victoria Daily Times* two days before the semi-final heats. To begin with, Halberg had always been unusually scrawny and gaunt, almost skeletal, owing to a childhood bout of polio, but what most people noticed first was his withered and immobile left arm. In his teens, like most young Kiwis, he had played rugby with a passion, but that had come to a jarring halt with a crash tackle from behind. Veins and arteries in his left shoulder had been cut, resulting in serious blood clots and significant permanent paralysis of his arm. During the months of rehab that followed he had struggled to re-learn how to walk, write and simply lift a spoon. Once recovered, the hyper-active Halberg was eager to get back into sports, but anything with contact or requiring arm agility were out. He turned to running and, under the watchful eye of legendary coach Arthur Lydiard, soon developed one of the great strides of his era. Hints of the gritty, iron-willed competitor he would become cropped up as he rapidly climbed the running ladder. Away from the track, he was as good-natured and friendly as any athlete, yet in the heat of a race he shocked even seasoned competitors with how intensely he pursued victory. "Do you know why I run?" he once growled at an interviewer. "I run because I enjoy beating other people." Vancouver was his first major games, and despite his undeniable talent, he was still adjusting to the pressures of elite racing, so as much as he bantered with Baillie and other competitors, inside he struggled to keep a severe attack of nerves in check. Although it was apparent that he was learning quickly in the pressure of international athletics, the question was not whether his skin was thickening but whether it was thick enough for the upcoming Mile.

John Landy, Victor Milligan (obscured) and Bill Baillie (right) finished in a dead-heat in the second mile semi-final, while Ian Boyd (left) trailed a few yards behind.

Halberg's partner-in-crime, Bill Baillie, could only be called a character. A boat builder by trade, he was unusually muscular for a distance runner. Lifting weights as a youth had given him a thickly sculpted upper body but also permanent curvature of the spine and a slightly hunchbacked posture. He spoke swiftly in a nasally voice, cramming in more words than time seemed to allow. He loved jokes, loved them even more over a drink, and had mastered the art of spinning enthralling yarns. He also had a weakness for pulling ridiculous stunts and pranks, once leading a group of athletes in an impromptu bowing exhibition in front of the Japanese emperor to the horror of royal protocol observers. In Tauranga he once sprayed cold water over a gymnasium full of sleeping athletes in the middle of the night before sprinting through the streets to elude his soaked victims. He was also supremely confident in his running ability, which sometimes manifested itself in well-placed verbal jabs toward competitors during races: "Shit! Ivan, is that you? Down a lap?" Crowds all over New Zealand, and later around the world, loved his antics and devil-may-care attitude. But here in Vancouver, Baillie was even less experienced than Halberg. Although he was his nation's half-mile champion, he had only been under Arthur Lydiard's training regimen for scant months and had never before ventured outside the confines of his island nation. No one could say how he would hold up to his first test of "big Games" pressure.

Northern Ireland's lone hope, Victor Milligan, bantered back and forth with the two young New Zealanders before adjusting his self-modified leather spikes, designed to protect a delicate ankle through another run. Milligan had grown up dirt-poor in a Belfast farming family before Franz Stampfl—the same coach who later guided Bannister to his historic four minute mile—identified him as one of the world's most promising young running prospects. By the time he reached university, he looked certain to be a future Olympian, but that is when injuries began to take their toll. First a pulled hamstring, then tendonitis limited his racing. "I was a bit of a fragile flower," he confirmed in a 2007 interview, but the worst was yet to come. In 1952 he became entangled with several runners in a Dublin race and suffered severe spike wounds and a torn Achilles tendon. Most felt his career was over, but he was treated by orthopaedic surgeon Dr. Kevin O'Flanagan, one of Ireland's most revered athletes, who immobilized Milligan's lower leg in a cast for several weeks to allow the sutured tendon to heal. Later Milligan underwent faradism treatment in which short bursts of low-frequency electrical current were sent into the damaged area to stimulate repairs of severed nerves and stretch the wasted muscles. After endless months of rehab, he was persuaded by friends to try a comeback, and driven by two years of pent-up energy, he attacked the track like a tornado. By the time he arrived in Vancouver, he had run in 14 major track meets that season, lowered his personal best mile time to 4min 6.7sec and elevated himself to dark-horse status behind Bannister and Landy. Milligan modestly laughed off such talk. "Me—I'm just going to hang on like grim death!" the lanky Irishman told a *Sun* reporter. Yet shortly after arrival, he seriously re-injured his right heel, shedding doubt on whether he would even be fit to run. In the ensuing days, the icepack became his best friend as he rested and worried, but he awoke the morning of the Mile semi-finals optimistic that he could challenge for a place.

And finally there was Richie—Richard Kirwin Ferguson, the forgotten man of Canadian track and field. Decades later he summed up his memories of the Miracle Mile in one line: "I was the person that wasn't supposed to be there." Because of injuries and the number of years that had passed since he had run a result that improved on his enormous promise as a teenager, observers had all but ignored him as an also-ran. Born in Calgary and raised in Edmonton and Toronto, Ferguson had first discovered his talent for running during his Boy Scout training. He had burst unexpectedly onto the Canadian track scene in 1950 as a wet-behind-the-ears 18-year-old, first by earning selection to the Canadian BEG team, then by running an impressive 4min 17sec mile at the Auckland Games. His potential appeared limitless. At the University of Iowa he had focussed on the less glamorous two-mile distance, twice winning Big Ten and NCAA two-mile championships while earning All-American honours, but to the press the two-mile lacked the prestige of the mile and so it was as if it had never happened. He then ran the 5000m for Canada at the 1952 Olympics but failed to finish his heat and press opinion of him soured. They also criticized him for quitting races on several occasions due to stomach ulcers.

Ferguson then turned to wonder coach Lloyd Percival, and his fortunes began to change, but wary Ontario track officials chose not to include him on the team travelling to Vancouver for the Canadian BECG trials because they reasoned he had given up too many times and would do so again. He was forced to pay his own way to the trials just for a chance to compete. In Vancouver he ran an unremarkable 4min 19sec mile, but it was good for third place and a Canadian team spot. With four weeks to prepare for the Games and little to distract him from Percival's gruelling training regimen, he went quietly about transforming himself, using the spurning by Ontario officials as motivation. As he pounded out the miles on UBC's Varsity Stadium track, one of the more improbable metamorphoses in Canadian track history took place. The weight of years of injury and neglect simply drained away like the sweat from his brow. His explanation at the time seemed more practical than metaphysical; as he told a *Province* reporter, "I just eat, sleep, and live track right now. With no studies to distract me, I couldn't help but improve."

The best part of this transformation was that no one else knew. As press and track aficionados dissected the field of Mile runners, looking everywhere but at the unrealized Canadian, he ran on, invisible and forgotten as he reinvented himself, propelled by this delightful secret. The signs were all there to be seen. In the 880yd heats, he blazed to the fastest-ever half-mile by a Canadian in a time of 1min 53.2sec, then dashed a half second quicker in the final, good enough for fifth. Even with such glimpses, he still felt like a man flying well below the radar. And he liked it that way.

For the semi-finals of the Mile, Games organizers had divided the big names between the two heats, hoping to balance the competitive qualifiers. The last thing anyone wanted was for the marquee Bannister-Landy match-up to be wasted in an insignificant semi. Thus, in the first semi Bannister and Halberg were matched up with an assortment of solid internationals, the most noteworthy being Disley, Macmillan, Law and Australia's Geoff Warren. Landy faced the tougher field in the second semi, which featured known contenders Milligan, Parnell, Baillie and Brasher.

Empire Stadium buzzed all afternoon leading up to the semis, and as the Bannister heat strode onto the track from the tunnel, the crowd roused to respond with polite applause. The race starter called the field to their marks and raised his silver starter's pistol. The crack of the gun caused a frenzied slashing of arms and legs as jockeying for positions began. Bannister avoided this initial scramble and casually followed behind. He had long ago determined he would do only the minimum required to qualify for the final. Disley won the early sprint to the lead and carried the pack through the first turn. Warren soon passed Disley and set a blistering pace, coming through the first lap in 58sec with Halberg 5yds back. Bannister led the remaining pack 10yds behind Halberg,

Canada's Bill Parnell (far right) leads Australia's Don Macmillan (second from right) and Canada's Rich Ferguson (centre) in the Mile at the 1950 BEG in Auckland.

content to let Warren stretch his lead. As the press later correctly speculated, the Australian was attempting to bait Bannister into running faster and wasting energy for the showdown with his teammate Landy in the final two days later. "I tried to make the race more honest—quicker—because I knew Bannister wouldn't run any faster than he had to," recalled Warren. "I couldn't tell Landy my plans because he'd have said, 'No, no you don't.' He would have hated it. So I kept my plans secret."

Warren dashed through the half-mile in a hair over 2min flat and promptly stepped off the track exhausted. "I looked back and no one was near me!" he exclaimed, still sounding shocked in an interview nearly sixty years later. "Bannister and the rest were 40 or 50yds yards back. They never took the bait. I felt like such a fool! It had all been for nothing. Much later I thought, how stupid. If only I'd tried just to qualify for the final, perhaps history would have been much different. I could have taken some of the brunt of the middle laps off the leaders. I could have given Landy a break, taken a bit of the heat off him. *That* was the time to do it, not the semi-final. But I didn't and we know what happened."

Halberg then took over the lead with a 20yd cushion on Ferguson, who had surprised everyone by moving into second. Bannister glanced over with a look that seemed to say, "And who were you again?" By the end of the third lap, a visibly strained Halberg still led, but he was faltering. The brisk early pace had taken its toll. Ferguson, running very strongly, closed the gap going around the turn to the back straight and charged ahead, head nodding as hard as his arms and legs were pumping. When he went by the New Zealander with the limp left arm, the crowd released a strong roar of approval. Bannister was now close behind as well. At this point a lesser runner might have cracked with the pack closing in so threateningly, but Halberg had mettle in that wiry body of his and a heart that wouldn't quit. He looked out of place among the more classic striders, but he was about to prove once again that he more than belonged. Glancing over his inside shoulder and seeing the pack on his heels, he found another gear and stayed with Bannister, running shoulder-to-shoulder as they entered the back straight. Law clawed his way into fourth ahead of a lagging Macmillan and a surging Disley. Down the backstretch they charged, strung out in a line, a yard or two separating each. Ferguson continued to lead around the final turn, running very comfortably, but then Halberg put on a burst and flew to the front. Ferguson let him go, conceding later he was amazed to discover his legs still had more left in reserve. He simply coasted to the finish behind Halberg, realizing he could perhaps beat him in the final and contend for a medal. Everyone else was surprised he had even qualified.

Looking unaffected by his now-famous cold, Bannister followed unconcerned 5yds behind, qualifying comfortably and nothing more. Sensing a runner on his inside shoulder, he saw it was his teammate Law. Moving over and slowing slightly, Bannister called out encouragement to the struggling lawyer. "Come on!" he urged him on repeatedly. Buoyed by the support, Law cruised to the final qualifying spot just ahead of Disley. Halberg's winning time of 4min 7.4sec marked the fastest Mile ever run in Canada to that point and made the 21-year-old the new BECG Mile record holder, slashing over 3.5sec off Parnell's 1950 time, though most felt his time was only a temporary post until

Opposite: Canadian team captain Bill Parnell of North Vancouver (left) was the defending BECG Mile champion and record holder.

Saturday's final. Ferguson, Bannister, Law and Disley had also finished below Parnell's shattered BECG record. Ferguson's 4min 7.8sec was more than 6sec faster than he had ever run before. Out of nowhere, he was now the fastest Canadian miler in history.

The Landy heat readied to go a short time later. Although less crowded with only seven runners, this heat appeared deeper in talent as Boyd, Baillie, Landy, Parnell, Brasher and Milligan all carried some sort of international reputation into the race. With the crack of the gun the pack sprang into action. Much like Bannister earlier, Landy stepped forward off the line rather nonchalantly and brought up the rear. The pack slowed considerably on the back straight, as Baillie, who seemed to feel a bit "toey," a Kiwi term for wanting to pick up the pace, took the lead. He led the field through a relatively slow first lap in 62sec, while Parnell continued to challenge on the outside. The crowd, awakened by the possibilities Ferguson had unexpectedly demonstrated in the previous heat, now showered cheers on Parnell. Running relaxed at the back of the pack, Landy quietly began moving up, picking off runners on the outside. Baillie, still leading, went through the half-mile mark in 2min 8sec, but the pace slowed as Parnell, Landy and Milligan jockeyed for positions close behind him.

With all the runners still bunched up, the third lap proved a chaotic brawl. Landy edged up on Parnell, who had looked so strong only a lap earlier but was now clearly struggling. Brasher, running without his customary horn-rimmed glasses, showed a surprising outside burst and slid into the lead, passing the entire pack on the corner. Baillie cut off Milligan, and both nearly tumbled to the cinders, but Baillie recovered

The three favourites in the Mile pose after the semi-finals, left to right: John Landy, Roger Bannister and Murray Halberg. Photo courtesy of Vonna McDonald.

quickly and, spurred by the contact, seized the lead again, passing the last-lap bell in 3min 12sec.

On the back straightaway, Brasher dropped back in the field, suffering from his ill-timed early sprint. Parnell, too, lost touch with the first five, his chances of replicating the magic of Auckland four years earlier rapidly dimming. Milligan, running very strongly, his delicate heel clearly no issue, broke on the outside and moved into the lead with a gliding Landy shadowing him in second. Boyd, hidden in the pack for much of the race, passed both Parnell and Brasher and moved into fourth. Milligan continued to stride beautifully away, gritting his teeth as the field rounded the final corner. Landy darted to the outside, running easily. He knew as long as this pace was maintained he would safely qualify, and when Milligan looked to his left, he was surprised to see the world record holder running with him effortlessly. As Landy eased up, Milligan followed suit, but Baillie charged through on the inside to nip both of them by a nose. All three—Baillie, Milligan and Landy—finished in a dead-heat, awarded the same time of 4min 11.4sec. Boyd galloped in two strides behind, certainly a surprise fourth place.

Parnell finished a dejected fifth, eliminated over two seconds back. "I remember the anguish and hurt on his face, trying so hard, but it just wasn't there," recalled Mario Caravetta, who had stolen away from his job at the stadium concessions to catch the race. "You could see he wanted it so badly and not that he'd given up—he was workin' like hell—but it just wasn't there. He didn't have it. And it wasn't through lack of trying or quitting." Largely ignored, Parnell trudged wearily away from the other competitors. For one of Canada's outstanding runners, it should not have ended like this. In the stadium tunnel, a lone reporter from the *Vancouver Sun* stopped him for a comment. "I've no regrets," Parnell began. "I've had a lot of fun in my 11 years in track and I've done everything I've wanted to do. I wanted to defend my Mile title at home, and I did." His gaze drifted off into the distance as he chose his next words carefully. "It would have been nicer if I had done better, but..." He paused, regaining his composure, although his sad eyes hid nothing. "I ran as best I could under the circumstances but I overlooked something, misjudged things. But that's my own troubles." With no further elaboration, he strode off. He was one of the class acts of Canadian sport, a popular past champion who deserved a better send-off. This was not how it was supposed to end.

A different scene ensued on the other side of the stadium. Reporters swirled around the qualified runners as they congratulated one another. CBC's Steve Douglas corralled Halberg, Landy and Bannister for a collective on-air interview. Young Halberg appeared nervous and fiddled with his jacket zipper. After he produced several uninspiring answers, Douglas turned to Landy. "How about Saturday's race, John?"

"Well, I'll be trying as hard as I can," Landy said. "I think I'll have to. The way they ran the other heat, I'll be flat out just to get a place."

Turning to Bannister, who was signing an autograph for a fan, Douglas followed with the subject on everybody's mind at that moment. "Doctor, how about Saturday's race?"

"Well, let's wait till Saturday, shall we?" Bannister parried with a grin.

With that, the world began counting down the hours and minutes toward the Mile of the Century in two days' time.

CHAPTER 9
FRIDAY, AUGUST 6, 1954

On Thursday night, after the excitement of the Mile semi-finals died down, John Landy went to bed in his Empire Village bunk, but he struggled to sleep, and around 3 a.m. he decided some night air might do him good. As he stepped down from the porch, the grass's light dew felt cool on his bare feet. He took a few more steps when suddenly a sharp pain stabbed the sole of his left foot. Pulling himself back up the stairs into the light, he could see that jagged shards of a photographer's discarded flashbulb were poking out of a deep two-inch slice on the arch of his foot just in front of his heel. Blood was flowing steadily from the wound. Carefully removing the glass, he went inside and was cleaning the gash at the sink when his roommate John Vernon stirred, saw the blood, and became immediately concerned. He offered to go for help and Landy agreed on the condition no one else should find out. Vernon dashed out, found a security guard and quickly located a doctor who saw Landy around 4 a.m. at UBC's Wesbrook hospital. Dr. M.J. Hiddlestone bandaged the cut and cautioned Landy against any running, but Landy remained determined, reasoning the cut was positioned in an area of his foot that didn't come into direct contact with the ground. Decades later he still adamantly down-played the cut's significance. "Well, there was a lot made of that," the Australian miler said in a 2007 interview. "I think we can forget that. It was most unfortunate, but it was a superficial cut. It made no difference."

Landy made Dr. Hiddlestone swear to keep his visit secret. But when he returned to his room, he and Vernon met fellow miler Don Macmillan and revealed what had happened to Landy. Beyond that, no one else was to know, though they were all aware that, living in such close quarters with other athletes and under the constant glare of the media's magnifying glass, it was inevitable that word would leak out. On Friday morning when Landy failed to show up for a National Film Board interview, *Montreal Star* sports columnist Andy O'Brien was sent over to his room. Caught unprepared, Landy jumped out of bed and O'Brien saw the blood on the floor. "Andy O'Brien broke into my room quite illegally," recalled Landy. "Of course, he thought he had the scoop of the century. I implored him not to mention it." Threatening that the race might be called off if word of the cut went public, Landy swore O'Brien to absolute secrecy. The sportswriter gave Landy his word and kept quiet—at least at first.

Later that day Landy revealed his secret to Murray Halberg and Bill Baillie, and Victor Milligan learned of the cut from the two New Zealanders. As far as anyone knows, that's as far as the secret spread before the Mile was run on Saturday. Still, it meant at least half of the eight men contesting the final were now aware. "Nobody knows except you blokes," Landy told them. "Just keep it quiet because it will not affect me in any way, shape or form." Despite several well-intentioned warnings from

Opposite: Gerry Buchanan was Canada's best amateur heavyweight boxer in decades.

them, Landy remained resolute that he would run, deep gash in his foot or not, but he also knew he couldn't reveal his injury publicly for fear people would perceive it as an excuse if he ran poorly. Already carrying a load of unthinkable pressure, he shouldered this added burden with quiet grace. As he spent the day quietly preparing for the biggest race of his life, those who knew of his predicament marvelled at his unwavering strength and courage.

✸

Several BECG sports wrapped up their final day of competition on Friday, August 6. One of these was lawn bowling. The home greens of the West Point Grey and New Westminster lawn bowling clubs had been hosting the lawn bowling events all week. In fact, the Doubles, which was held at West Point Grey, had been the first official Games sport of any kind to begin play, with North Vancouver's Sam Gardiner rolling the first bowl at around 10 a.m. on Friday, July 30, when the Opening Ceremonies were still 10 hours away. A record-breaking 61 bowlers from 11 countries had necessitated the extended schedule to accommodate 30 sessions of play and the two venues—Point Grey in Vancouver and Moody Park in New Westminster—and over the course of the week more than 3,000 spectators paid $1 for the general admission all-day pass to see the competition. The official history of the Games claimed it was "the biggest international occasion in the history of lawn bowling."

Although a few colonial reminders of the game's deep "old Empire" roots persisted, by 1954 the sport was in transition, moving towards a more inclusive future. For example, in the medal standings of the Fours competition, South Africa, Hong Kong

Lawn bowling offered perhaps the most relaxed competitive atmosphere of any Games event.

and Southern Rhodesia finished 1-2-3, the most unlikely medal grouping of the Games outside of Africa's sweep of the men's high jump. And the Hong Kong Fours lineup contained more team members of Portuguese heritage—Jose Alberto da Luz and the monumentally named Raul Francisco Eustaquio da Luz—than those of native Hong Kong descent. The silver medal they won was not only Hong Kong's lone medal in Vancouver but its first-ever in Commonwealth history.

However, those who wandered out to West Point Grey or Moody Park without any prior knowledge of the game or its rules may have been surprised by what they saw. Athletes sweating and straining in the sun were nowhere to be found. Instead, they would have seen teams of relaxed middle-aged—in some cases even elderly—men, dressed in snow-white shirts, slacks and shady fedoras. (One English Doubles competitor, Edwin Bateman, was 74—the oldest Games competitor ever in any sport.) As the matches progressed, women in heels and tastefully mid-calf skirts carried trays of cold drinks to the competitors, some of whom puffed on cigarettes as their bowls rolled across the green expanse like marbles on carpet. And they joked genially about how they would like to see Bannister and Landy perform under such brutal conditions. It was definitely competition but of the casual country-club sort. It was vigorous enough, however, that Welshman Obadiah Hopkins suffered a "mild heart seizure" on the eve of the Doubles competition that forced his team's withdrawal from play. But Hopkins proved a hard man to keep down, and he recovered in time to help his Welsh teammates to a ninth-place finish in the Fours competition.

Most of the competitors were more than satisfied with the bowls venues provided by Vancouver's BEG Society, although a few seemed perplexed by Canadian quirks to the game. In an article in the *Auckland Weekly News,* published four days after the Games ended, an unidentified Kiwi bowler provided stuffy insight into why he felt New Zealand had struggled to win in Vancouver. Under the headline "Unusual Greens," he wrote:

> They [the greens] are well covered—very well covered with inch-long grass—but they will not cut them. The greens are 126ft to 136ft long and there are no ditches. What is the use of trying to take a jack into a ditch which does not exist?... We are having great difficulty "getting up," but have made up our minds to throw the bowls as do our Canadian hosts. I cannot find words to explain how heavy the greens are, nor can I quote one at home which would give a comparable idea... The tournament committee of the N.Z.B.A. would have convulsions if championship competitors arrived to play as they do here. Anything goes in the way of dress... There is no bell to start or end the games. There are no umpires—the participants in any dispute have to settle it between themselves. And can you imagine what would happen in a "Dominion" if players defaulted without notice or played until lunchtime and forgot to come back... However, these are merely my impressions of bowls. Perhaps the Canadians have retained much of the enjoyment of the game that we have lost.

Perhaps some of the anonymous Kiwi's puzzlement about Canadians stemmed from watching Sam Gardiner, who had rolled the first bowl of the Games, and his partner, Dick Williams, both members of the North Vancouver Lawn Bowling Club, who

Canadian pair Dick Williams (left) and Sam Gardiner (right) were two of lawn bowling's most animated competitors.

were two of the more animated bowlers competing, though local spectators had grown to appreciate their antics. Gardiner was the least conspicuous of the pair, his ivory fedora complementing the thick pipe he kept clenched between his teeth at all times, puffs of smoke trailing behind him as he sized up his next shot. He had relocated from Sunderland, England, in 1909, and outside of lawn bowling, he ran a successful North Shore insurance company, though he often played a role in local theatre or opera productions.

By contrast, Dick Williams was a silver-haired dynamo. While some really enthusiastic competitors would go so far as to amble down the greens after bowling their wood and celebrate a successful shot with a polite cheer and handclap, Williams would gyrate like a belly dancer, shimmying and shaking, leaping like an antelope, using every ounce of energy to coax his bowl along the desired path and halt at the destination he had in mind. During a match at the Canadian trials a month earlier he had even completed a series of somersaults. Considering his profession, however, it's little wonder he was simply bursting with excess energy. For years he had repaired clocks and watches for Birks jewellers, spending most days hunched over his work table meticulously adjusting tiny gears, springs and sprockets. By the end of the workday his body and mind must have ached for movement—even in the unusual locale of a lawn bowling green. Another transplant to Canada, he had been born in Beaumaris, Wales, in 1898, emigrated in 1913, then served in the Canadian Army Medical Corps during the Great War. Lawn bowling had not been his first sport: during the 1920s his play with St. Andrews, Vancouver City and North Shore United soccer clubs had earned him selection to the Canadian national team that toured New Zealand in 1927.

To qualify for the Games in Vancouver, as well as taking part in club and city play-downs, Gardiner and Williams had endured 15 three-hour matches to win the provincial and national titles and followed this with another 8 matches during the Games, but Williams was still hopping, skipping and jumping as outrageously at the end of it all as the beginning. The North Vancouver duo had hit the ground running on the first day of play, scoring two wins. A 17-15 victory over Southern Rhodesia proved particularly dramatic as the Canadians had been down by a point on their final shot when Williams ran the jack (the white target ball competitors aim for with their bowls) through to score 3 and complete an unlikely comeback.

The second day proved a frustrating nightmare for the duo, and in one match after several closely missed shots, Gardiner approached the scene of the crime, wound up, and appeared quite serious about booting the offending wood across Burrard Inlet. Losses to Scotland and Hong Kong bookended a tie with the strong Northern Ireland pair of William Rosbotham and Percy Watson, who eventually took gold. For Watson, the win served as a satisfying redemption that had been 20 years in the making. At the 1934 BEG in London, the host English had edged out his Northern Ireland Fours team for the gold and he had been forced to settle for silver. Now two decades later Watson, a little greyer and wiser, could leave Vancouver with the gold in hand. No other Commonwealth athlete ever waited so long between medal wins. The Belfast Indoor Bowls Club building, renamed the Percy Watson Stadium in his honour, stands as a monument to him as the club's founder and the most patient of its sons.

Multiple matches take place simultaneously on the greens of the New Westminster Lawn Bowling Club.

On their final two days of play, Gardiner and Williams rebounded nicely to score four wins. With help from the Hong Kong team, which knocked off the Scottish, the Canadians leapt into silver medal position with a record of six wins, two losses and one tie, eliciting one last celebratory dance from Williams and another contented draw on his pipe by Gardiner. To this day their result remains one of Canada's best-ever in international lawn bowling.

In the Singles competition, while many had picked Glyn de V. Bosisto, the four-time Australian champ known in his country as "the Bradman of Bowls," or even New Zealand's James Pirret, the defending BECG Singles champion, as the favourites for the gold, Bosisto had a late collapse and Pirret had a slow start. Not many were bold enough to predict that Ralph Hodges, a mailman from Salisbury in Southern Rhodesia, would take it, but being used to evading snappy Rhodesian Ridgebacks on his daily mail route, Hodges quietly slipped past everyone with an impressive 8-1 record to take the gold.

✦

While the lawn bowlers were wrapping up play on Friday afternoon, a nearly full house was taking in the final day of the BECG fencing competition in Lord Byng High School's 1,200-seat gymnasium. Few locals could recognize a good *balestra*, the intricacies of the parry or a decisive *riposte*, or how competitors who had been struck with a successful *touché* didn't keel over mortally wounded, but that had not stopped the curious from trickling in, and over the course of the week a total of 3,100 spectators had paid the $1 general admission to watch and learn.

The school gym, with its basketball hoops, lent the international competition an endearing grassroots quality, but the organizers had laid down two *pistes*— the narrow, rubber-matted runways that constitute fencing's field of play—parallel to one another on the hardwood floor to allow two matches to proceed simultaneously. A new electronic scoring system was used in the epee events for the first time in Vancouver; tiny spring-loaded buttons installed on the tip of the blades sent electronic signals down a wire running underneath the competitors' armour back to a central drum, causing one of two light bulbs to flash and indicating which competitor had scored. The system was sensitive enough to distinguish between blows scored just 1/25 of a second apart and proved to be a far more reliable and accurate judge than the human eye. However, it also made opposing fencers look like dancing marionettes controlled by horizontal strings.

BECG fencers engage while an official watches for scoring blows at the Lord Byng High School gymnasium.

A FENCING FAMILY

Rene Paul was a second-generation member of an amazing family of fencers, his father, Leon, having founded both the Leon Paul Fencing Equipment Company and the Salle Paul Fencing Club that shaped British fencing for the better part of a century. Most leading British fencers trained there or sought the Paul family's wisdom on equipment and technique. Between Rene, his brother Raymond and his sons Barry and Graham, the Pauls brought 18 BECG fencing medals—13 of them gold—back to London, which must stand as some sort of family medal record. Members of the family also competed in 20 Olympic Games, 30 world championships, and won 25 national titles. A fourth generation has followed in the family business, and to-day the Leon Paul Company supplies cutting-edge fencing equipment to both the British and American national teams. The Pauls are often the first consulted when expertise or equipment is sought for the latest swashbuckling film. In several 1950s films Raymond doubled for Errol Flynn in sword fighting scenes, and more recently the Paul family consulted on the sword fights in the James Bond film *Die Another Day*, which featured Pierce Brosnan as Bond and Madonna as a sexy fencing instructor. This time, Raymond's son Steven, a six-time Olympian as both athlete and coach, doubled for Brosnan after instructing the actor for six months on the finer points of the sport. Rene Paul died in 2008 at the age of 88, but he had lived long enough to see his family's name become even more synonymous with the sport than anyone could have foreseen when he presided with such elegant panache over Lord Byng's gym in 1954.

Although England dominated the event in Vancouver, two Australian fencers did stand out. The dashing Melbourne swordsman John Fethers, who bore a striking resemblance to a young Errol Flynn complete with windswept hair and pencil-thin moustache, proved he was more than just a pretty face. By winning five medals, which included the individual foil silver medal and individual sabre bronze, he captured not only the most fencing medals in Vancouver but also the most medals of any athlete in any sport in the Games.

Ivan Lund, a Sydney bank clerk, won gold in the individual epee, marking the first time a non-English fencer had won a BECG gold medal. Over the course of four BECGs, Lund won thirteen medals (three gold, six silver, four bronze), making him the most decorated fencer in Commonwealth history and one of the most decorated Australian athletes in any sport. He served as Australian flag bearer at the 1958 BECG and 1964 Olympics, presented a statue of St. John Bosco, patron saint of sportspersons, to Pope John XXIII in front of 100,000 people at the 1960 Olympics and read the athlete's oath at the opening ceremonies of the 1962 BECG. To this day he is considered Australia's greatest fencer.

The English fencers were happy to adopt a BC Lions' cymbal-clapping wind-up monkey as their lucky charm and team mascot. "I hope you don't think us juvenile," 23-year-old English fencer Allan Jay admitted to a curious reporter. If anyone did, the English team's medal tally quickly quieted them: five of fencing's seven gold. Jay himself won the individual foil bronze while also helping England to gold in both team foil and

Following pages: Canadian fencers Elizabeth Hale (left) and Jeanne Gilbert (right) pose at Empire Village.

In some quarters the viewpoint was expressed that the calibre of the boxing was not, on the whole, up to Empire standards... a few of the contenders put on a show that could be equaled by novices. True, there were some flashes of brilliance and some enthusiastic belligerence that had the crowds in an uproar, but generally speaking, the whole show was nothing to get too excited about.

There may have been something to this damning critique. A Pakistani boxer named Ahmed Shah who was competing in the 112lb flyweight division had missed half the Games by the time he arrived on August 3, and he had brought only his boxing shoes. Other competitors took pity on the ill-prepared fighter, giving him a jockstrap, socks and shorts, and a coach gave him the undershirt off his back in lieu of a proper singlet just so the man could compete. Meanwhile, English boxing manager James Meech scored points with the press for the most original exit from the 1954 Games: falling out of a transom even before the Games began. In his column on July 27 the *Sun*'s Dick Beddoes called it the "Old English Rope Trick":

Mr. Meech could not be reached for an eye-witness account of his collision with the transom, but by all reports, he was beaten in straight falls.

He desired for reasons sacred unto himself to enter UBC's Memorial Gymnasium, which is reserved for boxing headquarters. His entrance was impeded by a locked door, but English ingenuity inspired him when he noticed a rope hanging from the open transom. He shinnied up the rope in record time for BEG climbers and almost had it made when, cuss it, the rope broke.

Meech suffered a chipped shoulder blade and fractured vertebrae and ended up in a Vancouver hospital. The British Amateur Boxing Association then rushed Jack Peel to Vancouver to take over as manager and assist with refereeing. Unfortunately, the *Vancouver Sun* singled out Peel's refereeing, along with that of Southern Rhodesia's Norman Nimmo, as "more amateurish than the fighters they handled."

Despite the best efforts of the ring crew, which included Canadians such as Jack Short, Bert Lowes and Dave Brown, all of them future hall of famers, the crowd at the Vancouver Forum still disagreed with virtually every decision. No single nation dominated. South Africa, Canada and England each carted home multiple medals, though most impressively, Scotland's three-man team won two gold medals and a silver. And while the boxing may have been lacklustre in spots, a few bouts and boxers ranked as the best of the amateur variety ever seen in the city.

The 156lb light middleweight division semi-finals on Thursday, August 5, was marked by one of the most unusual occurrences ever in a BECG boxing ring and led to a ruling that confused many and satisfied few. England's Bruce Wells, a London police officer and reigning European light middleweight champion, faced off against Maurice Tuck, New Zealand champion for five straight years, in a bout holding much promise. The swift-footed Wells was a classic flighty dancer, all jab-and-run, while Tuck was a plodding bomber with the ability to end a fight in a single punch. Midway through the fight, one of Tuck's rockets caught the Englishman on the chin. As Wells' legs buckled, he instinctively clutched Tuck and the two men cracked heads. The collision opened up "a wicked zig-zag" six-stitch cut in Wells' eyelid that bled profusely before he touched the canvas, while Tuck suffered a one-stitch slice above his own eye. The two fighters lay for a moment or two in a tangled, bloody heap, and after inspection by the ringside doctor who ruled both unfit to continue, the judges stopped the bout on the rarest of all finishes: a double technical knockout. The result eliminated both men from the tournament and meant the other semi-final between Edmonton's Wilf Greaves and Northern Rhodesia's Frederick Wright would become the division's gold medal match. Meanwhile, as Wells had been ahead of Tuck on points at the time of their collision, officials awarded him the bronze medal even though technically he had not won a single bout. After retiring from the ring, Wells became a movie and television stuntman and worked on the *Doctor Who* series.

Although they had been given an unexpected extra day of rest before their match, on Friday night Greaves and Wright squared off with a lot more on the line. A fresh-faced, 18-year-old high schooler, Greaves had a lot going for him: surprising strength, the ability to take a punch and a mighty wallop with either fist. In the opening round he relied on the left, popping Wright on the chin with stinging hooks. In the second round, Wright had the edge, shutting the young Canadian down. In the deciding frame, Greaves changed strategy and relied on crisp jabs, snapping Wright's head like a puppet, a strategy that ultimately won him the fight. The *Sun*'s Jack Richards wrote, quite rightly, that the schoolboy's winning formula came down to "heart and hooks." Vancouver's Tommy Paonessa, perhaps the most knowledgeable ringman on the West

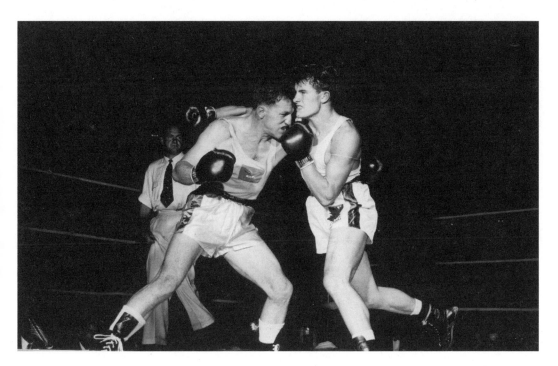

Canada's Wilf Greaves (right) spars with Northern Rhodesia's Frederick Wright (left) in the light middleweight final.

Coast and unofficial Canadian co-coach, jumped into the ring at the announcement and grabbed Greaves in a jubilant bear hug. So there it was: a peach-fuzzed high schooler took gold, second-place silver went to a boxer who had lost his only match, and the bronze medalist had finished his bout bleeding and lying on his back. After engineering this cruel masterpiece, the boxing gods must have been gleefully cackling up in that musty boxing ring in the sky.

When Wilf Greaves later entered the pro ranks, he was managed by Jake Mintz, who had guided Ezzard Charles to the heavyweight championship. Greaves won the Canadian middleweight title in 1958 and two years later upset future world champion Dick Tiger for the British Empire middleweight belt. In 1961 he battled the great Sugar Ray Robinson but took a knock-out blow in the eighth round of their scheduled ten-round fight.

The 178lb light-heavyweight division at the BECG featured the biggest upset of the entire tournament. Tony Madigan, who was representing his native Australia at the Games, was also the reigning British light-heavyweight champion and the odds-on favourite in the gold medal final against South Africa's Piet van Vuuren. But van Vuuren surprised everyone by carrying the bout and even dominating stretches. Little argument came when judges awarded the South African the decision, forcing Madigan to settle for silver. The *Sun*'s Richards declared Madigan "one of those fighters who is always a bridesmaid but never a bride." Perhaps Madigan kept that clipping as future motivation for he never again lost a Commonwealth match. After winning light-heavyweight gold four years later in Cardiff, he successfully defended his crown in Perth in 1962, becoming the first boxer in Games history to win back-to-back gold medals in the same division. He retired as the most decorated boxer in Commonwealth Games history. But an interesting career side note took place between Madigan's gold medal victories: at the 1960 Olympics he scrapped to a bronze

PRINCE PHILIP'S BOYS

Philip's penultimate day in Vancouver, Friday, August 6, proved his busiest. He began with a speech expressing his admiration for Canada at a luncheon at the Hotel Vancouver attended by 1,200 persons and telecast on CBUT. A visit to Empire Pool to take in the afternoon's swimming and diving events was followed by an exclusive gathering at UBC president Norman MacKenzie's tony Marine Drive residence. But the day's highlight came later at Empire Village, where Philip met many of the athletes and dined in the cafeteria with representatives of all 24 competing nations. While strolling through the courtyard afterwards, he spoke freely with a friendly throng of athletes. One of the more memorable exchanges occurred when he stopped in front of New Zealand welterweight boxer Mike Hannah, who sported two black eyes and a fat lip.

"How did you get those?" asked Philip.

"I was a boxer," said Hannah, still smarting from his early elimination.

"Who beat you?" the Duke enquired.

"One of your boys, sir," Hannah replied, referring to an English boxer.

"You're all my boys," Philip assured him with a sympathetic smile.

in the light-heavyweight division, losing his semi-final to the eventual gold medalist, a skinny unknown from Louisville, Kentucky, whose fists and feet were matched only by the speed of his mouth. That young boxer's name was, of course, Cassius Clay, later known around the world as Muhammad Ali.

The BECG boxing competition ended on a high note with the over 178lb heavyweight division final. Canada's hope in this division rested with its best amateur heavyweight in decades, Gerry Buchanan of Montreal, a curly-haired blond bomber with the hardest punch in the Games. Buchanan had easily dispatched George Jenkins of South Africa on a TKO in his opening bout on Thursday night, a bloody mismatch that officials prolonged to the second round after Jenkins had already kissed the canvas three times. The other preliminary bout had featured England's brawling Brian Harper squaring

Canadian boxing team co-coach Tommy Paonessa of Vancouver (right) was one of the most knowledgeable ringmen on the West Coast. Photo by John McGinnis.

off against the Australian Steve Zoranich in a match that lasted all of 2min 41sec before the referee awarded a dubious knockout win to Harper. The Englishman, who would become known as "the British Bulldog"—because as he told an interviewer in 2008, "I not only looked like a bulldog but fought like one"—had cheaply decked Zoranich from behind after the referee separated the two fighters when they became locked in a clinch. Somehow the obvious foul was not detected, and another Harper barrage sent the Australian backwards to the canvas. Zoranich got to his feet in good shape well before the ten-count, but to the shock of the crowd the referee ruled it a knockout. A stopwatch at ringside timed the supposed "ten-count" at only six-and-a-half seconds. Many called it the worst refereeing job of the Games. Referring to the one-armed referee, who had a hook in place of one hand, the *Daily Mirror*'s Peter Wilson wrote that the ref had "a more lethal hook than [Zoranich] will ever possess" and added that the plundered Aussie "will take an awful lot of persuading that the days of the pirates are past."

This ruling left Buchanan and Harper to duke it out for heavyweight gold on Friday night. On paper there were all the ingredients here for an attractive match-up. Buchanan was a dogged Highland steer with a steel chin that could absorb three solid shots in the time he needed to unload his neck-snapping cannonball special, a punch that had sent many fighters to the canvas swimming in their own drool. Harper, on the other hand, possessed the best all-round combination of size, speed, strength and toughness of any amateur boxer in the Commonwealth. He rarely ventured into a ring as the second-fittest man, and he certainly was not above resorting to tactics like that cheap shot on Zoranich to gain an edge. He also had good genes. His father was Jack

London, a stylish professional who had won the British heavyweight crown during WWII. After quitting school in Blackpool at 16, Harper had learned to brawl by going downtown on weekends and picking fights on the street. Then while serving his mandatory two years of national service in the RAF, he took up boxing for the sole reason that boxers got better food and more time off, and he progressed rapidly into one of the more fearsome foes between the ropes.

Throwing a dash of spice into the mix was some pre-fight bad blood. Buchanan had rubbed some observers the wrong way by boasting he would waltz his way to the gold medal. Harper felt the mouthy Canadian should simply shut up or sod off, take your pick. Put a bulldog in the ring with a bull and you may not have the most orthodox match-up, but you will certainly have a fight, and after the opening bell, both fighters tried to end it in the first flurry. Looking for an early edge, Harper targeted a healing scab on Buchanan's cheekbone, a remnant of a training mishap, and during a clinch he used his glove's laces to rake away the tender flesh so that Buchanan emerged with a streaming wound. There would be more back alley stuff, including thumbs to Buchanan's eyes and continual head butts, but Harper always remained discreet enough to get away with it. He would then fall back upon his superior foot and fist speed to get inside on Buchanan and repeatedly score legal blows. It infuriated the Canadian, who swung back wildly but found mostly air. At times it resembled something you might see down in the shadows of the dockyards on a foggy Friday night. There seemed to be nothing sweet and very little science to the butchery these two were determined to inflict on each other.

In the second round Buchanan put in a warrior's effort, upping his work rate. Hardening his defensive stance in the face of Harper's infuriating tactics, he patiently waited for the right moment to strike back. His reward was at least three bone-powdering wallops that straightened up the Englishman. The crowd—a beaming Prince Philip among them—roared louder with each blow. At one point, Buchanan appeared to have Harper in dire straits, but the bulldog showed he was as wily as he was wild. After receiving a particularly unfriendly love tap from Buchanan, Harper played dead, feigning being struck by a phantom low blow. The ref didn't take the bait, but it allowed Harper time to regain his bearings and exit the round upright.

Harper rallied in the third round while by this time Buchanan looked spent. Now the tough Canadian could only protect his face by leaning forward, head down. Harper, sensing the kill, bashed and swiped relentlessly, peppering shots at the top of Buchanan's exposed skull. However, the exhausted Montreal boy refused to quit, and as the round wound down, he found enough energy to mount one final charge, driving the scrappy English bulldog back. At the bell both men's shoulders sagged, their faces drawn tight with fatigue.

The largest indoor boxing crowd in Vancouver's history erupted in a prolonged standing ovation for the efforts of two men who had soldiered through nine agonizing minutes of total war. In his *Daily Mirror* column the venerable Peter Wilson ranked it "as good an amateur heavyweight battle as I have ever seen," while others called it simply the greatest boxing match in BECG history. There would have been no dispute from any of those on hand that night who continued to shower the ring with applause until throats became hoarse and palms tingled. And when officials raised Harper's arm as the winner by decision, the crowd offered no disagreement. "The Blackpool Rock,"

THREE LEGENDS

Counterbalancing the failures in the boxing ring was the expert involvement in the management end of the boxing competition of three future Vancouver sports legends. Jack Short, best known for broadcasting 43 seasons of horse racing at Vancouver and Victoria tracks, helped out with the ring announcing; by 1976 when Short closed his final day of racing with his signature "Adios amigos!" he had called nearly 50,000 races during his career. Bert Lowes also sneaked his foot into the door of international refereeing and judging at these Games, although unluckily he seems to have refereed every bout that went controversially awry. However, in later years he refereed or judged at four more Commonwealth Games and three Olympics, becoming the first Canadian referee to attain international accreditation with the International Amateur Boxing Association. Short and Lowes were joined on the ring crew by Dave Brown, who over a 25-year period became one of Canada's most consistent refs, and until his retirement in 2000 it was Brown that the World Boxing Council relied on for world title fights all over the world. His resume included refereeing the second Muhammad Ali-George Chuvalo fight at Vancouver's Pacific Coliseum in 1972; Ali thought so much of Brown's work he gave him his satin boxing shorts, which were still sprinkled with drops of Chuvalo's blood.

now sporting a purple shiner under his left eye, had been the aggressor and carried two of the three rounds. Afterwards, Buchanan understandably felt shortchanged by the result and looked to confront Harper about his less-than-simon-pure tactics. In a 2007 interview Tommy Paonessa recalled the aftermath of that fight. Paonessa, who had worked Buchanan's corner during the match, was by now a trim 101 years of age, but he recalled every detail of the event clearly. "Gerry [Buchanan] was that mad," he said, "and he was going to try and do something about it, but I stopped that and thank god I did because it would have been a helluva mess up there." Buchanan's ire had been particularly raised when he learned one of the judges who had voted in favour of Harper was English. "The English judge shouldn't have been in there—not while an English fighter was in a fight," Paonessa explained. "If I had known at the start, I would've raised hell, but I didn't know and when he announced it, well, it was too late. That was it." Having been an excellent fighter himself through the 1920s, once appearing on the undercard of a Jack Johnson bout in Chicago and then working his way back home with the Barnum and Bailey Circus as a ferris wheel ticket taker, Paonessa knew first-hand how much hung on a judges' tight decision. "The fight [between Harper and Buchanan] was just so damn close," Paonessa lamented, his voice trailing off at the memory.

The trajectories of Buchanan's and Harper's respective careers went in completely different directions after Vancouver. Buchanan turned professional soon after the Games and won all four of his pro fights, including a TKO of the Australian heavyweight champion in New Zealand. As he had played some football in his early years, while he was Down Under he tried out with the venerable All-Blacks of New Zealand rugby fame but in the

Following pages: Canada's Gerry Buchanan (left) tangled with England's Brian Harper (right) in an electric heavyweight final.

CHAPTER 10
SATURDAY, AUGUST 7, 1954

By mid-morning on Saturday, August 7, thousands of cars were crawling along east Vancouver streets towards Empire Stadium, while city traffic cops did their best to alleviate the congestion. To the south more than 500 vehicles an hour streamed across the border from the US, and soon all 7,000 stadium parking spots at 50 cents a pop were filled. At 11 o'clock, the stadium's gates opened, and although fire wardens attempted to organize people into orderly lines, the gates were soon choked by a great mass of humanity heading for their seats. Another 5,000 people, many of them waiting outside the gates since dawn, crowded around the four sales booths in the hope of snagging the last remaining tickets. They were out of luck. A loudspeaker announcement that all seats and even standing room tickets had been sold out days earlier caused a mass groan, but when the ticketless turned back to the scalpers who had been offering $5 bleacher seats for $50 on the way in, they discovered their prices had doubled.

Many finding their seats that day carried a copy of the morning's *News-Herald*, which summed up the excitement gripping the populace: "This is it. THE DAY Vancouver and the whole world has been waiting for." CBC broadcast legend Ted Reynolds, interviewed in 2004 for a CBC documentary on the Games, remembered the feeling in the air as unlike any he would experience in his next five decades of covering sports around the world: "The atmosphere going into the stadium that day, it was a carnival, it was a festival, and it was going into the unknown." The first spectator in his seat, young Ellery Littleton, who had been allowed early entry because his uncle was working as a track official, recalled much the same when interviewed for a *Vancouver Courier* retrospective in 2004. "It was nuts, like a rock concert, slightly out of control," he said. "It was really wild, electric and barely contained." Adding to the charged ambience, a helicopter jointly chartered by *Sports Illustrated* and *Life* magazines hovered noisily overhead snapping aerial photos. Afterwards it was set down on a nearby golf course to be ready to rush copy and photos to Seattle from where they would be wired to headquarters in New York.

Throughout the morning the temperature rose steadily. The forecasts in the Vancouver papers had been for a surprisingly low temperature for early August—somewhere in the mid-to-upper 60s F. (about 19° C.)—but later estimates placed it in the mid-70s to the mid-80s (24° to 29° C.). Officially it peaked in the early afternoon at 82° F. (28° C.), though out on the exposed pavement of Vancouver's streets it felt closer to a humid 100° F. (38° C.). Later many would cite August 7 as the hottest day of the year in Vancouver. Stadium concessions capitalized on the plight of spectators in the exposed seats, selling hundreds of gallons of "orange drink" the day's best seller. Also popular were the colourful paper "coolie hats" that dotted the stands like a rainbow.

Opposite: Roger Bannister (top, in white) watches helplessly from trackside as English teammate Jim Peters struggles on the track.

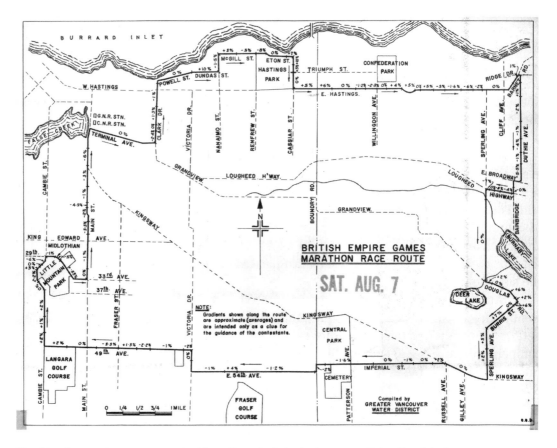

The 26-mile marathon route stretched from Burnaby Lake in the east to False Creek in the west.

in green shorts and white singlet elbowed his way between Peters and Cox. The Englishmen, noticeably agitated by the appearance of this "race crasher," immediately stepped off the track. The newcomer, however, remained standing poised at the line. Confused officials attempted to find his correct starting position while the crowd and competitors watched, amused and baffled. "Where's your number?" officials asked, seeing none on his singlet. But the man spoke no English and through sign language gestured he had stepped down from the crowd. Then he began pleading with officials to let him run. "Incredible as it might seem," Australian marathoner Allan Lawrence told Rob Hadgraft, author of *Plimsolls On, Eyeballs Out*, "some of the Canadian officials initially thought it would do no harm to let him start the race as 'he would soon get tired and drop out.' Jim Peters would have none of it and kept appealing, 'Remove this madman!'"

Most of the waiting marathoners appeared visibly annoyed at the needless delay in the baking sun. Sweat already glistened on their faces, and they had not even begun the race. Officials finally came to their senses and informed the man he could not run, which plunged the situation into the truly wacky. Upset at this news, the man ran around in circles, waving his arms and gesticulating wildly. Then, crying, he threw himself on the ground and pounded the track with his fists. To top off the tantrum—or

The marathon field completes a lap of Empire Stadium's track before exiting to Vancouver's scorching streets.

protest, no one knows which to this day—he proceeded to turn somersaults before officials led him away. Newspapers later identified the man as Victor Zajelinik, a Yugoslavian immigrant who had been barred from running at the BECG trials for failing to meet residency qualifications.

The sideshow over, officials got the field away on the second try without further disruption. The crowd gave the competitors a nice cheer as they trotted one lap of Empire's track. To guard against the blazing sun now directly overhead, several runners, including Barry Lush of Canada and Joe McGhee of Scotland, wore hats, and McGhee also had a handkerchief tied around his neck. To the crowd's delight, three Canadians led by Gerard Cote of Quebec, a four-time Boston Marathon winner, fronted the field before they all climbed the steep hill to the stadium gate and disappeared out onto Vancouver's searing streets. They would not return for well over two hours as they followed the roughly circular route that would take them as far east as Burnaby Lake then all the way west to Little Mountain and Queen Elizabeth Park before they worked their way back to the stadium. However, the punishing conditions these 16 men would suffer over those 26 miles of pavement would exhaust most of them to depths they had never known before. For many it would prove to be the toughest run of their lives.

✺

After the marathon runners departed, the spectators in Empire Stadium turned their attention back to the oval below them where the finals of the pole vault, hammer throw, and the women's broad jump would take place. It was in the midst of these events that Prince Philip arrived. His day had begun at the Vancouver General Hospital where he opened and then toured the new Health Centre for Children, now known as the Children's Hospital, and from there he had gone up to the Capilano Golf Club in West Vancouver's British Properties for a lunch reception. When his convertible entered the stadium in early afternoon, he climbed out and mingled with the athletes down on the infield, among them Canadian pole vaulter Bob Adams, who for reasons known only to himself, was carrying a black velvet Mexican sombrero. Philip turned the gem-encrusted hat over in his hands admiring it, while thousands watched curiously to see if he might place it on his head, but decorum prevailed—he did not. He and his entourage then proceeded to the royal box, which had been constructed about 15 rows up in the west-side covered stands so that it overlooked the finish line. The box was already crammed with enough dignitaries, officials and celebrities to round out a solid parade. Prominent among them sat Premier Bennett, Lord Alexander, Mayor Hume and BEG president Major Jack Davies, all of them eagerly awaiting the Prince's arrival.

The men's 440yd final was the last race run before the Mile on that hot afternoon. Terry Tobacco of Cumberland on Vancouver Island who had made such an impression on the crowd two days earlier was lined up in lane two; Kevan Gosper of Australia stood in lane four. They were the two to watch. At the gun, both men burst from the blocks with strong starts. Heading into the first corner, Tobacco kept his eye trained on Gosper who was staggered ahead of him two lanes to his right. New Zealander Don Jowett, gold medalist in the 220yds two days earlier, ran in lane three between them. Tobacco seemed perfectly positioned, able to watch his rival and match his speed, while Gosper, up ahead, would be unaware of Tobacco's progress. Through the turn and entering the back straight, Tobacco looked strong, striding along smoothly, and both he and Jowett ate into the stagger on Gosper up ahead. Already Empire Stadium's 35,000 spectators were shrieking for the young Canadian, Tobacco's own family among them, having taken the ferry to the mainland to be here for this. And back in the Three Sisters Café in Port Alberni, everyone was yelling at the black-and-white Sylvania television set, urging him on.

But now Tobacco was breathing hard and pumping his arms, the pace feeling slightly faster than he was used to. Although the pain from a pair of blisters on his left foot—one later revealed to be the size of a fifty-cent piece—bit with every step, the sight of Jowett and Gosper running up ahead forced him on with a grim sense of purpose. At the 220yd mark—halfway home—the tenor of the race changed sharply, courtesy of Gosper. While most quarter-milers save any kick remaining for the final straight, Gosper settled on a different strategy, hoping the element of surprise might work in his favour. Fearing both Jowett's faster natural speed and the unknown potential of the "wonder boy" Tobacco, he decided to kill off both threats with an early burst. He recalled telling himself, "Go, go hard with your arms and the legs will follow!" and entering the turn, he poured on the pace, catching the others off guard and opening up a wide gap. Surprised, Tobacco and Jowett darted after him, desperate to match his speed, but it was already too late.

Australia's Kevan Gosper (right) happily strides home as the 440yd winner ahead of New Zealand's Don Jowett (second from right) and Canada's Terry Tobacco (second from left). Photo courtesy of Vonna McDonald.

"I felt the power and the rhythm of my body interacting perfectly," Gosper wrote in his book *An Olympic Life*. "As I shot into the home straight, I thought: 'Easy, you've got it. Don't do anything stupid.' As I closed in on the tape, I could feel the thrill and elation rising in my whole body." A wide smile covered his face as he crossed the line in 47.2sec, just a tenth off the BECG record he had set in the heats.

At the end of that race Terry Tobacco looked human for the first time that summer. Although Jowett had passed him in the final 50yds to add silver to his earlier gold, Tobacco still held on for bronze in 47.8sec, but he looked noticeably disappointed with the outcome. It had, however, been a remarkable run for this young man as nobody had expected him to advance past the Canadian trials just a month earlier. And even if his BECG story had ended right there, it still would have been a good one. Yet as it turned out, Cumberland's "Kid Comet" had saved an exclamation point for the 4x440yd relay at the very end of this remarkable day.

and lay there. I swore I'd give it up. I said I'd never do it again." But he got up. Around the 18-mile mark as he passed Langara Golf Course on 49th Avenue, the crowd lining the road began cheering as a runner approached him from behind. Lawrence, the Australian, had somehow rallied. "Lawrence... passed me smoothly and confidently, and the gap opened astonishingly quickly," recalled McGhee. "I couldn't do a thing about it. This was the beginning of my personal crisis. Certainly I felt bad, but the trouble was more psychological than physical. I simply could not visualize myself completing the eight miles ahead."

However, McGhee came upon Lawrence again near Queen Elizabeth Park. The Australian was sitting on the curb, finished. "Keep going, Jock!" Lawrence shouted as McGhee trotted by. The encouragement helped him temporarily, but soon thoughts about dropping out returned. When he hit the 20-mile mark on Main Street, even the sight of the North Shore Mountains towering over downtown Vancouver provided no lift. But that was when he saw Scottish team manager Willie Carmichael at the roadside hollering support. "I was hoping desperately that Willie would be merciful, take the decision for me and pull me out," he recollected. "His response was simply to scowl and gruffly urge me on. I swerved, half-twisted to glare back at him and found myself running into a high, jaggy hedge. The prickles and my resentment of Willie stung me into a short-lived burst of speed."

Trailing behind McGhee but steadily gaining ground were the determined South Africans Jackie Meklar and Jan Barnard. Meklar worked as an apprentice in the printing industry and did his training by running to and from work, clocking nearly 200 miles a week. Even with that kind of remarkable mileage, Vancouver's marathon course was testing him to his outer limits. Between the 15- and 22- mile marks he didn't see anyone. "I felt extremely dejected as I knew I wasn't running well," he told Rob Hadgraft years later. "I was given my drinks at most of the feeding stations, but no official offered any indication as to position or what was happening up ahead or behind, which was remarkable."

Two solid hours into their brutal march, Peters, as expected, remained far in the lead, Cox trailed in second with McGhee, Meklar and Barnard following at varied intervals behind them. Plucky Canadian Barry Lush was running in a respectable sixth place. Although the race was not over yet, these men were already survivors. The course and conditions had laid waste to nearly half the field by this time, sending many off in ambulances and medical cars. More drama awaited those who remained. And although the 35,000 people in Empire Stadium were receiving regular marathon updates over the PA, as the minutes ticked down to 2:30 and the start of the Mile, they became increasingly less absorbed in the marathon's outcome.

✸

Shifting his normal race day schedule forward by an hour, Bannister had awakened at 7:00 and had a light breakfast. After a brisk 45-minute walk, he had rested in his room before having an early lunch at 10:30. Landy had slept until 10:00, but soon after rising he noticed blood seeping from the cut on the sole of his left foot. Knowing he could not run with his foot in this condition, he returned to the university hospital and somehow managed to slip in unnoticed. Dr. Kenneth Young, director of student medical services, told him that he definitely should not run, but Landy remained determined and swore the doctor to absolute secrecy. Dr. Young inserted four stitches to close the gash and applied a piece of adhesive tape for added protection. Around 11:30 Landy had a pre-race steak at the Village cafeteria and departed for Empire Stadium by bus.

Bannister travelled to the stadium by car with English teammates Ian Boyd and David Law who were also running in the Mile. The trio arrived early, parked discreetly in the shade of some trees and waited there nervously until an hour before the race's 2:30 p.m. start time. When they joined several of the other finalists in one of the changing rooms, few words were spoken. Still coughing occasionally, Bannister carefully tightened his leather racing spikes, the same pair he had worn for his historic four minute mile at Oxford earlier that spring. Landy purposely came in later, and as he slipped his feet into the same spikes he had worn for his world-record run in Finland, he took care to conceal the bandage on the bottom of his left foot. But the world's most famous milers were not the only ones in that field dealing with maladies: Victor Milligan was still troubled by his touchy Achilles tendon, while Richie Ferguson quietly suffered with his gastric ulcer.

Bannister appeared on the infield for warm-up 40 minutes prior to race time, and as he jogged several comfortable laps with Boyd and Law, the crowd cheered wherever they passed. Landy emerged 20 minutes later to mass applause. He put himself through a warm-up, light by his standards but enough to erase any doubt in his mind that his stitched foot would be fine to run on. Boyd, who had been jogging with his teammate Bannister, joined Landy for several runs and wished him luck. Bill Baillie offered Landy his front-running services to aid the Anzac cause, but Landy politely declined. He remained determined to set a scorching pace himself in the hope of burning off Bannister's rocket-like finishing burst. "I thought—that's the way I run," Landy told the *Melbourne Age* in 2004. "I'll take him on and try to run him into the ground."

After weeks of build-up, the race tactics of the two men had become common knowledge. Landy would lead from the front, while Bannister would conserve and try to sprint from behind. Yet lost in all the pre-race talk of what Bannister and Landy might or might not do was the fact that six other men, all of them among the best milers in the world, were also in this race with plans of their own. David Law knew he had little chance of staying with the leaders, so he intended to support his teammate Bannister. Boyd felt unusually stiff and tired after running the 880yd heats and final as well as the Mile semi-final two days earlier, but he hoped to hang in there and give a good account of himself. Baillie, too, was realistic about his chances. "I'd only just qualified," he recalled in a 2007 interview. "I was hoping to do around 4:10. I wanted to do as well as I could but knew I couldn't hang onto 61sec laps all the way or be able to run close to four minutes like John or Roger."

Baillie's New Zealand teammate Murray Halberg felt wracked with anxiety and later remembered nothing prior to toeing the start line. "That probably is partly due to the fact I was not in control of my abilities, my emotions," he recollected in a 2007 interview. "Please, I'm not using this as an excuse. This is just how I was, see?"

Victor Milligan, a more seasoned runner, remembered that he and Halberg had felt—as many did—that the bronze medal was up for grabs between them. "Halberg and I had decided that one of us was going to be third because we reckoned we couldn't beat Bannister or Landy," he recalled in a 2007 interview. "I ran to beat Halberg and he ran to beat me, I think."

The one man most people tended to forget was Richie Ferguson, which seems odd now as he was the lone Canadian running in front of a Canadian crowd. Many predicted he would finish well back in last place but that the public should feel satisfied one of their own had even made it into the final. Ferguson, though, was not just happy to be there. He knew Landy would take off quickly so he intended to stay as close to Bannister as possible. Remarkably, for an unranked Canadian in a strong international field, he also believed he could stay in that position. "I felt after the mile heats I could beat Halberg," Ferguson told a *News-Herald* reporter the day after the race. "So I thought that if he was going to run third then so was I—even if it was a photo finish."

✪

At 2:00 p.m. Pacific Standard Time, tens of millions around the world began tuning in televisions and radios to BECG coverage from Vancouver. The race, the showdown, the Mile, was almost here. An estimated North American television audience of 70 million watched on NBC and CBC. Worldwide radio coverage in at least three languages included over 20 million across the US and millions more in Europe, who listened in the hours approaching midnight. Scores of Australians and New Zealanders set their alarms to ensure they didn't oversleep and miss the race, which was broadcast live at 7:30 Sunday morning.

The NBC broadcast featured a panel of commentators, including the world's third-ranked miler, Wes Santee, who watched on a studio monitor at New York City's RCA Exhibition Center. The network had abandoned a curious scheme to broadcast the Mile on split-screen—Bannister and Landy on one side and Santee on the other, running against the clock in Virginia. The CBC's live "BEG Actuality" television broadcast with commentary by Steve Douglas didn't actually hit the screen until 3pm—30 minutes after the race's scheduled start time, but this was as 'live' as live television got in 1954. (One of the few commercials CBC aired during the Mile was for the Sylvania "Superflash bulb," which even Landy with his flashbulb-gashed foot would have found ironic if he had known.) The CBC had used three cameras, an unheard of number for 1954, to cover Games week, but for the Mile cameraman Ken Bray was getting ready to film on a brand new Marconi Mark II broadcast camera using a single shot for the entire race, a remarkable feat of camerawork for the time.

Chris Chataway was one of the many crowding Empire Stadium's broadcast booth that afternoon, having been invited there by Vancouver radio station CKWX because of his unique perspective on the Mile. No one knew the strengths and weaknesses of the competitors as he did, having run against both Bannister and Landy in their historic races earlier that spring, but because of the draconian amateur rules of the day, technically Chataway was not allowed to broadcast without permission from English track officialdom. However, "when the commentator without prior notice announced just before the gun that I was going to give race commentary," Chataway recalled in a 2007 interview, "I thought to hell with it and just did it. My sin was compounded by accepting a case of champagne sent round to our room afterwards by the radio station. Surprisingly I never heard from the authorities."

Down on the infield an army of green-uniformed volunteers and blue-blazered officials tended to last-minute details. Future BC Lieutenant-Governor Garde Gardom buzzed around the field coordinating details with other volunteers and officials by using a brand new device known as a walkie-talkie. Other officials sported another innovation: the loud hailer megaphone. Recorders checked over their equipment in order to be prepared for timers to sprint over with official timing slips, from which they would get the numbers to pass to nearby BC Telephone staff manning the "Round-Robin" teletype machine that would distribute the information first throughout the Games' network of venues and then around the world. The 179 loops of wire for telephones, switchboards, telegraph, radio and television would provide the fastest coverage for any sporting event ever held to that point.

At the same time a crew of Omega technicians and official timers completed their final checks on the 25 carefully calibrated stopwatches, each valued at $500, that would be used to time the Mile. At the finish line the timers climbed to their places on a sloped ladder rising from the ground to 15 feet, four holding watches to time the first-place finisher, three the second-place, three the third and one each the remaining five places, while three timers stood at the 1500m mark in case a world record was run there. A fully electronic timing system was also set up, including an early "phototimer" used for photo finishes, although its results were considered unofficial and used only for research and comparison.

A rumble slowly built in the bleachers as the runners made their final preparations at the start/finish line while they awaited official instructions. Bannister and Landy shook hands just prior to stepping onto the track. The other runners exchanged final words, many shaking hands as they pulled off track suit tops. Landy moved apart, pacing anxiously.

The official race starter, the veteran Vancouver Police sergeant Cookie Ryan, blew his whistle, and the competitors lined up three yards behind the start line. The crowd hushed. Bannister checked his spikes, testing their grip in the cinders. He and Milligan shook hands before moving to their lanes. Baillie stepped into place last, stalking behind the others, eyeing the line of competitors.

Sergeant Ryan pointed his starting gun skyward. "On your marks."

The eight men walked to the start line in unison. Bannister pushed back his hair and stole a final glance at Landy. Several seconds later Landy looked over in Bannister's direction. Three competitors stood between them at that moment, but clearly both knew that would not be the case for long. John Landy had drawn lane one on the inside, and now he stood waiting for the starting gun in evergreen shorts with competitor number 300 pinned to his white singlet. His legs were so darkly tanned the white track spikes on his feet stood out in stark contrast. To his right, the lone Canadian, Richie Ferguson wearing number 154, stood hands on hips, looking calm and purposeful. "I was completely relaxed," Ferguson recalled. "Maybe too much so." Next to him was Murray Halberg in New Zealand all black, number 548. Then came Northern Ireland's Victor Milligan, white top and red shorts, number 632. The three English runners in white shorts and singlets followed in a row: Roger Bannister, number 329 and the oldest man in the field at age 25; number 331 Ian Boyd; and number 346 David Law. On the farthest outside was number 544 Bill Baillie, at 19 the youngest, also in New Zealand all black.

"Get set."

The eight starters in the Miracle Mile, left to right: Bill Baillie, David Law, Ian Boyd, Roger Bannister, Victor Milligan, Murray Halberg, Rich Ferguson and John Landy.

Each man leaned forward expectantly in standing starts, except the New Zealanders, who both crouched in sprinter's stances. Thanks to weeks of bottled anticipation, the moment stretched on and on until the jarring *crack* of the gun blew the lid off and sent them away. Each man scrambled off the line, spikes sending up dusty puffs as they dashed for position. On the outside Baillie launched to a fantastic start and had sprinted 2yds into the lead by the first turn. "I thought, Well, I'll see if I can help John as far as I could go," Baillie recalled. "Instead of just staying at the back and running at my own pace, I wanted to be up with them and be part of the atmosphere and the feeling. As a result, I went off fast."

Halberg followed close behind him. Landy and Law, running shoulder-to-shoulder, made contact with one another and the Australian accidentally stepped on the back of the Englishman's heel. Law shot a sharp glance at Landy, took an awkward stride, and suddenly his left track shoe flew off his foot toward the outer lanes of the track.

Perhaps spurred on by losing his shoe and finding himself running with one bare foot, Law caught up to Halberg and Baillie before the end of the back straight and took the lead into the turn. Landy went with him while Bannister trailed a yard back. Ferguson, Boyd and Milligan brought up the rear. Landy's Australian teammate Don Macmillan, kneeling at the 220yd mark, yelled out his split times: "28.9!" and "Three yards behind!" *Too slow*, thought Landy. He shifted gears and stepped up his pace.

"I could see him coming," Ellery Littleton told the *Vancouver Courier* for a story published in 2004. He had been sitting in the front row at the stadium's north end that day. "There was a look in [Landy's] eyes that said, 'Do I take the lead or not?' It was just a momentary look and then away he went. I could not hear him touch the track. He had such a light pace."

Landy accelerated smoothly past the New Zealanders and Law on the outside and moved into the lead on the turn. This is what the crowd expected to see: the world record holder in front. To millions watching at home, CBC's Steve Douglas made the call: "And Landy has made a move early that has the crowd gasping just a little bit and wondering what kind of pace he is going to try and set." Down the

Broadcasting to listeners on CKWX, Chataway had sounded concerned for his friend. They had gone over Bannister's race plan together again and again in training. Both knew Landy would run from the front, but neither had expected him to push so hard. Now as his friend began to fight back, Chataway's evident relief poured forth into the microphone in his rich Chelsea accent:

> But now Bannister is closing. Bannister is closing on Landy with two-and-a-half laps of this race gone. Um, there can only be 5... 5... 6yds between them. Landy looks to me as if he's tiring just a little, perhaps a shade. Roger Bannister is striding magnificently there.

Fifteen yards behind, Ferguson watched as Bannister began reeling Landy in, and even as he fought to stay in third place—"really a big surprise," said Chataway on-air—he felt a sense of awe at the way Bannister was digging himself out of a hole that would have buried any other runner on the planet. "Roger [was] like a runner with a spring inside, just waiting to uncoil," Ferguson told the *Province* 20 years later. "He was uncoiling but not yet all the way."

As the roar of the crowd grew, perhaps sensing Bannister's move, Landy's aura of invincibility showed its first cracks. He shot a quick glance over his inside shoulder as he entered the back straight on the third lap and then another on the corner entering the home straight. Neither time could he see his rival, but by the shrieking of the crowd, he knew Bannister must be very close. "That really sent a shiver down my spine," he said later.

As the final lap bell sounded, Landy blazed through the line in 2min 58.4sec with Bannister only 2yds behind, but Bannister was now "so absorbed by the man-to-man struggle" that he missed the PA announcer's lap time announcement. Time no longer held any meaning for him. All that existed at that moment was the tanned Australian running effortlessly up ahead and the problem of how to get in front of him. Ferguson remained 15yds behind in third, so far back the CBC cameras could only fit him into wide panning shots, and Milligan, who had moved past Halberg into fourth, was nowhere to be seen in the picture. With only a lap to go and just a couple of strides separating the two greatest milers in history, it appeared anyone's race, but Chataway, the one man who had raced both of them in recent months, made a bold prediction over the airwaves:

> With one lap to go, this must be the greatest mile race that any of us have seen. John Landy, still in first place, striding easily, but I feel it's Roger Bannister's race. I feel *certain* it's Roger Bannister's race. Here he is in second place, striding very easily and I think soon we shall see the famous Bannister spurt.

By now the crowd was on its feet, screaming itself hoarse. They weren't just roaring for Bannister and Landy, but also for Ferguson, the Canadian in third running the race of his life. Everything else in the stadium stopped. Concession staff hurdled over their deserted counters and ran to the stadium entrances to watch the final lap. The Canadian men's 4x110yd relay team, preparing outside the stadium, halted their warm-ups and sprinted inside. On the infield, competitors in the hammer throw, pole vault and broad jump stopped everything and turned to watch. New Zealand's Yvette Williams, on her way to winning two more gold medals that afternoon, stood at the broad jump pit, transfixed, hands covering her mouth as she held her breath.

The crowd noise, a thunderous, rolling crescendo, was deafening. Chataway, virtually yelling over the noise into the microphone, exclaimed at one point: "The crowd are going *absolutely mad* here!" To some degree, each of the seven remaining milers had experienced large, loud crowds before, but this was unlike anything any of them had ever heard. The noise felt disorienting, confining, almost crushing. Young Halberg, now struggling in fifth place, recalled that:

> The sensation was such of a noise, a crowd, the occasion, all combining to give the feeling of not being able to control the situation. It was like being tumbled and in danger of drowning in the heavy surf. The harder I tried to fight it, the worse it got.

Landy could no longer hear himself breathing, let alone hear Bannister's footsteps just behind him. Coming into the first corner of the final lap, his shadow stretched out in front of him. A quick inside turn of his head revealed Bannister's shadow a little farther back, but as he rounded the corner into the back straight, the shadows fell out of his line of view and he no longer knew where Bannister was. He decided it was now or never and quickened his stride, hoping to add to his leading cushion and lose Bannister for good. Bannister, feeling dangerously depleted, held on as Landy's lead grew again by a yard or two. But Bannister remained determined. "I fixed myself to Landy like a shadow," he recalled.

At the end of the backstretch, Landy could feel Bannister on his heels and knew he was in trouble. Bannister was too close and must be kicking soon. In the stands the wild, thrashing banks of humanity were urging them both on. Entering the turn, Landy took another quick peek over his inside shoulder: "I was wondering: *When is it going to come?*"

Bannister, too, was feeling the strain. "I felt there was a dangerous moment on the backstretch when John made his move," he remembered. "I knew I had to keep close without using my reserve energy." So he clung to Landy, steeling himself for the coming moment of truth when "my mind would galvanize my body to the greatest effort it had ever known. I knew I was tired. There might be no response, but it was my only chance."

Around the turn at the 1500m mark, Landy still led, running 3min 41.9sec, only 0.1sec slower than his world record, but he was barely hanging on now, and his once-fluid stride had begun to tie up and slow marginally. Bannister, on the other hand, amid the frenzied howling from the stands was somehow keeping his focus, and he finally made the decision to sprint with all that remained in him. Ross McWhirter, writing in *Athletics World* magazine described Bannister's move as being "like a high horsepower car building up the revs—and in he slammed the clutch ..." Never had Bannister left his finishing kick so late in any race. "I chose the time when I thought he would least expect me, which was on the end of the last curve," he explained. "By overtaking him there, I was actually running extra distance, but I thought that it would take him by surprise."

Those spectators who were crowded just inches off the track received faces full of cinders flung off Bannister's spikes as he accelerated. The stands seemed to shake as the overpowering thunderclap of excitement drowned out everything else. And then came the defining moment of the race, the months of build-up, the whole 1954 Games, perhaps even that era in all of sport anywhere. Bannister, gaining with each hurtling stride, surged past Landy on the outside. And at the same instant Landy looked back again over his inside shoulder. He saw no sign of Bannister. "It was a look of hope," Landy said later, hope that his back straight burst of speed had been enough. He turned back just as a blurring white figure streaked by on his right.

Landy later claimed he looked back in an attempt to see the third-place runner, though in truth, he knew "it was just a matter of time" before Bannister passed him, and the shock on his face said it all. It was akin "to a blow in the stomach." Landy's head turn also fractionally delayed his reaction to Bannister's sprint. "It was my tremendous luck that these two happenings—his turning around and my final spurt—came almost simultaneously," Bannister admitted in *The Four Minute Mile*. Ferguson, clinging to third place halfway around the turn and about 40yds behind, saw it all. "The sun was coming from the rear across the inlet, and I'm sure John was looking for Roger's shadow," he recalled. "But at that precise moment, Roger was at his shoulder, and the two shadows were one." Bannister was 90yds from the finish when he charged past Landy, the Englishman's mouth agape, gasping for air, hair flapping in the wind. Landy, who was run out, had no response.

Sun photographer Charlie Warner, sitting on the grass on that final corner, was ready with his trusty Speed Graphic. The length of time it took to reload film in that camera meant he could get only one shot per lap. Earlier in the race he had noticed Landy glance behind and thought that it might make an interesting photo. "I was keeping my fingers crossed that he would look back again," recalled Warner. "On the fourth lap, by God, he did and that's when I grabbed the shot. At the time I was pretty sure I'd gotten it all right." He wouldn't know for sure until he got back to the darkroom.

The crowd, having wrung every last decibel out of their lungs over the past 60sec, now exploded in one massive detonation. The broadcast footage that has survived vibrates momentarily at this point; amateur footage taken by excited spectators in the stands shakes crazily. In both, spectators can be seen wildly shouting and punching the air with triumphant fists. In living rooms and bars across the continent, millions watching on television jumped on sofas, pushed their stools back and yelled at the screen. Most announcers became just as caught up in the drama and lost all semblance of partiality. You could almost envision the CBC's Douglas on his feet cheering wildly as he described the race's climactic moment: "Bannister is kicking very definitely! He's passing Landy! Landy looked the wrong way!" A few feet away in the press box, Chataway yelled above the din into his microphone, the genuine exhilaration over his friend's victory shining through:

Opposite: One of the most famous sports photos of the 1950s, shot by *Vancouver Sun* photographer Charlie Warner. Bannister sprints by Landy on the final corner as Landy looks back over his other shoulder. Photo courtesy of Charlie Warner.

Roger Bannister has come into the lead! Roger Bannister is striding away!
The most magnificent win! Roger Bannister has five yards on John Landy!
Six yards! Seven yards! The race is all over!

Bannister crashed through the two-ply baby wool finish-line string, his face turned
up to the sky, exhaustion written on every strained line. Landy followed 5yds behind,
characteristically looking as fresh as when he started four laps earlier. It marked his first
mile defeat in two years.

Perhaps the only portion of Empire Stadium not cheering madly was the small
Australian contingent that watched from the athletes' section in the southwest bleachers.
"There were tears up in the stands among us when he didn't win," remembered team-
mate Geoff Warren. The reaction was much the same Down Under and was put best by
Landy's friend Robbie Morgan-Morris: "When Landy lost in Vancouver, the whole of
Australia cried." John Vernon, one of the few who knew of Landy's cut foot, felt utter
"disappointment. But knowing the circumstance there was a feeling of great pride in the
way John had performed."

Immediately after crossing the line, an exhausted Bannister collapsed into the
arms of Leslie Truelove, knocking the English team manager's glasses askew. With the
help of a policeman, Truelove propped Bannister up, then hefted him into his arms and
carried him away from the gathering swarm of officials, timers, other athletes, photographers and reporters, who stormed the track so quickly that every finisher after Landy
was impeded to some degree, running headlong into a milling throng of several hundred
as they tried to reach the finish line. "It was chaotic," confirmed Doug Clement. "There
was no real security, there was no real control over the crowd. People were running into
the infield." As the mob on the track expanded, Landy walked away alone, head down.
Jack Harrison, in his full Vancouver City Police uniform, went to Landy and put his
arm around him. Landy asked him, "Did we break four minutes?" Harrison nodded and
Landy breathed a sigh of relief and looked pleased. When his teammate Kevan Gosper
ran up, the first thing Landy said was, "I did my best."

Another delirious ovation erupted once the mostly Canadian crowd realized the
man in third place was one of their own. Ferguson struggled down the straight 35yds behind Landy. "The last 75 yards… were the longest of my life," Ferguson told the *Province*
20 years later. "Maybe it was anti-climactic, with the race won well up ahead of me. And
I think I felt a twinge of disappointment for I'd gotten to like Landy and wanted him to
win." But Ferguson had held off the hard-charging Milligan by 5yds. The Irishman finished stronger than anyone outside of Bannister. "I thought I ran a great last lap, a well-
judged race," he recalled in a 2007 interview. "But Ferguson never died! He just hung
on. I didn't know him from Adam, nor did Halberg, so Ferguson was the real upset in the
mix. And I just didn't catch him."

Following Milligan in rapid succession were Halberg, hampered by nerves but just
inches ahead of Boyd, whose legs were aching. Baillie came down the straight in seventh
and faced a wall of humanity blocking his path. In a 2007 interview he recalled, "I was
pushing my way through people to get over the line and almost had to stop because of the
amount of people physically on the track."

Bannister crosses the finish line five yards ahead of Landy to win the Miracle Mile. Photo from author's collection.

Ferguson caught up to Landy soon after finishing. "He looked disgusted with himself—not just disappointed," he remembered. "He grabbed my hand and mumbled congratulations as we jogged along." Bannister recovered after a few moments, but as congratulatory hands stretched out to him, he pushed them all away and jogged after the one man he respected more than any other. Approaching him from behind, he put his arm around Landy's shoulders. "Bad luck, John," he said. "Congratulations." As they shook hands and embraced, Landy said, "You were colossal, Roger. I feel quite good up here," he said, patting his chest, "but I went in the legs." They held one another up, arm in arm, still breathing hard, as cameramen snapped away. Bannister had done his best to soften the defeat, which Landy—crushed—appreciated. "He was very gracious about it, very nice—considerate," remembered Landy. "We had a good relationship—still do—and, you know, it was one of those things. Somebody had to win. It wasn't me." As the mob closed in around them, Bannister gestured to Landy. "Come on, let's jog," and the pair went off together to cool down. As Ferguson jogged along the backstretch, the crowd gave him an ovation reserved for the truly beloved. "I guess it was my turn, and for me that was a very emotional moment," he reminisced. "I knew I'd never experience its like again."

With the victor decided, one question remained: how fast had they run? The stadium PA announcer brought the still-buzzing crowd to near silence as he called for attention.

Following pages: Bill Baillie (left) congratulates Bannister and Landy after the mile as they stand arm-in-arm.

"The winner of event number six, the One Mile, competitor number 329, Roger Gilbert Bannister of England, in a time of *three* minutes and..." Like Norris McWhirter's famous cut-off announcement three months earlier at Oxford's Iffley Road, no one heard the rest as 35,000 sets of lungs bellowed their approval: the third four-minute mile in history was confirmed. Bannister's official time, the second fastest behind Landy's world record, was listed as 3min 58.8sec. More importantly, his Vancouver victory validated his Oxford four-minute mile. Never would he be remembered as just a "test-tube miler" who'd concocted one "artificial" paced record.

When the jubilation began to subside, the announcer continued: "The time of second-place finisher, competitor number 300, John Michael Landy of Australia, was *three*..." Again the crowd exploded and drowned out the rest. Purists could quibble about fractions of seconds, but for the majority in that stadium all that mattered as they screamed and clapped, jumped for joy and waved their fedoras was the fact they had just witnessed history—the first time *ever* two men had run one mile in less than four minutes in the same race. The stopwatches recorded Landy's official time as 3min 59.6sec.

And then, unbelievably, came the announcement of Ferguson's third-place time of 4min 4.6sec, a Canadian national record, which brought the loudest response of all. No one had predicted he would finish as high as he did. *No one.* Many had pegged him to finish last. For the record, he ran 9sec faster than his previous mile best before the Games, and 15sec faster than his third-place finish at the Canadian BECG trials just a month earlier. His run must stand as one of the great Canadian track and field performances of all time.

The CBC had first dibs on interviewing the milers down on the infield. Asked if he had been confident he could beat Landy, in a classy move Bannister, coughing repeatedly from his lingering cold, heaped praise on his beaten opponent. "Well, it's a strange mixture," he said. "You have confidence in your own ability and respect for your opponent. I have tremendous respect for John Landy. I knew that if I did beat him, it would take everything I'd got. I think he felt the same way."

When asked about his front-running strategy, Landy said, "I had no alternative. I tried to run a lone wolf race. If I couldn't shake Roger off, I had to lose, and when I looked down on the final back straight and I saw him with me, well, I knew it was curtains." Both men had high opinions of the Canadian. "Ferguson should have a great future," said Bannister, and Landy agreed. Maybe the most surprised were Milligan and Halberg, the men Ferguson edged out. "Halberg and I were speechless," Milligan recalled, laughing. "We just looked at one another and said, 'Who the hell is Ferguson?'" At the time Ferguson said he was the one who felt "speechless," but looking back later, he maintained a surprisingly high standard for himself. "I think I should have extended myself more," he said. "I may not have been better than third, but I may have made it closer." However, no Canadian in the stands that day was complaining about his performance.

�֍

As the capacity crowd in Empire Stadium came down from their euphoric four-minute roller coaster, most would have been content to simply let the remaining track events drift peacefully by. Nothing could possibly top the Miracle Mile. But less than 30min later, another event would sear itself into the memories of those in attendance even more vividly than Bannister and Landy's epic struggle. In the excitement almost everyone had forgotten about the poor marathoners out on Vancouver's baking streets. The buzz generated by the Mile had barely subsided when Jim Peters appeared at the stadium gates.

The marathon route's final five miles leading to Empire Stadium had been torture for Peters. While the mile-long downhill slope on Main Street might normally have brought him relief, on this day that relief was offset by the crushing heat. And when he turned off Main onto Terminal and reached the second-to-last feeding station, he was offered nothing more than another dry sponge. However, his fear of Cox in hot pursuit behind him fended off any thought of wilting in the sun. He could not let up now. So on he plodded, suffering with every step.

After 22 miles on the road, the short rise up the Terminal viaduct to Clark was a killer. But he ran down Clark, turned east onto Powell, refusing to slow past the industrial buildings, while the rumble of trains in the nearby railyard echoed in his ears. Another significant climb on Dundas did more damage, but there was a nice downhill stretch on McGill going past the horse paddocks of the Hastings Racecourse. Peters felt wretched, but at least Empire Stadium's twin roofs beckoned just ahead. He was almost home. But as he pushed up the hill to the stadium, visions of Cox chasing close behind continued to eat at him.

What Peters did not know was that he was so far ahead that he could have comfortably walked the rest of the way. Cox, who had been struggling mightily for some time, had actually dropped out near the 25-mile mark on the uphill climb on Dundas. Totally exhausted by the heat and the breakneck pace, he had run into a telephone pole and fallen into a ditch unconscious. "I was really lucky I hit that telegraph pole because I would have carried on and probably killed meself," he said later. "I would have carried on whether it killed me or not. We were so close I could see the stadium from where I collapsed." An alert Mountie found him and radioed for help, and while ambulance staff attended to him, he regained consciousness. His first question was: "How did Bannister get on?" Told that Bannister had won, Cox replied, "God bless him." Then his racing instincts returned to the task at hand. "I can't let England down," he said. "I've got to finish. Get the shoes off me. My feet are burning." Apparently he intended to finish barefoot. An ambulance wisely took him away, his day done a mile short of his goal.

Joe McGhee, now in second place some three miles and over 15min behind Peters, was fairing little better physically. Worse yet, he now found himself locked in a cat-and-mouse duel with the fast-closing South Africans Meklar and Barnard.

As Peters approached the stadium, he became vaguely aware of something wrong. "As I went up the hill I wobbled a little," he wrote in *In the Long Run*. But this was more than a "wobble" as at least one witness saw him collide with a lamppost. Clearly he was in some distress.

After watching the Mile, Geoff Warren had gone to stand on the hill outside the stadium to encourage Peters on his way in, but he found the street eerily quiet. A lone volunteer waited at the northeast gate to indicate the way in. Then Warren saw Peters. "As he came towards me," he recalled in a 2013 interview, "he was already in a bother, still running, glassy-eyed, and didn't acknowledge my call: 'Come on Jim! Come on,

Just minutes after the Mile, Jim Peters enters Empire Stadium's gates and begins the descent down the ramp to the track.

you're nearly there!' He didn't seem to see me even though he passed within only a few metres, veering from side to side." Peters' physical appearance gave Warren a chill. "He looked like a concentration camp victim. His bones were sticking out and his eyes and skull looked thin. It was a horror sight."

Peters had reached the stadium in 2hr 23min—near but not on the world record pace as some sources incorrectly reported. Based on his training, he believed himself capable of a time nearly 8min faster—in the 2hr 15min range—under favourable conditions. Clearly, conditions were not favourable that day. As the gate swung open to admit him, the PA announcer intoned, "Jim Peters, about to enter the stadium. He's not in good shape." Several witnesses recall that the announcement sounded almost as if he had been cut off, but it may only have been that the announcer was in as much shock as everyone else.

Peters wobbled a little at the top of the steep ramp down to the track, and he remembered feeling an unnerving "giddiness," something he typically encountered when looking down from any height. The thought crossed his mind that he should wave to the crowd as he usually did entering a stadium at the end of a race, but he decided to take no chances and simply finish this murderous run off. He found his rhythm again and began awkwardly teetering toward the oval. And that's when everything seemed to stop, the entire stadium focussing on the pale little man dressed in all-white in sharp, shocking contrast to the black asphalt on which he stood. Probably owing to his peculiar head-bobbing, even more pronounced by his extreme fatigue, the crowd momentarily hesitated. Was he okay? Some mistakenly thought he might be clowning around. "I thought he was putting on a show," said Mario Caravetta. Then, realizing Peters was fighting exhaustion, the crowd let loose a strong roar of encouragement, and he continued ambling down the slope with the eyes of 35,000 people upon him.

And then Jim Peters fell. The crowd released a collective gasp and a sudden hush blanketed the stands. "That deathly silence... it was unreal, something I'd like to forget—but I'll never forget it," recalled Halberg.

"I just couldn't understand what had happened," Peters said later of his somersault near the foot of the ramp. "For a moment I was completely bewildered. Then I made up my mind I was going to finish." Shakily he picked himself up, and the crowd applauded his courage. He must have stumbled over something on the ramp, right?

But after a few more steps Peters collapsed again. From that point on, he slipped in and out of consciousness. "I do remember coming into the stadium and falling for the first time on the sharp incline," he recalled. "I thought of 1908 and Dorando Pietri and the very next race I was due to run [at the European championships in Berne]." Up in the royal box, Lord Alexander must have been squirming uncomfortably. It had been just the previous day that he had told Peters of witnessing Pietri's collapse at the 1908 Olympics.

Peters later recalled falling three times. In reality, it was closer to 12, although some claim it was as high as 20. Over the next 10min—but again, estimates vary greatly—he managed to stumble and crawl just 200yds of the track, when normally he would have pounded out *two miles* in the same amount of time. "Everybody was mesmerized," remembered North Vancouver sports historian Len Corben, then just a boy. "When you're in a situation like that, time kind of stands still, almost like in a car accident." Watching Peters in this state was truly horrible, but most couldn't take their eyes off him. Many commented they felt they were witnessing the final stages of a man running himself to death before their very eyes. And they were right. Peters' skin was a ghostly, glazed white with just the slightest hint of sickly yellow, which was magnified grotesquely by the glare of the bright, beating sun. No longer running, he shuffled drunkenly, legs rubbery, arms swinging limply, everything uncoordinated, and a blank, emotionless stare upon his face. "He looked as if he was in a trance," remembered Kevan Gosper. He tripped, twisted, fell on his back, picked himself up, then pitched face-first to the cinders, badly cutting his lip. When he picked himself up again, it was clear he had lost all bodily coordination as he turned over on both ankles with each step. At one point, though there was a water fountain beckoning like an oasis just a few feet off the track, he crawled on his hands and knees and seemed to be calling out for help like a man lost in the parching desert. "I thought I could see the tape, you know, sort of a mirage," he said in an interview with the *Vancouver Sun* days later. "I thought I'd made it, but the tape didn't seem to be coming any nearer."

At first the crowd had roared each time he rose and collectively groaned when he fell. Peters vaguely recalled this. "I could hear a noise, that's all. Sort of a cheer." But soon the entire stadium fell into shocked silence, amazed something like this could be happening in front of them. Everyone wanted to stop it, but no one seemed to have the wherewithal or authority to do so. And so it went on.

Gradually Peters worked his way to the oval's west side straight, then suddenly veered toward the stands, his dragging feet kicking up white puffs as he crossed lane lines. The crowd gasped as he collapsed once more. Peters said later he had seen the shade of the stadium roof and was seeking refuge there from the relentless sun. By now a massive crowd of volunteers, officials and other athletes were following his progress from the infield—trying to get close but not too close. The pole vault competition came to a standstill as the horde that was following Peters clambered over the runway and through the sawdust landing pit. Officials commandeered the pole vault bar and even the vaulters' poles to create a makeshift barrier to keep the crowd at bay. A police officer shoved a photographer off the track, sending him tumbling over a rope barrier into a heap on the grass. Another officer trailed behind Peters, with Boy Scouts following along behind him carrying a stretcher. With tears in his eyes, the 6ft 7in English shot putter John Savidge got down on hands and knees at the track's edge next to Peters and pounded the cinders with his fists. Some heard him yelling, "Get up, Jim, get up!" but Warren, now among the mass of people beside the track heard Savidge say, "Give up, Jim!" Either way Peters didn't hear him. As he recalled later, "I knew I'd taken more punishment than I ought to have done. But there was no question of surrender." Reactions of other witnesses ran the gamut. Some wept, others turned away unable to watch and a few were visibly sick, including one reporter who vomited at trackside. For Bannister, just minutes after achieving victory in the greatest race of his life, the sight of Peters in this condition was horrifying. "Stop it, for heaven's sake!" he called out. Ian Boyd, who had heard the warnings given to Peters that morning, could only shake his head at the sight before him now. Many of the other milers still down on the infield saw things unfold first-hand, too. "It was horrible, like something out of the Colosseum," remembered Landy. "And ironic that it should happen immediately after the Mile." Halberg recalled feeling "sick. It was truly sad." And Baillie remembered that "we were almost in tears. I remember just holding my breath. It was unbelievable."

Terry Tobacco was in a training room receiving a rubdown before his next event, the 4x440yd relay. "I could hear the crowd going 'Uhhh!... Ohh!... Uhhh!'" he recalled. "I went outside and the English were saying, 'Don't touch him! Don't touch him!' He was staggering and falling down and crawling and all the things you don't expect a human to endure... What the hell are we doing here? Are we trying to *kill* this guy for the sake of the flag?" Sitting up in the athletes' stand, Doug Hepburn turned to Lorne "Ace" Atkinson and said, "Boy, I'm glad I'm a weightlifter because it's over quick." And Chris Chataway, who had watched in horror from the broadcast booth, remembered that it was "like watching lions eat Christians in a Roman amphitheatre." Not far away in the royal box, Prince Philip turned his head away from the scene several times and exclaimed, "How awful!"

One of the most emotional at trackside was Peters' English teammate Dorothy (Odam) Tyler, high jump silver medalist, who had known him for years. "Stop it! Stop it!" she cried. "For God's sake, someone help him!" But those with the ability to assist were waved away by officials who feared their intervention would disqualify Peters. Several doctors in attendance, including Scottish team captain Ewan Douglas, pleaded with them to remove Peters from the race before he further endangered his life. The English team officials heard the recommended action but refused to allow it.

Ultimately, a most unlikely individual took matters into his own hands and ended this disaster before it became any worse. The English team's masseur, Mick Mayes, an elderly, silver-haired man wearing a gleaming white lab coat, was standing at the west side finish line next to Bill Parnell. "I said to him, 'Micky, somebody should end that,'" recollected Parnell. "He said, 'I'm going to.'" With those words, Mayes pushed through the crowd, his ankle-length lab coat billowing out as he moved, and stepped onto the track just beyond the finish line. It made for one of the most dramatic sports photos ever taken. Mayes stood there, arms outstretched, gently coaxing Peters in, a look of sincere compassion on his face that seemed to say, 'Come now, son, your work today is done.' Peters, seeing Mayes' inviting arms, picked up his awkward pace and collapsed into them. His horrendous battle was over.

Mayes carried him to the waiting stretcher, saying on the way, "Well done, Jim, you've done it." Savidge assisted and, while attempting to comfort Peters, gently kissed him on the forehead. Once placed on the canvas stretcher, Peters lay groaning, writhing and foaming at the mouth while English officials, first aid attendants and police huddled around him. The situation looked grave. "It was a hell of a scene, one of the most horrific in athletic history," Chris Brasher told the authors of *Fast Tracks* many years later. "They took his brain temperature right there and it was about 107 or 108 degrees. It is something that is still absolutely unbelievable in medical circles. He was on the verge of cooking his brain."

The crowd uneasily applauded the fallen runner's extreme courage, but one final cruel twist remained. As ambulance attendants carried Peters away, the stadium PA provided grim news: Peters had been disqualified for receiving assistance. "The finish line... is on the other side of the track," explained the announcer. Peters had actually been 200yds short of his goal. After everything that had transpired, it seemed like some kind of sick joke. The crowd, stirred out of another shocked silence, lustily booed.

For nearly six decades, debate has persisted over that finish line. Why was the finish line for the marathon the only event to be situated on the stadium's east side? Most people, even the well-informed such as Bill Parnell, were confused at the time. "I thought [the west side finish] was the finish line because all the finish judges were there!" he said in a 2007 interview. "*Why* they would take that marathon and finish it on the far side of the stadium when everything else was finishing [on the west side] was a mystery. I don't know whether anybody's ever explained it."

The next question is: Did Peters know the true marathon finish line was another 200yds around the track? The answer is most certainly yes as officials had shown all the competitors the start and finish lines prior to the race, and Peters acknowledged this in interviews at the time. In the last years of his life, he revealed his memory of the finish:

After collapsing a dozen times on the track, Peters (left) staggers towards the inviting arms of the English team's masseur, Mick Mayes (right).

"In my heart I knew that I had not touched the winning tape, and when [Mayes] got hold of me, I just lapsed into unconsciousness."

So perhaps the more pertinent question is: Did Mayes know where the true finish line was when he pulled Peters from the race? Two days after the race *The Globe and Mail* reported that after Peters had first collapsed, Leslie Truelove summoned Mayes from the locker room, and he ran to the correct marathon finish line on the track's east side and waited. Soon after, Truelove ordered Mayes to the west finish line. Peters himself contributed to the confusion on this point in his biography: "I honestly believe that when Mayes did it [pulled him out], he thought I had won the race." Parnell's eyewitness account, however, stands as the most conclusive proof that Mayes knew he was ending Peters' run early. The English masseur, who is the only person who really knew the truth on this point, died a few years after the 1954 Games.

Attendants carried Peters into a stadium dressing room where a group of six doctors and nurses tended to him on the stretcher and gave him oxygen. He regained consciousness for a moment. "Did I win?" he asked a nurse.

After failing to complete the 26-mile marathon by just two hundred yards, Peters lays unconscious on a stretcher before being rushed to the hospital.

"You did very well," she said smiling. He passed out again, apparently relieved.

As Peters was struggling to cross the finish line he would never reach, the four next closest marathon competitors—Scotland's Joe McGhee, South Africa's Jan Barnard and Jackie Meklar, and Canada's Barry Lush—were engaged in a wearied battle of their own on Vancouver's east side streets. They were almost three miles behind Peters.

McGhee found himself in dire straits as he ran down Terminal Avenue. Even worse, threatening footsteps behind him were growing louder with every stride. At the base of the Terminal viaduct, he tripped on the curb and nearly fell. Any disruption to a runner's rhythm after a distance of 22 miles can be disastrous, and the thought of lying down and giving up crossed his mind. To top off his crisis, he sneaked a look back and saw the South Africans Barnard and Meklar only 50yds behind and closing.

In subsequent retellings over the years the story of McGhee's mishap at the base of the Terminal viaduct grew legs so that it was said McGhee fell into a ditch and lay there a beaten man until "an old Scots lady revived [him] with the exhortation that the honour of Scotland was at stake." The truth is that McGhee simply found the inner will to rally. "At that very moment my own personal miracle occurred," he told *Scotland on Sunday* forty years later. "I suddenly realized I was going to finish those last three miles, and with that realization, my energies and my racing instincts came surging back."

The revitalized McGhee threw himself into the turn onto Clark and cranked up his pace. Having learned from spectators along the route that Cox had been taken away by ambulance, he knew he stood in second and was determined not to let that silver medal slip from his grasp. He was now hugging the edges of the crowded pavement in an attempt to lose Barnard and Meklar, but he barely avoided disaster when he collided with a group of spectators and nearly went down. The increased pace finished off Barnard, who dropped back after 23 miles. Though tiring himself, Meklar left his teammate behind with some encouragement, saying weakly, "Go on, keep going."

Over the next two miles, Meklar, the man who ran to work and back each day, put in a yeoman's effort, refusing to let McGhee escape from view. But the Scotsman expanded his lead on Powell and slammed the nail into Meklar's coffin on Dundas, the route's most punishing climb. "At the top of this hill," McGhee told *Scotland on Sunday*, "I knew the route turned left for a short distance [onto Nanaimo] before abruptly swinging right again [onto McGill]. Bursting from the crowd, I spurted flat out to reach the further corner before my pursuers rounded the first. Then I settled down into a more comfortable racing pace."

The South Africans never came any closer than that, but McGhee never risked a glance back for fear it might provide them with hope. On the hill outside the stadium, word reached him of Peters' collapse. "My first reaction was one of complete panic," he remembered. Then he looked back and saw no one. "I knew then I could not be beaten and I never felt better in any race."

Sixteen minutes after Peters entered, Scotland's Joe McGhee trots around Empire Stadium's track in the lead.

Sixteen minutes after Peters had stumbled down the stadium ramp, McGhee, in his navy Scottish singlet, white shorts, and a white bandana tied around his neck, trotted in. "Vividly I can remember seeing the smile on [Scottish team captain] Ewan Douglas's face," McGhee said. "It could have been disbelief. Then he did a dance which struck me as being extraordinary for such a huge fellow." He remembered his team captain dancing "dolphin-like" and springing "up and down waving his arms" to urge him on. The crowd hesitated, cautious after what it had witnessed with Peters just minutes earlier and wondering whether McGhee too might falter. When it was clear he was trotting comfortably, the entire stadium broke into roaring applause. "My ears were literally popping with the din as I raced around the track towards the tape," McGhee recalled. He crossed the finish line—the correct one—in a time of 2hr 39min 36sec, over 9min slower than the BECG record, demonstrating just how punishing the route and conditions had proved on this day. But overshadowed by Peters' collapse, McGhee remains among the least applauded of all marathon victors.

Barely a minute later, Meklar emerged at the stadium gate, unsure of his position. The crowd gave him a strong reception as a reward. "When I finally ran into the stadium, I was told by excited spectators I was about to finish second, but I couldn't believe it," Meklar recounted to the author of *Plimsolls On, Eyeballs Out*. "Only when Vic Dreyer, who'd just finished second in the hammer, dashed across the track and yelled at me, 'Jackie, you're lying second!' did I think it might be true. Suddenly I no longer felt distressed and sprinted that last lap on the track. I was so relieved I felt I had just woken from a bad dream." Officials clocked Meklar's solid run in 2hr 40min 57sec.

Outside the stadium, 18-year-old Barnard of South Africa and Barry Lush, the Ontario dairy farmer, became involved in a late dash for the bronze medal. While the heat had hit Barnard hard in the final miles and he had struggled to keep moving, Lush had maintained a steady pace, never leaving the top-ten all day and doing so without taking a single sip of water the entire race for fear it might upset his stomach. Now he found himself gaining on the fading South African. Informed by the crowd lining the road that the runner up ahead was sitting third, Lush made his push to overtake in the last mile. Organizers had kept the course clear of traffic "for a good part of the race," but by the time the runners entered east Vancouver, cars were pulling out of driveways in front of them and each man had to be alert. "I got behind this driveway and I could see this policeman standing up ahead," Lush remembered in a 2013 interview. "He was facing me and waving very frantically to the left. I thought he was waving to the car ahead because he was mad at the car's driver for being right ahead of me. The car driver turned and I turned." This was a big mistake, and as a result, Lush ran 75yds down the wrong road before the cop hollered at him to stop: "Come on back, you've gone wrong!" Lush turned and ran doggedly back to the main street, but he knew his fate was sealed. He estimated that he "was probably 400yds from heading down into the stadium" when he took that wrong turn, and that inadvertent detour effectively ended his chance of catching up to the flagging Barnard. "He ran well," admitted Lush of Barnard. "But... I should have been third."

Barnard was in terrible shape when he stumbled into the stadium to snag the bronze in 2hr 51min 49.8sec. The day's brutal conditions had caused him to run 26min slower than the South African national record he had set earlier in the year. His exhaustion was

Canada's Barry Lush, seen here running at the 1955 Pan American Games, finished fourth in the 1954 BECG marathon.

most evident later when he was carried to the podium on a stretcher and held upright by two police officers for the entire medal ceremony.

A minute after Barnard arrived and just as the Canadian anthem was being played for Canada's gold medal-winning 4x110yd relay team of Don Stonehouse, Bruce Springbett, Harry Nelson and Don McFarlane, Lush followed him into the stadium. His singlet was flapping loose at the waist, but he still wore his white newsboy cap, and the crowd gave him a hearty cheer. The race had taken its toll on him, too. "I pushed hard," he recalled. "I don't remember coming into the stadium." The crowd roared again when he trotted in front of the royal box and waved his white cap joyfully before tipping it courteously in the direction of Prince Philip. On the final straight, he tossed the hat into the stands before crossing the line in 2hr 52min 47.4sec. He doesn't remember that part either.

Two more competitors managed to complete the course within the next ten minutes: George Hillier from St. John's, Newfoundland, and Robert Crossen from Northern Ireland. But that was it. The true conqueror on this day proved to be the sun. Of the 16 original starters, only six managed to complete the 26-mile 385yd race.

✺

After the marathon medal ceremony, the focus of the crowd gradually returned to the last of the track and field events wrapping up on the field below. One of the highlights of those closing hours was the final event—the men's 4x440yd relay with Terry Tobacco anchoring the Canadian team. As strong as Tobacco had appeared in individual quarter-mile races, he had always saved his best for relays. "By far the best races I ever ran were with a running start," he recalled. "I always ran really well from way back, 18 or 20yds behind, catch up to everybody, hang on for quite a while, and then still have a bit of a kick to go. It was always neat for me to be able to catch up to somebody and just run on his shoulder and beat him."

Relays forced Tobacco to ratchet up his effort-level a notch or two and extend himself beyond his capacity regardless of the pain. "Some guys could finish a race and jog around the track totally fresh," he explained. "When I finished a race I ended up on my knees, puking all over the place. I was sometimes deathly sick. I couldn't even stand up... I could give it everything I had, just do myself in, completely wiped." (Years later doctors discovered he had a split diaphragm, likely a result of over-exerting himself too many times on the track.)

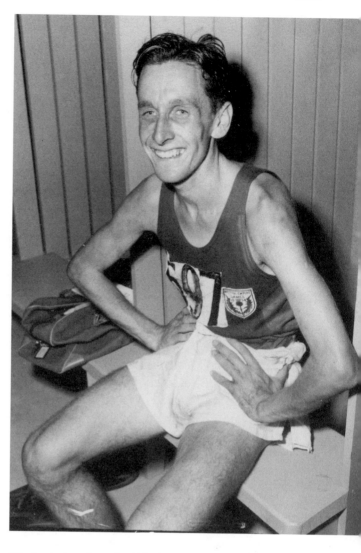

Glowing in the aftermath of his victory, Joe McGhee was the fastest of only six runners who completed the race.

Six countries entered teams in the 4x440yd relay, but from the gun, Australia, Kenya, Gold Coast and Jamaica were battling for scraps. Canada's Laird Sloan and England's Peter Higgins immediately pushed the pace and opened a small gap of separation on the others that only grew. At the first baton exchange Canada owned a slight edge. A half-mile specialist, Vancouver's Doug Clement was always in tough against England's Alan Dick, a fleet 440yd finalist. Riding on the roar of his hometown crowd, Clement gamely clung to the Englishman after he was passed, as Dick's greater natural speed opened up an 8yd lead. On the third leg Toronto's Joe Foreman sprinted off after Peter Fryer and by the last bend had cut the gap to a yard. Then disaster struck. Foreman was absolutely gassed and his legs began tying up as he struggled up the home straight to the exchange zone. Fryer pulled away smoothly and handed off to the English anchor Derek Johnson who sped off with determined purpose. Waiting for Foreman, Tobacco bounced up and down eagerly, inching forward, urging his fading teammate on. Foreman, however, was done, totally run out and as he stretched the baton to reach Tobacco, he fell face-first to the cinders, and Tobacco all but came to a dead stop to grab it. Now the headway Foreman had gained on the English lead was lost and then some, but Tobacco charged off like a man possessed. He was at least 12yds behind Johnson with less than a lap to work with. The crowd bellowed and rose from their seats, thousands echoing Tobacco's name into one thundering indecipherable uproar, pushing the young phenomenon forward. Foot by foot, he clawed into Johnson's lead, the din rising higher and higher as he closed the gap. On the back straight Tobacco whittled the deficit to just 2yds. By the final corner he had pulled level, poised to pass on Johnson's outside shoulder, but the Englishman had not won the 880yd gold earlier in the week for nothing. He had kept something in reserve and now he upped his work rate. Tobacco went with him, but whenever he pushed, Johnson pulled ahead a little faster. It was a skill he had mined throughout his running career, and it was said he had never been passed in a relay.

Perhaps Tobacco came closer than anybody to passing him on this day, but in the end, Johnson held off the determined young Canadian by 4yds, the English team taking gold in 3min 11.2sec. Both England and Canada smashed the existing BECG record by over 5sec. Timers unofficially clocked Johnson's anchor leg at 46.9sec and could barely believe the 46.4sec their stopwatches read for Tobacco. It was just 0.4sec off the world record and the fastest lap by any competitor in the Games.

After that, high praise for the previously unheralded Cumberland lad arrived from impressive sources. "Watch that boy Tobacco," said Jamaica's Olympic gold medalist Les Laing. "Before long he'll be running quarters in 46 and a fraction. I look for him to be a standout at the 1956 Olympics in Australia." Kevan Gosper, who had been closer to Tobacco's runs than anyone in Vancouver, told reporters, "I've been trying to break 47sec for a long time and here this 18-year-old comes along and breaks it in that relay run. You admire some athletes for their ability and that's it. I sat across from Terry at the final banquet and I admire him as a person." Perhaps the highest compliment of all. came from Roger Bannister himself: "There is a future champion." But the last word on the subject belonged to the young man himself, still a year from high school graduation, who had run like a seasoned pro. "It was a tremendous thrill running before that huge crowd," he marvelled to reporters. "I won't forget today for a long, long time."

Once all the track and field events were complete on that Saturday afternoon, Prince Philip took his place at the lectern in the royal box for his Closing Ceremonies speech. He concluded with a special word for the competitors:

> You have often been told that we are a family of nations. Now I am sure that
> every one of you who lived in the Athlete's Village will be able to go home and
> say that you *know* we are a family of nations...

As the thousands exited Empire Stadium's gates, few could have fully appreciated the historic afternoon—historic week—they had just witnessed. That would come with time, the deeds of Bannister, Landy, Peters and others growing more heroic with each passing year and each retelling. On their own, both the Mile and the Marathon stand as landmark, once-in-a-lifetime-if-you're-lucky events to witness. Six decades later the fact they took place on the same afternoon less than half an hour apart seems almost unbelievable. To give some idea of their lasting impact, you only have to look at the 2014 *London Telegraph* article ranking the greatest moments in Commonwealth Games history over the preceding 84 years. Number one and number two on the list? Bannister and Landy's Miracle Mile and Jim Peters' ill-fated marathon.

To this day, the pull and resonance of the 1954 BECG remains amazingly strong. Many of the athletes and spectators interviewed for this book commented on it. A few felt proud of the fact. Some, like John Landy, gently mocked the long passage of time since that week. "Are you still running that Miracle Mile?" he asked with a chuckle in a 2007 phone call. "It must be very grainy now." When told that several places such as the BC Sports Hall of Fame, Royal BC Museum and Museum of Vancouver are still showing the film, he laughed full out. "Gosh," he said with a hint of wonder. "*Pretty grainy.*" Maybe. Yet there was pride in his voice.

EPILOGUE

Before the dust had settled on the cinder track after the running of the Mile, hundreds of writers were already putting their stamp on what they had just witnessed. The praise was almost universally euphoric. "Bannister Wins Greatest Mile Race of All" heralded the *Times* of London. The *Melbourne Age* called it "the race of all time" and "the world's greatest ever athletic spectacle." The *Sydney Morning Herald* claimed, "Nothing like this race has been seen in the history of athletic competition." Jim Vipond of *The Globe and Mail* deemed the race "the most publicized sports event of any era." The *New York Times* said, "This is competitive sport at its very best." As was his wont, mercurial *Vancouver Sun* sports editor Erwin Swangard outdid everyone in the hyperbole department: "Saturday Vancouver was the centre of the universe." For once no one argued with him. The Mile of the Century even hatched at least two more effusive nicknames—"Magic Mile of Miles" and "Mile of the Millennium"—but ultimately it was "Miracle Mile" that stuck to what many still consider the greatest footrace of all time.

All Vancouver and Victoria papers, as well as most major papers across Canada, carried front-page coverage and race photos, as well as in-depth features that spilled from the sports pages into other sections. Even more startling was US coverage. In most major US markets, the Mile wasn't just the top sports story of the day, in many it ranked as the top news story. Race headlines and photos ran in the *New York Times*, *Boston Globe*, *Los Angeles Times*, *Washington Post*, *Chicago Tribune* and *Christian Science Monitor*, to name but a few of hundreds. Perhaps not so surprisingly, the *Vancouver Province* beat all of them to press for the biggest sports story of the year. By rushing copy and film negatives across town as soon as the race ended, the *Province* was able to publish a late edition that newsboys were hawking outside Empire Stadium by the time the over 35,000 in attendance filed out of the gates. Above a dramatic photo of Bannister breasting the finish tape, the headline in 2in type read: "BANNISTER WINS."

Charlie Warner spent half the night in the *Sun*'s darkroom processing his film from the day's work. "You were never really sure until you got back to the darkroom," he recalled in 2007, referring to the shot of Landy's head-turn as Bannister sprinted by. "I held my breath." The photo, shot from ground level, made Bannister and Landy appear massive, looming over the crowd in the background. Warner recognized the shot as a good one, but tired and looking ahead to his next assignment, he simply dropped it off among many others on the *Sun*'s photo desk and left without a second thought. "It wasn't until I got back and saw the papers that I realized the impact of it." Warner's photo ran on the front page of the *Sun*, *Globe and Mail*, *Toronto Star* and many international newspapers, including the first news page of the *Times* of London. Some film cameras had caught the head-turn, but Warner was the only still photographer to catch it. The National Headliner Awards in Atlantic City voted it the best sports action photo of 1954,

Opposite: After recovering in hospital for five days, Jim Peters returned home to his family in London under the care of teammate Dr. Roger Bannister. Photo from author's collection.

and in a rare move, the *Sun*'s management encouraged Warner to copyright it in his own name. Now considered the quintessential photo of the 1954 Games and one of the most famous in sport regardless of era, it has appeared in hundreds of publications all over the world.

Meanwhile, for some reporters, coverage of the marathon and the Peters drama far overshadowed the Mile. And as they tried to summarize and comprehend what they had witnessed, virtually all focussed on Peters' collapse, which meant that in many accounts the winner of the marathon, Joe McGhee, was virtually ignored. The *Sun*'s front page on Monday, August 9, was typical: four photos of Peters in various stages of collapse dominated above the fold with Warner's famous Bannister-Landy photo and all the Mile stories pushed below it. "Spectacular as the Mile was, for sheer drama, the 26-mile marathon dominated the Games," stated *Time* magazine. The *Sydney Morning Herald* said, "Never in modern times has a sporting crowd witnessed a more sickening sight." The *Edmonton Journal*'s sports editor Hal Pawson wrote: "Recall the most brutal prize fight you have ever seen. Recall a gory bullfight if you will, recall what you will in sport, and you won't come close to matching this for naked cruelty and primeval barbarity in one great man's battle to make courage master exhaustion." The *Province*'s well-travelled reporter Ross Munro went even further:

I've never seen anything more gripping—or more heart sickening. It was wonderful and it was terrible.

In nearly twenty years reporting human triumphs and tragedies in peace and war in many parts of the world, I've never witnessed anything like the exultant drama of Dr. Roger Bannister's victory in the mile. Nor have I witnessed such an anguished sight off a battlefield as Jimmy Peters' tortured struggle down the track at the end of the marathon... I've never seen such a ghastly look in any face with the exception of those of wounded or dying men in battle.

Dozens of accounts and recollections illustrated similar emotional mixtures. Ultimately Peters gained more notoriety from this race, the one he failed to finish, than any other he ran.

❂

On Monday, August 9, *Montreal Star* reporter Andy O'Brien broke the story about Landy's cut foot, and it appeared in the *Vancouver Sun* the same day. O'Brien had kept his word to remain silent prior to the Mile, but with the race over he could contain himself no longer: "I believe the sports fans of the world agree it should be told." At first Landy denied anything was wrong. When a *Sun* reporter asked him to prove it by removing his shoe, he stamped his heel hard against the ground while repeating, "There's nothing wrong with this foot, see?" But as photographs and stories of Landy's foot ran on front pages around the world, speculation built to a veritable frenzy. Landy came clean on August 10. "I kept quiet about it because I didn't want people to think I was crying about the result." Naturally the press speculated whether the injury had played any role in the Mile's outcome. Landy remained adamant the cut should not be misconstrued as any excuse for his performance. "It's obvious that you don't run like that when there is anything wrong with you," he told them. Fourth-place Mile finisher Victor Milligan agreed. He had trained with Landy before the race, had known of the cut beforehand and had seen Landy run up close. "I think [the injury] had an effect, but not a material effect," he argued. "I don't think it changed the course of the race."

In an interview over 50 years later, Landy continued to downplay the injury. "It was a superficial cut. People made a fuss about it because I got beaten, but frankly, it made no difference. I didn't even recall having cut my foot until about ten hours after the race." More than anything, Landy's decision to keep his injury quiet leading up to the race revealed his exemplary character. If he had used it as any sort of crutch before or after the Mile, maybe his performance would have been viewed even better than it already was, but then maybe he would also be viewed as less of a person.

Jim Peters remained in Shaughnessy Hospital for five days after the marathon. When he arrived there, the doctors listed his condition as critical. Nurses quickly snipped off his plain white singlet and placed him in an oxygen tent where saline solution and dextro was fed into him, but he vomited repeatedly and passed in and out of consciousness. It took several hours before any sensation returned to his legs and six hours for a leg cramp to straighten. That evening when he came briefly to, he looked over at the patient in the next bed. Seeing it was Stan Cox, he exclaimed, "What the hell are you doing here?" For 48hrs both men remained on a drip feed of salt, saline and glucose. "Brought us back to life!" Cox recalled much later.

Watched over by several doctors, including the newly minted MD Roger Bannister, Peters gradually recovered. Bannister summed up Peters' condition as "heat exhaustion—fluid loss through sweating." Peters' attending doctor at Shaughnessy, Dr. R.B. Kerr, described his condition as "severe exhaustion," but although some strange readings of his pulse rate were noted, no evidence of any cardiac damage could be definitively determined. His condition raised enough interest in the medical field that specialists came from as far away as New York to study the effects of the run on his body. Some years later, Glen Smith, stroke of the 1954 Canadian eights rowing crew, did some of his post-graduate medical training at Shaughnessy Hospital where he saw Peters' medical records. "They still had some of his electrolyte test results and electrocardiograms," Smith explained. "He was closer to death than a lot of people understand. He was hypo-potassiumaemic [an electrolyte imbalance], which is a very unstable situation for a runner to be in. He could have died."

A day after his collapse, officials finally allowed Peters to see a few select visitors including several of the marathoners. Barry Lush had the opportunity to sit with him that day, and one thing Peters said stuck with Lush decades later. "It just exhausted me," Peters told the Canadian fourth-place finisher. "I gave it all I could and I couldn't give it anymore." On doctors' recommendations, Peters formally withdrew from the European championships scheduled for later that month, one of the toughest decisions of his life. At this time he also wrote the final entry in his training journal; it read: "Tragedy. Collapse with sunstroke on stadium after world class run. Three mile lead." Apparently he did not suffer any significant lasting injury from the BECG marathon, but Peters often noted he felt "giddiness" thereafter and what he referred to as "my Vancouver headache." In the following years although he occasionally ran lightly on his own, ultimately the Vancouver marathon stood as his last competitive run. He retired with the world's best marathon time as well as four of the six fastest clockings ever.

However, even while Peters was still recovering in hospital, debate and criticism of several aspects of the marathon raged in the press. Some questioned the course's number of hills. Others condemned officials for running the race at the hottest time of day. Many felt Peters had been let down by both race officials and his own team; on August 10 the *Seattle Post-Intelligencer*'s Emmett Watson questioned the competency of both:

> What [Peters] was doing had nothing to do with sport or competition. He was a man who had lost all the dignity of being a man. No prizefighter would ever be subjected to that. But they subjected Peters, those stupidly cruel, dense, gutless amateurs crouched on the sidelines, egging him to get up, to finish, to go on... you can make it... finish... you can win. Win what?
>
> Why didn't the utterly incompetent people who followed Peters stop him before he got into the Stadium? Why didn't any one of a number of pompous badge-wearers (some were doctors) step in and use the authority they claim for those badges?
>
> One man, a resident of Canada, said later: "It was horrible. I expected any moment they would call out the lions."
>
> They wouldn't call out the lions. Too many officials were on the field.

Virtually everyone felt that to some degree Peters' own breakneck pace had contributed to his downfall. For forty years marathon winner Joe McGhee, later a lecturer in English at the University of Aberdeen, refused to comment on the race, but when at last he did, his intelligent analysis carried weight:

> It is not enough to point to the weather conditions and the hilly nature of the course. After all, these were the same for everyone, and when you race you are competing not only against other runners but the elements and course as well. You have to adapt accordingly. I personally ran half a minute slower per mile than I was capable of. Peters obviously did not. A "glorious failure" is all very well, but it does not disguise the fact that Jim Peters, the best and most experienced marathon runner in the world at the time, lost because he ran an unintelligent race.

Geoff Warren, who had trained with Peters and discussed race strategy beforehand, felt Peters *had* taken into account the heat and hills: "Jim had made allowances, maybe not quite enough, but so close to right." Jackie Meklar, who would become a five-time winner of the 89km Comrades ultra-marathon, agreed. Taking into account how far Peters was in front of him (5 miles) and just 5min off the world record pace in horrendous conditions, Meklar told Peters during a visit years later: "Jim, your last race was the greatest of your long career."

Some of the controversies surrounding the marathon persisted for decades. One revolved around the cause of Peters' collapse, and in 2008 three doctors—Dr. Tim Noakes, a University of Cape Town professor of sport science, Dr. Dan Pedoe, the long-time medical doctor of the London Marathon, and Jackie Meklar published a study of Peters' 1954 medical condition in the *SAMJ Forum*. Their "speculative" conclusion—which they described as "ultimately unsatisfactory" as it came 54 years after the fact—found that the combination of high body temperature, high levels of sodium in the blood, and low sugar and water levels may have caused a brief brain dysfunction that could explain why Peters collapsed and seemed to lose all control of his body.

The other controversy concerned the length of the marathon route. Peters maintained long after the race that he felt his body reached the 26 mile 385yd distance well before Empire Stadium, inferring that if the course had been the proper length, he would have finished, perhaps not even collapsed. Vancouver marathon officials adamantly maintained the course had been carefully measured to the correct length. So, who was right?

I decided I could shed some light on this point by completing a simple, yet physically taxing, experiment. Using 1954 marathon maps and plotting the route on today's roadways, I walked the entire 26-mile course with a measuring wheel in one long day in December 2013. After adding the 250yd partial opening lap the marathoners completed at the beginning of the race before leaving the stadium, plus an estimated 40yds for the steep ramp out of the stadium, I began my measurement at the northeast corner of where Empire Stadium once stood. I walked the route measuring each mile along the same roads Peters and the rest of the marathon field ran nearly 60 years earlier, hugging corners wherever possible, just as the runners would have, to get the most accurate measurement. In only one instance did recent road improvements force me from the 1954 route: where Highway 1 now runs through the Burnaby Lake area, I had to estimate the distance and carry on with my measurement on the other side of the highway. After nine hours I arrived back at my starting point, dragging two badly blistered feet. According to my measurement, I would reach 26 miles partway down the ramp into the stadium. By adding the remaining ramp distance and the 400yd partial lap of the track to the finish line, I concluded that the marathon route was over-length by about 50 or 60yds—but no more. Even allowing for a slight margin of error in my measurement, I am certain that the route was not over-length by any significant amount, definitely not the full mile that Peters claimed repeatedly in his book, *In the Long Run*. And even if the course had been 50 or 60yds shorter, Peters would still have collapsed short of the finish line. I followed up my measurement by checking the route using Google Earth, which came to much the same conclusion, effectively disproving the myth of the over-length Vancouver marathon course.

Perhaps the most lasting legacy of Peters' collapse would be the changes in marathon rules concerning start times and feeding stations. After 1954, marathons were generally held in cooler hours, either early in the morning or later in the evening, and the placement and staffing of feeding stations became standardized. Thanks to the ordeal Peters suffered before the eyes of the world, the safety of athletes competing in endurance events became paramount.

Five days after his collapse, Peters had recovered enough to go home. Bannister, who had stayed behind to help care for him, accompanied him on the flight. As officials led Peters through the hospital to a private car, patients, nurses and doctors leaned out of doorways and gave him three cheers. He appeared pale and a bit shaky and sported badly chapped lips and a bandaged hand. At the airport before leaving, he told reporters, "I wouldn't have cared if I had died if I had won the race for England."

"Jim doesn't mean that," said Bannister, standing behind him on the plane steps.

"Yes I do," Peters insisted. "It would have been worth it—any race would be when you were running for your country. The people who cried to have me pulled out of the race, they were very kind. But I would have been most annoyed, most annoyed. Other chaps have done more for England in the war and all."

Landy left Vancouver two days later. With the police pipe band playing the farewell tune "Will Ye No Come Back Again," he climbed the steps to his plane. Near the top, he turned and said, "I've had a tremendous time in Vancouver. Naturally I am sorry to leave, but someday I may return..."

Except for a brief meeting at the 1956 Olympics, 13 years went by before Bannister and Landy met face-to-face again, and fittingly it occurred in Vancouver. Before they spoke at a Sportsmen's Dinner at the Hotel Vancouver, a film of the Miracle Mile was shown, and the 800-person dinner crowd rose and cheered wildly as the race's dramatic final lap played out on-screen. Bob Hope, the evening's emcee, took in the incredible scene before him and mouthed one word: "Beautiful." Third- and fourth-place Mile finishers, Rich Ferguson and Victor Milligan, had also been brought back for the event, and rounding out the reunion was David Law, who was by coincidence in town on business. He turned up carrying the track shoe he lost on the Mile's opening lap.

The following evening prior to a BC Lions football game at Empire Stadium Bannister and Landy were honoured with the unveiling of a 3m bronze statue of the race's crucial moment. The Mile statue, erected atop a concrete pedestal, had been three years in the making. Lions general manager Herb Capozzi had conceived the idea and the *Sun*'s Denny Boyd had written a column calling for a monument to the Mile at Empire Stadium: "The world will never forget the Miracle Mile. But Vancouver will if something isn't done." Readers mailed in a small mountain of cash and *Sun* publisher Stu Keate rounded up former members of the BEG Society to beat the corporate bushes for further donations. They raised over $18,000, which allowed Vancouver sculptor Jack Harman to turn Charlie Warner's iconic photograph into majestic everlasting bronze.

In June 1983 when Landy returned again to Vancouver, he was interviewed by a *Vancouver Sun* reporter and when the subject of the statue came up, he said:

> You know, mate, history is a funny thing. As long as they talk about that race, they'll say I lost it because I turned to look for Roger... It didn't matter that I turned. It didn't slow me or break my rhythm, but it's made me into a piece of history. Lot's wife looked back and she was turned into a pillar of salt. I looked back and was turned into a pillar of bronze.

And in a 2007 interview when he was once again reminded of the statue, Landy laughed and said, "Haven't torn it down yet?" Far from it. After 26 years of prominence at the PNE entrance on the corner of Hastings and Renfrew, the statue was relocated in 2015 to the newly opened Empire Fields sports park, just a few feet from where the Mile's famous moment took place.

By an odd coincidence, just two months before the statue's unveiling, Jim Peters had also returned to Vancouver for the first time since his unforgettable marathon collapse. Brought back by *Province* columnist and BC Sports Hall of Fame curator Eric

Located at Empire Field sports park, Jack Harman's three-metre-tall bronze statue commemorates the Miracle Mile's climactic moment.

Whitehead, he was the feature attraction at the BC Lions' "Hall of Fame Game" at Empire Stadium. Mayor Tom Campbell proclaimed it "Jim Peters Day," reportedly the first time an individual had received this honour. There would be no statue for Peters—not even a small plaque—but he would be given the opportunity to finish the race he failed to complete 13 years earlier. At halftime the crowd turned toward the stadium's northeast gate to see Peters in the same shorts and shoes he had worn in 1954, standing at the top of that daunting ramp. Much like that hot August day, the stadium hushed. "It was like the ghost came back," he recalled.

With no sun, just the glare of the stadium's night lights to worry about this time, he began to jog down the ramp. The crowd came to its feet. Some wept openly. Others stood silently and applauded. The emotion of the moment, of the 13-year-old memory of this courageous man's battle with exhaustion, seemed to touch everyone, Peters included. "The roar of the crowd gave me a fantastic feeling," he said. "It was the feeling I used to get when I won the big races and never in my fondest dreams expected to hear for myself again."

At the exact spot on the track where he first collapsed waited BEG Society chairman Stan Smith and Peters' 13-year-old daughter, Jennifer, who had never seen her father race as she was born just weeks before his 1954 run. She placed a garland of flowers around his shoulders and he continued to jog on. Holding the tape at the finish line were the two officials who had waited there 13 years earlier. Peters sprinted through the line elated. Asked later what went through his mind as he completed his run, he said he saw his English teammates and Joe McGhee watching him, cheering him on, looking as they had in 1954. It was as if they were running that marathon over again, except this time they got the ending right. "I never thought I'd see this stadium again," he said, visibly moved. Neither did anyone else.

❂

Despite initial fears the Games would run a deficit of nearly $100,000, when all revenue and expenses were tabulated, a modest profit of $32,000 was realized. However, some controversy persisted for months after the Games about a perceived $150,000 deficit. In a complicated way, this was both a deficit and not a deficit. It just depended on your interpretation of Stan Smith's explanation of the financial situation. According to the minutes of the final BEG Society Board of Trustees meeting on May 17, 1955, Smith explained that when "contracts were let for the Stadium... he had made it very clear the BEG would assume responsibility for not more than $1,365,000. The original estimates came nearer the two million mark, but in collaboration with the PNE and Vancouver City Council these were considerably reduced, though they still included night lighting of the field and roofing, which were not required for the Games. The BEG Society, therefore, assumed a "moral obligation" to pay the extra $150,000 owing *only* if funds eventually permitted, but the Society did not assume legal responsibility for these extras. Thus the profit of $32,000!

Ultimately, it was the Mile frenzy that had rescued the BEG Society's bottom line. Still, the overall Games' attendance had proven disappointing. Just under 160,000 people attended events, half the number of the 1950 BEG in Auckland, a city half the size of Vancouver. Many factors had kept the hoped-for crowds away. Ticket prices for most events ranged from a reasonable $1 to a moderately high $3.50, but the best seats for track events cost $5, a steep price when the average BC worker's weekly salary in 1954 was only $64. Understandably many irate Vancouverites vented about this, and on August 7 the *Province* printed the view of one disgruntled citizen:

> It seems mighty peculiar to me as a family man and owning a small business that although we donated to the BEG through the business and advertised same in the store window, we find the price of BEG tickets beyond our means. The BEG is a supreme public event which we may never get the chance to see again, so, Mr. Promoter, with so many empty seats, why are we denied this?
>
> Another Disappointed Would-be Spectator

Lack of night-time events, employers unwilling to give workers time off and chilly weather on several days all played a role in keeping the crowds small. However, the biggest factor in keeping spectators away proved to be the new medium of television, which according to some estimates cut attendance by over 10 percent. The CBC's fledgling Vancouver station, CBUT channel 2, went on-air in December 1953, just seven months before the Games, and with prices for television sets finally falling to attainable levels for most of the middle class—a shiny 17-inch black and white RCA could be bought in Vancouver for $198.50—many chose the summer of 1954 to buy their first set and watch Games events from the comfort of their own living rooms. And even if the new models seemed pricy, some TV dealers offered rental sets for $15 a week. Contrast that with the $10-$20 needed for reasonably good seats to witness a week of track events at Empire Stadium.

Although some claimed the Games actually caused their businesses financial loss rather than the economic spur they had been promised, the key legacies remained significant—if harder to quantify. First, Vancouver was elevated as a destination on the world sports map. It was now a city capable of hosting big events successfully. It was no coincidence that in the 20 years after the Games, the city became home to three major professional teams that are now deeply entrenched in the fabric of Canadian sport: the CFL's BC Lions, the NHL's Vancouver Canucks, and the NASL/MLS's Vancouver Whitecaps. Second, the Games effectively engaged a significant percentage of Vancouver's and BC's population unlike any event before and most that have come after. Third, on an individual level, the lasting effects for those involved elevated many to places of honour: at least 50 individuals who took part in the Games in some capacity ended up inducted into the BC Sports Hall of Fame and another 15 in Canada's Sports Hall of Fame. As well, hundreds of thousands of British Columbians became engaged and inspired by watching some aspect of the Games in person or on television or by following events through the press or on radio.

And finally, no one could discount the physical legacy left in the form of athletic facilities built expressly for the Games and then used to benefit professional and amateur athletes for the next three decades. By 1983, however, these physical legacies were decaying, if not already dead—none more obviously than Empire Stadium, the Games' crown jewel. Rushed to completion in record time using cheap building materials, the "Old Fair Lady of Renfrew Street" did not age well. The field, built on an ancient streambed, became a quagmire. "The drainage system underneath had never been properly connected," said revered sports columnist Jim Kearney. "The guys installing it, if they ran into a boulder, they just drove to the other side and continued it." Fellow Hall of Fame columnist Jim Taylor recalled a story that "when they sank the first piling, they lost it! Which should have been a clue, you know?" Barely a year after the Games, the city sued the architects, Marwell Construction and the PNE over $56,000 damage to Empire Stadium's field. In the early 1970s they covered the grass with blacktop and teams played on artificial turf. A decade later the building of BC Place Stadium rendered Empire obsolete.

It was into this state of change in 1983 that the Miracle Milers were brought back to Vancouver to be on hand for Empire Stadium's nostalgic curtain call: a mid-week Whitecaps game. Stories were shared of Grey Cups, of Pele and Franz Beckenbauer, of the Lions' roar and the Whitecaps' wave, of international rugby and soccer, of sprinter Harry Jerome, of the annual inter-high school track meets, of the Beatles and Elvis, of the Queen and the Pope—of everything that had come to pass within this once-gleaming emerald of a stadium. No event, however, had surpassed The Mile, so it seemed entirely fitting at Empire Stadium's final event that Bannister and Landy were introduced one last time at the site of their finest hour. Now in their fifties, these two distinguished gentlemen giants of the sports world, who had gone on to impressive careers in vastly different fields, stood quietly on the infield as a ceremonial mile race was run in their honour. "What remarkable citizens of the world these two men had become," recalled Ted Reynolds. "It made you feel proud knowing their greatest moment had taken place here in Vancouver and we saw it live."

Local politicians and PNE officials allowed the Games venue that had put Vancouver on the map to rot for another decade until it served as little more than an overflow parking lot for the PNE and a haven for pigeons. In 1992 it was demolished and the site became a community playing field. Despite the fact three statues dedicated to track athletes exist within Vancouver's boundaries—a claim few cities in the world can make—since that time a modern track and field facility has not existed in the city.

The other sports venues built specifically for the Games fared no better. After the rowers left town and the rowing facilities on the Vedder Canal were dismantled, no regatta ever dared battle the canal's unpredictable waters again. And despite Tommy Taylor's fervent efforts to promote Burnaby Lake's development over the Vedder, it was not until 1973 when Burnaby hosted the Canada Summer Games that a FISA standard rowing course was developed on Burnaby Lake. Although heavily used for two decades, by the early 1990s the lake had once again become clogged with vegetation and sediment build-up. Today the lake sees some limited use, while a lake-saving dredging plan sits on a government backburner amid environmental concerns.

The China Creek cycling track remained the heart of Vancouver cycling for many years after the Games. Thousands turned out for regular international meets and a generation of BC cyclists learned to keep their speed up and lean into the steep corners. But a decade of rain wreaked havoc with the track's cedar surface, and by the mid-1960s China Creek had begun to rot. Although the sport's popularity waned, the track and its small group of cycling die-hards carried on until 1972 when China Creek's death knell appeared imminent. That was when Tony Hoar and Ace Atkinson organized enthusiasts to form the Cycle Track Racing Action Committee (C-TRAC), which successfully raised enough money to restore the track to racing condition. Eight years later the Vancouver Park Board sold the property for $2.75 million to provide a site for Vancouver Community College. A final ceremonial lap by Atkinson, Hoar and five other riders who had competed on the track during the 1954 Games was held on September 3, 1980, just before the bulldozers went to work.

Ironically, the most embattled BECG venue, Empire Pool, lasted the longest of all Games facilities. After six days of BECG swimming competitions, the pool opened to the public, and boys and girls paddled and splashed up and down the lanes, trying their best to be the next Henricks or Crapp, Harrison or Grant. And some eventually would. However, within five years of the Games, the pool had become obsolete as international meets now required eight lanes, two more than it was built with, and the switch to metric distances worldwide meant that the 55yd pool could only be used for local competition and training. After that, it largely served as a community recreation pool. Today Empire Pool appears fated for demolition to make way for a new modern aquatic centre. On the other hand, Percy Norman did eventually get his pool in the Little Mountain area, although he was not around to see it. While fighting the pool war in 1954, the face of Vancouver swimming had also been battling terminal cancer, although it was a heart attack that took him three years after the Games. The Percy Norman Pool was built in 1962 as part of the Riley Park Community Centre and replaced after the 2010 Olympics with the 60,000 square foot Percy Norman Aquatic Centre across the street. Norman may have lost the initial swimming pool battle but he ultimately won the war.

☿

In the years since the Games it has become a well-worn joke that if you added up all who claimed to have been there in person the day the Mile and Marathon were run, the seating capacity of Empire Stadium would have required expansion north of the 250,000 range. It became one of those where-were-you-when? signpost moments for British Columbians, perhaps unsurpassed until February 2010 when the Winter Olympics came to town. Each generation has its defining moments and for Vancouver and British Columbia in the fifties, Saturday, August 7, 1954, was it. Lives changed that day. Lifelong memories were forged, while the post-Games careers of many of the athletes who captivated the crowds in 1954 proved to be even more remarkable than their performances in the Games. Some found success, some met misfortune, and some delved into fields far removed from sport. And although another Games participant or two fades from the picture with each passing year, their stories persist.

Mike Agostini continued to streak through the track world after tearing up Vancouver with his mouth and feet. In 1956 he set a 220yd world record (20.1sec), equalled the 100yd world mark (9.3sec) and ran for Trinidad at the Melbourne Olympics. He continued to spend his summers in Vancouver while attending Fresno State College, and when Trinidad offered no support for its athletes, he ran for Canada at the 1958 BECG, picking up a 100yd bronze medal. After retiring from sports, Agostini moved to Sydney, Australia, and worked as a schoolteacher, a journalist, a broadcaster, published athletics magazines and Australian Broadcasting Corporation Olympic guides, ran a printing company, marketed drinks and synthetic running surfaces, organized Australia's first series of "fun-runs" and the Sydney Marathon and authored several books on the afterlife and the paranormal. A born salesman, he reputedly became a multi-millionaire but went broke chasing one too many of his far-flung ideas. Agostini still lives in Sydney; to hear him spin tales, his enthusiasm tripping over itself, remains a rare treat.

Australian world record-holding sprinter Hector Hogan rebounded from his disappointing performance in Vancouver to nab a 100m bronze medal at the 1956 Olympics in Melbourne. It marked the first time an Australian man had won an Olympic sprinting medal in 56 years. Two years later his health began to deteriorate rapidly and he was diagnosed with leukemia. Hogan lay dying in a hospital bed in Brisbane on September 2, 1960, listening to a radio broadcast of the 100m final at the Rome Olympics, a race he should have been running in. By the time the sprint ended just over 10sec later, he was gone. The seven-time Australian 100yd champion was only 29 years old.

In 1956 after Canadian officials reaffirmed Jackie MacDonald's amateur status, she became the first female thrower to represent Canada at the Olympics, throwing a personal best in the shot put (14.31m) to finish tenth overall. In 1958 she captured a BECG bronze medal in shot put to cap an excellent international career. In 2010 she joined 18 other Canadian Olympians—most of them her 1956 Olympic teammates—to carry the Olympic Torch in Trail, BC. Although she long ago came to peace with the decision of officials to remove her from the 1954 Games, that traumatic incident remains a tender subject to this day.

By the end of 1954 New Zealand's Yvette Williams, the only athlete to win three individual-event gold medals in Vancouver, had retired from athletics. She worked many years as a PE teacher and coached track and field at Pakuranga Athletic Club, which she helped form, besides playing basketball into her fifties. She was inducted into the New Zealand Sports Hall of Fame and named the nation's athlete of the 1950s decade and Otago sportsperson of the century. Many still rank her as New Zealand's all-time greatest female athlete.

Chris Chataway broke the four-minute barrier himself in 1955, finishing second in a race behind Hungarian Laszlo Tabori. Later that year he lowered his own Three Mile world record by another 9sec. He retired from athletics at age 25 and moved into broadcasting and was the first individual on-screen newsreader for Britain's ITN. While serving as a Tory MP in the governments of Harold Macmillan and Lord Home, he was credited with introducing local commercial radio to Britain. Later Prime Minister John Major appointed him chairman of the British Civil Aviation Authority; he was knighted for his services in 1995. In his fifties he returned to running regularly to improve his health and for the first time truly enjoyed it. In his 80th year he ran the half-marathon Newcastle-to-South Shields Great North Run and clocked in at 1hr 52min, a time that beat 80 percent of the field. Sir Christopher Chataway battled cancer for the last two years of his life and died in London at the age of 82 in 2014.

Although strongman Doug Hepburn delivered the BECG weightlifting gold medal for Canada, the gym that he claimed Mayor Fred Hume had promised him never materialized. (Hume denied making such a promise.) After an unsuccessful try-out with the BC Lions and a short run of moderate success in pro wrestling, he began drinking and sank into a deep depression. When things were at their darkest, he checked himself into New Westminster's Hollywood Hospital and had his alcoholism treated with LSD; the radical procedure proved successful as Hepburn never drank again. He ran and lost gyms, bred huskies, sold mail-order strength courses, invented fitness equipment, wrote poetry, lost weight to become a lounge crooner, recorded several radio-friendly Christmas songs, studied Eastern spirituality, became a philosopher and built arm-wrestling machines. The one constant in his life was weightlifting, and he continued to lift into his seventies, routinely breaking Masters age-class world records. He was inducted into both the Canadian and BC Sports Halls of Fame. He spent the final years of his life in an apartment overlooking Stanley Park and died of a perforated stomach ulcer in 2000. Today many still consider him the grandfather of modern powerlifting.

Two years after Irene MacDonald's second-day diving collapse, her "thin skin" looked tougher than steel armour up on Melbourne's Olympic springboard. Although fighting excruciating bursitis in her shoulder, she delivered a historic bronze medal, Canada's first-ever Olympic podium finish in *any* women's aquatic event. Four years after her BECG bronze in Vancouver, MacDonald upgraded to silver in Cardiff, a result earning her Canada's female athlete of the year status. But the media crucified her sixth-place finish at the Rome Olympics as a failure and she retreated to Vancouver. She retired following the 1960 Olympics due to a detached retina. Over the next 35 years she developed into one of the world's leading diving coaches, became an internationally respected judge and a popular CBC commentator alongside Ted Reynolds. Four separate halls of fame honoured her. She never located her birth parents, and she developed an aggressive form of Alzheimer's in her early sixties. Her last public appearance came as an honoured guest at the 1994 Commonwealth Games' diving competition where Reynolds, her long-time co-worker and friend, spoke to her for the last time. "I just wanted to make sure she realized what a tremendous contribution she made to her sport in Canada," he said. "I hope she realized she had made a marked impression."

The victory of the 1954 UBC-VRC eights crew proved just the beginning of a Canadian rowing dynasty. At a reception later in the Games, an impressed Prince Philip suggested to Frank Read he bring his crew to the famed Henley Regatta. A year later they accepted his invitation and defeated the defending champion USSR Krasnoe Znamia crew in the semi-finals. Despite a narrow defeat to the University of Pennsylvania in the final, the 1955 regatta was remembered thereafter as "the UBC-VRC Henley." A year later UBC-VRC crews went to Melbourne and brought home Canada's first-ever Olympic gold medal in rowing as well as a silver. In Cardiff in 1958 they took a fours silver and eights gold then added an eights silver in the 1960 Rome Olympics, Canada's only medal of the Games. Even after Read retired, success for the program he assembled continued with another pairs gold medal at the 1964 Olympics.

Man-for-man the 1954 crew produced more doctors, lawyers and engineers than perhaps any other similar-sized team in Canadian history. Team captain Tom Toynbee developed one of Canada's largest wholesale lumber businesses and later invested in Saltspring Island's historic Mouat's Store. For over 50 years Ken Drummond worked as a geologist for Mobil Oil and the National Energy Board, while also playing a major role in the Hibernia project off Newfoundland. Doug McDonald ran a Saltspring sawmill and Garibaldi's Alpine Lodge before managing a bulldozing business that prepared many of Whistler-Blackcomb's early ski hills. After graduating in dentistry from Montreal's McGill University, Herman Zloklikovits shortened his name to Kovits and worked as a Chilliwack family dentist, living within sight of the Vedder. Glen Smith practised as a medical doctor in Prince George and a throat and neck specialist in Burnaby before managing three hospitals in Saudia Arabia. A brilliant engineering student, Laurie West briefly coached UBC's rowing program. After graduating in engineering physics, Mike Harris worked for Canadair before joining the RCAF to fly F-86 Sabre fighter jets in Europe and to work for the US Air Force on the precursor to the space shuttle program. Later he flew experimental aircraft at the Cornell Aeronautical Laboratory and instructed young test pilots on how to fly them for the Air Force, Navy, Marines and FAA. Phil Kueber practised corporate and securities law for 35 years in Calgary, owned a thoroughbred horse racing stable, and founded the Calgary Rowing Club. Bob Wilson became successful in the oil business running a parts distribution company worldwide; he finally settled in Calgary. Cox Ray Sierpina became a successful West Vancouver chartered accountant. Team manager Don Laishley attended MIT before operating one of the world's largest forestry consulting companies and later managing 2.5 million acres of forest for Champion International, then the world's largest paper company. For his services to the UBC-VRC rowing program, Frank Read was named UBC's first winner of the "Honourary Alumnus" award in 1957. He served as the BC Sports Hall of Fame's inaugural chair in 1966, the same year the 1954 UBC-VRC eights crew became the first team inducted.

Australia's "Lithgow Flash," Marjorie Jackson-Nelson, retired after her three sprint gold medals in Vancouver to operate a sporting goods store with husband Peter Nelson. After he succumbed to leukemia in 1977, Jackson-Nelson fundraised several million dollars for leukemia research in his name. She remained involved in several Australian sports organizations, worked as Australia's team manager at the 1994 Commonwealth Games and served as a member of the Sydney Organizing Committee for the 2000 Olympic Games. She was chosen as one of the Olympic flag bearers at the Opening Ceremonies. Honours bestowed on her include the Order of Australia, the Order of the British Empire, the Royal Victorian Order and the Olympic Order given by the International Olympic Committee. She has also been honoured on an Australian postage stamp and with a statue in her hometown of Lithgow. From 2001 to 2007 Jackson-Nelson served as governor of South Australia.

Two years after Kevan Gosper won the 440yd final in Vancouver he added an Olympic silver medal in the 4x400m relay (in which he ran alongside his 1954 BECG teammate, the 440yd hurdles champion David Lean). But perhaps no athlete who competed at the 1954 BECG rose higher in world sport in later years. While working as a top executive for Shell in Melbourne and London, he had an impressive career with the International Olympic Committee, rising to vice-president. He served as vice-president of the Sydney Organizing Committee for the 2000 Olympic Games, inaugural chairman of the Australian Institute of Sport and president of the Australian Olympic Committee from 1985-90.

After Terry Tobacco's improbable double-medal performance in Vancouver, the *Province* newspaper named him BC's athlete of the year and a slew of American universities courted his running talents. He opted to attend the University of Washington, while for the remainder of the decade ranking as Canada's top 400m/440yd runner and in the top five in the world. Although an Olympic medal contender at two separate Games, the achievement ultimately eluded him; he came closest in 1956 when he led the Canadian 4x400m relay team to a fifth-place finish. In the semi-final anchor leg, however, he clocked 45.3sec, which was faster than the 400m gold medal-winning time. After claiming another 440yd BECG bronze medal in 1958 and running at the 1960 Olympics, Tobacco retired to focus on teaching at Victoria-area secondary schools and running a commercial fishing boat in the summers.

Each of Tobacco's 1954 relay teammates went on to interesting post-athletic careers. Joe Foreman became a prominent lawyer in Sarnia, Ontario, while Laird Sloan of Montreal earned five engineering degrees and worked on the Avro Arrow before that remarkable aviation program was halted. He later helped design and build NASA's Mission Control Center in Houston, Texas. After graduating from the University of Oregon, Doug Clement became a general practitioner in Richmond, but encouraged by his mentor, Bill Bowerman (University of Oregon coach and founder of Nike), he soon limited his practice solely to the emerging field of sports medicine. With several UBC colleagues he founded BC's first sports medicine clinic in 1979 and in 1992 received the Order of Canada for his contributions. Clement and his wife, Diane, a top Canadian sprinter herself, founded the Richmond Kajaks track club, which developed countless university athletes and 55 Olympians. In 1985 the couple were part of a group that approached the *Vancouver Sun* to establish an annual run to promote healthy living; the Sun Run is today one of the world's largest timed 10km runs, with nearly 50,000 participants annually. Both Doug and Diane have been inducted into the BC Sports Hall of Fame.

Lorne "Ace" Atkinson retired from international cycling after riding Canada's top result at the Games but continued competing locally until 1964 when, at age 42, he won the BC 2000m tandem track event. He organized countless BC cycling events while coaching top riders to the international level and operating Ace Cycles on West Broadway. Ace earned induction into the BC Sports Hall of Fame and in his later years served as Vancouver cycling's unofficial historian, keeping meticulous scrapbooks. He continued to cycle well into his ninth decade, leaving younger riders in his wake on 50km Sunday pleasure rides to Horseshoe Bay and back. When the Olympic Torch Relay paused outside his bike shop in 2010, he held the Olympic flame from his wheelchair. The smile on his face said it all. Ace Atkinson passed away three months later at the age of 88.

English marathoner Stan Cox, who collapsed into a ditch in the final miles of the 1954 marathon, brought his impressive 17 years of international competition to a close in 1956, although he remained involved in running as a field event judge. At the 1957 AAA junior championships he was in the field measuring javelin tosses when the next competitor threw. That javelin, he recalled later, "went straight through into my chest about an inch away from my heart. What saved my life, I had a ballpoint pen in my blazer pocket. It hit that, smashed it, and went off it the right way. If it had gone the other way, I'd have been a dead man." The horrific accident made international news. To make matters worse, doctors treated him with penicillin, not realizing he was allergic. Fortunately, he recovered fully and later worked as an assistant computer analyst for Standard Telephones & Cables, an early adoptee of computers. Cox led fitness walks into his early nineties, and as one of Britain's last surviving 1948 Olympians, he wanted to carry the Olympic torch when the Games returned to London in 2012. Sadly, he died at age 93, one month before the Games opened. The torch relay passed through his hometown the day of his funeral.

Perhaps no other group went on to more varied and interesting lives than the eight men who ran in the Miracle Mile. David Law, who failed to finish after losing his shoe on the Mile's first corner, won a 1500m bronze medal at the 1955 World Student Games in Spain. But he curtailed his running after that as it competed with the increasing demands on his time to complete his law degree at Oxford. He practised as a solicitor in his hometown of Sheffield until retiring in 2002. He was diagnosed with Parkinson's and died in 2011 at the age of 80.

Bill Baillie, the youngest of the milers, ultimately competed the longest. After Vancouver he represented New Zealand at three more BECGs and achieved a sixth-place finish in the 1964 Olympic 5000m. He also broke world records at 20,000m (59min 28.6sec) and total distance run in one hour (12 miles 960yds 7in) and won 12 national titles at widely varied distances. His last serious competition came at the European Ironman in Germany at the age of 65, where he completed the 3.8km swim, 180km cycle, and 42.2km marathon in just over 12hrs to win his age group with another world-best time. He was inducted into the New Zealand Sports Hall of Fame in 2011. He worked as a boat builder, a timber machinist, and then a sales rep for a chip and particle board company. Later he and his wife ran a taxi business from their home in Auckland. When John Walker ran his 100th sub-four-minute mile in 1985, Walker invited Bannister and his wife to New Zealand for the occasion, and Baillie chauffeured the Bannisters around in his cab, allowing him the opportunity to reconnect with the miler he had chased in Vancouver.

Sixth-place Mile finisher Ian Boyd ran for Britain in the 1956 Olympic 1500m final against fellow Miracle Mile alumni John Landy and Murray Halberg. In 1961 Boyd moved to New Zealand where he worked at Victoria University of Wellington and became influential in the national athletics scene. He later served as chair and president of Athletics New Zealand and sat on the New Zealand Olympic Committee for over two decades. For his years of service he was named a life member of Athletics New Zealand, a member of the New Zealand Olympic Order, a Veteran of the IAAF, and an Officer of the New Zealand Order of Merit. He remains involved in New Zealand athletics to this day.

Murray Halberg was disappointed with his performance in Vancouver and at the 1956 Olympics, but after Chris Chataway suggested he switch to longer distances, he won the Three Miles at the 1958 BECG, took a dramatic 5000m gold medal at the 1960 Olympics and defended his BECG Three Mile title in 1962 by winning another gold. He also became the first New Zealander to run a sub-four-minute mile and then broke three world records in 19 days in 1961. In 1963, after attending a disabled children's fundraiser in Toronto, he returned to New Zealand and formed the Halberg Trust (now known as the Halberg Disability Sport Foundation) to assist disabled children through sport. He resurrected the national sports awards as the foundation's fundraising arm and used the funds raised to create equal opportunities for athletes with disabilities. Knighted in 1987 and more recently appointed to the Order of New Zealand, Halberg remains one of the most revered athletes in New Zealand sport.

Although Victor Milligan didn't know it at the time, the Mile was literally the last race he ever ran. In 1955, having won a scholarship to study engineering at Indiana's Purdue University, he was mountain climbing in Wyoming's Grand Teton national park when a handhold gave way. He fell approximately 120ft down a cliff, landed head-first on a rocky slope and tumbled to a stop in a snowbank. He sustained a double skull fracture, broken bones in his shoulder, neck and back, and partial paralysis on one side of his body. Newspapers prematurely reported him dead, but after months of therapy at the Montreal Neurological Institute, he regained full use of his limbs. As a Toronto district engineer, he helped design the Don Valley Parkway as well as many banks, dams and bridges. In 1960 he helped form Golder and Associates, one of the world's top engineering firms, and his work took him to all corners of the globe. "One day in Tehran, long before the Shah left, I was lining up for a hotel room," recalled Milligan. "I looked over and it was Chataway. I said, 'My God, what are you doing here?' He said, 'I'm looking for a damn room, have you got one?'" They both laughed, marvelling at life's amazing reconnections. Milligan retired in 1994 as Golder's president, chief executive and chairman, having earned election to both the Canadian and British Royal Academy of Engineering. Victor Milligan died of a heart attack in 2009 while travelling in West Africa.

Rich Ferguson's bronze medal in the Mile earned him the Lionel Conacher Award as Canada's athlete of the year for 1954. But the Miracle Mile was his last major international race. He returned to the University of Iowa to complete his business degree and by the early 1970s had worked his way up to president of Spalding Canada. When he grew tired of working for large corporations, he moved to southern California where he ran a successful Palm Springs printing company until his death from cancer at the age of 54. In interviews over the years Ferguson had hinted at his dissatisfaction with the focus placed on Bannister and Landy in the Mile. "There were three medals awarded," he said in 1983, "and I got one of them. There are only two names on the statue. It would have been nice… " Perhaps this book will help shine the spotlight a little more sharply on one of the most surprising—and forgotten—Canadian athletic performances ever.

Late in 1954 a package arrived in Jim Peters' mail box postmarked "Buckingham Palace." Greatly moved by Peters' courage, Prince Philip had sent a 1954 BECG gold medal encased in a plexi-glass stand with an engraving: "This Gold Medal was given to H.R.H. THE DUKE of EDINBURGH at Vancouver and presented by him to J. PETERS as a token of admiration for a Most Gallant Marathon Runner." It became Peters' most prized possession. With running no longer the focal point of his life, Peters filled the void with family and his growing business as a dispensing optician, yet he was uncomfortable with the way his running career had halted so abruptly. "My only regret is that although I won more than 200 races in my career," he told *BC Sports News* in August 1967, "it seems I shall always be remembered for the race I did not win." However, the impact of his larger marathon accomplishments did not go unnoticed. Once, years after he had retired, while making a guest appearance at the Netherlands' Enschede Marathon, 20 African runners swarmed him for his autograph, each holding a copy of his book, which they still used as their training guide. And 42 years after their first meeting at the 1954 BECG, Peters reunited with Joe McGhee at the 1996 London Marathon, and they relived memories of that fateful day on Vancouver's blistering streets.

In 1993 Peters was diagnosed with terminal cancer, but he refused to give in easily. He fought the disease for another six years before his death in 1999. In one of the final interviews of his life, a reporter informed him that a recently published marathon history had called him "the greatest marathon runner ever." In his typical down-to-earth manner, Peters replied, "Well, I'll be blowed. That's lovely." To this day no runner has lowered the world-best marathon time by a larger margin—a massive 7min. At the time of his death the IAAF saw fit to honour Peters alongside Ethiopia's Abebe Bikila and Portugal's Carlos Lopez as the three greatest marathoners in history.

After his loss to Roger Bannister, John Landy pulled out of all European events and retreated to teaching at Geelong Grammar School's isolated Timbertop campus. For seven months, he never ran at all, then slowly he began jogging again over the surrounding hills and rediscovered the joy he had once felt in running. In his first mile race since Vancouver, he laid down the first sub-four-minute mile on Australian soil, then ran another a short time later. Then, with bad press circulating about the 1956 Olympic preparations in his hometown of Melbourne, he went on a US tour to promote the Games, and on California's rock-hard tracks, he ran two more sub-four-minute miles, giving him six in two years. Then battling injury and immense pressure, he gutted out a dramatic 1500m bronze medal at the 1956 Olympics. He retired from running a year later.

For 22 years Landy worked for Australia's Imperial Chemical Industries, the last 11 managing their biological department. Throughout his life he has remained a devoted naturalist and conservationist; he wrote two award-winning books about aspects of Australia's environment, featuring his own photography, and lent his support to many environmental organizations and causes, playing a major role in increasing the state of Victoria's national parks five-fold. He still keeps a large butterfly and moth collection.

In 2001 John Landy began a five-year term as governor of the state of Victoria. Since then he has enjoyed a relatively quiet retirement, living mostly at a vacation home north of Melbourne and tending to his large gardens. His honours include the Order of the British Empire, the Order of Australia and the Royal Victorian Order. When the 2006 Commonwealth Games came to his hometown, he was chosen to present the Queen's Baton to Queen Elizabeth. Besides the Miracle Mile statue in Vancouver, there is a statue in Melbourne's Olympic Park dedicated to the moment in 1956 when he selflessly turned back to assist the fallen runner Ron Clarke during a national championship race. But the disappointment of finishing second to Bannister has never left him. "I keep running that Vancouver race in my mind on the theory that if I re-run it a thousand times, the results will at least once be reversed," he told a *Vancouver Sun* reporter in 2004. "But it hasn't happened yet." And to John Bryant, the author of *3:59.4: The Quest to Break the 4 Minute Mile,* he said in 2004, "Buzz Aldrin, Tenzing Norgay and me. It's nice we haven't been completely forgotten. Perhaps we should have had some sort of club named after the men who got there second." John Landy remains among the most respected and revered Australian athletes of all time.

After his brilliant Mile victory in Vancouver, Roger Bannister ran only once more competitively; later in August 1954 he won the 1500m comfortably at the European championships, and *Sports Illustrated* named him their inaugural Sportsman of the Year. Besides a few notable writing sidelights—his 1955 book *The Four Minute Mile* remains one of sport's great reads—he dedicated himself fully to his medical career, devoting himself to researching the mysteries of the human nervous system. He wrote and edited numerous textbooks and some 80 research papers, including the definitive book on autonomic nervous system disorders. He retired in 1993, by then firmly established as one of the world's foremost neurologists. In 2005 the American Academy of Neurology honoured him for lifetime achievement in medicine. "I feel my medical career is more significant than my running," Bannister emphasized in 2007.

However, Roger Bannister also served as the first chairman (1971-74) of the British Sports Council (now Sport England) where he worked to increase the number of sport facilities across the nation from 20 to over 400. He became a committed advocate for drug-free sport and initiated some of the earliest testing for performance-enhancing drugs. For his contributions to sport and medicine Bannister was knighted in 1975. From 1976 to 1983 he led the Berlin-based International Council of Sport Science and Physical Education and served as master of Oxford University's Pembroke College from 1985 to 1993. He continued to run recreationally almost daily for 20 years after Vancouver, but in 1975 a drunk driver slammed into his car, and his right ankle was shattered. Thereafter, he walked with a limp, and since running was too painful, he rode his bicycle for exercise instead. More recently, Parkinson's has left him wheelchair-bound. Bannister stayed close friends with Chris Chataway and Chris Brasher for decades after their running careers were over. He also maintains a special bond with Landy, who attended the 50th anniversary celebration of Bannister's four-minute mile at Oxford in 2004. They remain good friends to this day.

Despite the steady lowering of times for all running distances, those who have run the mile in under four minutes still stand as a rather exclusive club. By 2004 just over 2,000 runners around the world had broken four minutes. (More people have climbed Mount Everest.) As the first man through the sub-four-minute door, Sir Roger is still the object of the public's fascination. He receives hundreds of autograph requests by mail every year, as well as dozens of requests for interviews from news outlets. He responds to all of them personally. He was honoured with a commemorative British 50-pence coin in 2004 and the singlet he wore in Vancouver now resides within the Smithsonian's collection. Speculation was rife in the lead-up to the 2012 Olympic Games in London that Bannister would light the Olympic cauldron during the Games' Opening Ceremony, but fittingly his leg of the torch relay took place on Oxford's Iffley Road, site of so much personal history. Sir Roger Bannister remains one of the great ambassadors of world athletics, celebrated as a heroic gentleman amateur with the courage to push himself beyond known limits.

❂

In 2010 Vancouver hosted the Olympic and Paralympic Winter Games, the first sports event held in British Columbia that truly surpassed the 1954 BECG in every way. Others had come close—the 1994 Commonwealth Games in Victoria chief among them—but like 1954, the 2010 Games had worldwide impact. Other parallels linking the two events are the bitter controversies over venue placement, an athlete's tragic in-competition accident that shocked the world, and the much-hyped match-up that exceeded all expectations on the final day. There was one more aspect that surprised most in 2010, though not those who had experienced the Games in 1954. Dr. Doug Clement, who had been a member of the Canadian team then, came back in 2010 along with his athlete wife Diane, but this time they were there to serve as Olympic ambassadors and mayors of the Paralympic Athletes Village at False Creek. When interviewed for this book in 2007, three years before the Olympics were to open, Dr. Clement predicted the drama that lay ahead for Vancouver:

> For the month around the British Empire Games, Vancouver was just abuzz with excitement and spirit, which I think will be duplicated in the 2010

Olympic Games. Most people don't have a clue about how exciting that gets, not only for competitors but for everybody living in the area. It will be a topic of conversation that just will not go away. It dominates everything for that period of time, which you have to go through to experience and believe.

Of course, Dr. Clement was proven completely right. In 2010 Vancouver dropped its characteristic laidback disinterest and proved to be a city that got behind big events to an extraordinary extent. Vancouverites painted the town Canadian red, welcoming the world with open arms, red mittens and warm smiles. The spirit with which they took to the Games stunned even hardened Olympic observers, and that spirit became infectious as hundreds of thousands celebrated victories on downtown streets, high-fiving strangers amid impromptu street hockey games. And the spirit that swept over Vancouver in 2010 could very well have been the biggest legacy left behind by the 1954 British Empire and Commonwealth Games.

In 1954 some extremely prescient ad writer had produced a slogan promoting Vancouver's first Games: A Week You'll Remember a Lifetime! Most advertising slogans never live up to their message or they become so sanitized they lose any real meaning. This one rang truer than most. Ask those who were there. Read their stories. They've carried with them the spirit of that unforgettable week in Vancouver their entire lives and spread it around the world.

Opposite: When Roger Bannister (left) and John Landy (right) returned to Vancouver in 1967 for the unveiling of their bronze statue, comedian Bob Hope (centre) emceed the dinner ceremony. Photo from author's collection.

RESOURCES AND RESEARCH

ARCHIVAL SOURCES

BC Sports Hall of Fame Archives

1954 British Empire and Commonwealth Games Written Documents
Scrapbook Collection, Various
Audio Interview Collection
>   Jack Bain, 1980; Irene MacDonald, 1980; Paul Nemeth, 1990; Jim Peters, 1996; Fred Rowell, 1992; Stanley Smith, 1973

British Library

Sheila Lerwill Audio Interview, 2002

Chilliwack Archives

British Empire and Commonwealth Games Society (1954) Rowing Events
Engineering Committee minutes and correspondence, 1953-1954

City of Vancouver Archives

British Empire Games- Budget, 1954
British Empire Games- Director's meetings, 1954
British Empire Games- Executive Committee minutes, 1952-1953
British Empire Games- Rowing Committee minutes, 1954
British Empire Games- swimming pool, 1951-1954

Jim Peters Family Collection

Jim Peters Personal Training Journals

University of British Columbia Archives

Frank Read fonds

BOOKS

Agostini, Mike. *Sprinting*. London: Stanley Paul, 1962.

Bale, John. *Roger Bannister and the Four-Minute Mile: Sports Myth and Sports History*. London: Routledge, 2004.

Bannister, Roger. *The Four Minute Mile*. New York, Mead, 1955.

_____. *Twin Tracks: The Autobiography*. London: The Robson Press, 2014.

Bascomb, Neal. *The Perfect Mile: Three Athletes, One Goal, and Less Than Four Minutes To Achieve It*. New York: Mariner Books, 2004.

Brasher, Christopher. *Sportsmen of Our Time*. London: Victor Gollancz Ltd., 1962.

Breen, David, and Kenneth Coates. *Vancouver's Fair: An Administrative & Political History of the Pacific National Exhibition*. Vancouver: University of British Columbia Press, 1982.

Brunt, Stephen. *Facing Ali: The Opposition Weighs In*. Toronto: Alfred A. Knopf Canada, 2002.

Bryant, John. *3:59.4: The Quest to Break the 4 Minute Mile*. London: Arrow Books, 2004.

_____. *Chris Brasher: The Man Who Made the London Marathon*. London: Aurum Press Ltd, 2012.

Carver, John Arthur. *The Vancouver Rowing Club: A History, 1886-1980*. Vancouver: Aubrey F. Roberts Ltd., 1980.

Clarke, Ron, and Norman Harris. *The Lonely Breed*. London: Pelham Books Ltd., 1967.

Clerk, Blair M., and Norah M. Scott. *The Official History of the Vth British Empire and Commonwealth Games: 1954*, Vancouver, Canada. Vancouver: British Empire & Commonwealth Games Canada (1954) Society, 1954.

Cox, Michele. *Sunrise From The Summit: 18 Inspiring New Zealand Sportswomen Share Their Stories*. Auckland: Harper Collins Publishers (New Zealand) Limited, 2007.

Cunliffe-Jones, Peter. *My Nigeria: Five Decades of Independence*. St. Martin's Press, 2010.

De Beaumont, Charles Louis. *Fencing: Ancient Art and Modern Sport*. Oak Tree Publications, 1979.

Denison, Jim. *Bannister and Beyond: The Mystique of the Four-Minute Mile*. New York: Breakaway Books, 2003.

Dheenshaw, Cleve. *The Commonwealth Games: The first 60 years, 1930-1990*. Victoria, BC: Orca Book Publishers, 1994.

Fraser, Fil. *Running Uphill: The Fast, Short Life of Canadian Champion Harry Jerome*. Edmonton: Dragon Hill Publishing Ltd., 2006.

Gilmour, Garth. *A Clean Pair of Heels: The Murray Halberg Story*. Auckland: A.H. & A.W. Reed, 1963.

_____. *Arthur Lydiard: Master Coach*. Cheltenham, United Kingdom: Sportsbooks Limited, 2004.

Gordon, Harry. *Young Men in a Hurry: The Story of Australia's Fastest Decade*. Melbourne: Lansdowne Press, 1961.

_____. *Australia and the Olympic Games*. Queensland: United Queensland Press, 1994.

Gosper, Kevan, with Glenda Korporaal. *An Olympic Life: Melbourne 1956 – Sydney 2000*. St. Leonards, New South Wales: Allen & Unwin, 2000.

Hadgraft, Rob. *Plimsolls On, Eyeballs Out: The Rise and Horrendous Fall of Marathon Legend Jim Peters*. Essex, UK: Desert Island Books Limited, 2011.

Hall, Ann M. *The Girl and the Game: A History of Women's Sport in Canada*. Peterborough, Ontario: Broadview Press, 2002.

Henry, Tom. *Inside Fighter: Dave Brown's Remarkable Stories of Canadian Boxing*. Madeira Park, BC: Harbour Publishing, 2001.

Hewson, Brian. *Flying Feet*. London: The Sportsman's Book Club, 1962.

Hoby, Alan. *One Crowded Hour*. London: Museum Press Limited, 1954.

Johnson, Len. *The Landy Era: From Nowhere to the Top of the World*. Melbourne: Melbourne Books, 2009.

Kearney, Jim. *Champions: A British Columbia Sports Album*. Vancouver: Douglas & McIntyre Ltd., 1985.

Kelso, John (Jack). *The History of the Ocean Falls Amateur Swimming Club, 1926-1974*. Vancouver: University of British Columbia School of Human Kinetics, 2004.

Kennedy, Margaret, and Gordon Kennedy. *Stadium Stories: The Empire Stadium Scrapbook*. Vancouver: Stadium Productions Ltd., 1992.

Krise, Raymond, and Bill Squires. *Fast Tracks: The History of Distance Running*. Brattleboro, Vermont: The Stephen Greene Press, 1982.

Landy, John. *Close to Nature: A Naturalist's Diary of a Year in the Bush*. Melbourne: Ringwood, 1988.

_____. *A Coastal Diary: A Study of One of Australia's Wildest and Most Beautiful Coastlines*. Sydney: Macmillan, 1993.

Lewis, Steve. *Ken Jones: Boots & Spikes*. Cheltenham, UK: SportsBooks Limited, 2011.

Mossman, Gary. *Lloyd Percival: Coach and Visionary*. Woodstock, Ontario: Seraphim Editions, 2013.

Oliver, Brian. *The Commonwealth Games: Extraordinary Stories Behind the Medals*. London: Bloomsbury Publishing Plc, 2014.

Ottah, Nelson. *The Trial of Biafra's Leaders*. Fourth Dimension, 1980.

Palenski, Ron, and Terry Maddaford. *The Games*. Auckland: MOA Publications Ltd., 1983.

Peters, Jim, "Johnny" Johnston, and Joseph Edmundson. *In The Long Run*. London: Cassell & Co. Ltd., 1955.

_____. *Modern Middle and Long-Distance Running*. London: Nicholas Kaye Ltd., 1957.

Phillips, Bob. *Honour of Empire, Glory of Sport: The History of Athletics at the Commonwealth Games*. Manchester: The Parrs Wood Press, 2000.

_____. *The Commonwealth Games: The History of All The Sports*. Manchester: The Parrs Wood Press, 2002.

_____. *3:59.4: The Quest for the Four-Minute Mile*. Manchester: The Parrs Wood Press, 2004.

Siollun, Max. *Oil, Politics, and Violence: Nigeria's Military Coup Culture* (1966-1976). New York: Algora Publishing, 2009.

Sirotnik, Gareth. *Running Tough: The Story of Vancouver's Jack Diamond*. Vancouver: The Diamond Family, 1988.

Smit, Barbara. *Pitch Invasion: Three Stripes, Two Brothers, One Feud: Adidas, Puma, and The Making of Modern Sport*. London: Penguin Books Ltd., 2006.

Smith, George. *All Out For The Mile: A History of the Mile Race, 1864-1955*. London: Forbes Robertson Ltd., 1955.

Solomon, Robert. *Great Australian Athletes: Selected Olympians 1928 – 1956*. Marrickville, New South Wales: Southwood Press Pty Ltd., 2000.

Stampfl, Franz. *Franz Stampfl On Running: Sprint, Middle Distance and Distance Events*. London: Herbert Jenkins, 1955.

Stell, Marion. *Half The Race: A History of Australian Women in Sport*. North Ryde, New South Wales: Angus & Robertson Publishers Pty Limited, 1991.

Thurston, Tom. *Strongman: The Doug Hepburn Story*. Vancouver: Ronsdale Press, 2003.

Young, Derrick. *The Ten Greatest Races*. London: A.C.M. Webb (Publishing) Ltd., 1972.

Zeiler, Lorne. *Hearts of Gold: Stories of Courage, Dedication and Triumph from Canadian Olympians*. Vancouver: Raincoast Books, 2004.

INTERVIEWS

(Conducted in person, by phone, by email, or by written correspondence)

Ackles, Bob, 2008
Agostini, Mike, 2010
Atkinson, Lorne, 2007
Baillie, Bill, 2007
Bannister, Sir Roger, 2007
Boyd, Ian, 2007
Brown, Dave, 2005
Burrows, Vicky, 2007
Capozzi, Herb, 2008
Caravetta, Mario, 2007
Chataway, Sir Chris, 2007
Clement, Doug, 2007
Corben, Len, 2007
Corlett, Yvette (Williams), 2007
Cox, Stanley, 2007
Drummond, Ken, 2007
Eccleston, Faye (Burnham), 2007
Farley, Jack, 2008
Fieldgate, Norm, 2008
Frew, Keith, 2008
Gardom, Hon. Garde, 2007
Gilchrist, Lenore (Fisher), 2012
Gilchrist, Ron, 2012
Good, Jr., Bill, 2013
Halberg, Sir Murray, 2007
Harris, Mike, 2007
Henricks, Jon, 2009
Hird, Alan, 2004
Hopkins, Thelma, 2013
Hume II, Fred, 2007
Hunt, Helen (Stewart), 2007
Jackson-Nelson, Marjorie, 2013
Kearney, Jim, 2006
Kovits, Dr. Herman, 2007
Kueber, Phil, 2007
Laishley, Don, 2007
Landy, John, 2007
Law, David, 2007

Lush, Barry, 2013
MacDonald, Jackie, 2007
Maltman, Frieda, 2007
McDonald, Doug, 2007
McDonald, Vonna, 2007
McFarlane, Don, 2013
Miller, Eleanor (McKenzie), 2012
Milligan, Victor, 2007
Neale, Kaye (McNamee), 2007
Nelson, Harry, 2013
Onyeama, Henry, 2013
Paonessa, Tommy, 2007
Parnell, Bill, 2007
Parnell, Joan, 2009
Reynolds, Ted, 2007
Richards, Dal, 2007
Robson, Jim, 2008
Sierpina, Ray, 2007
Simicak, Alice (Whitty), 2013
Smith, Dr. Glen, 2007
Sparks, Robert, 2008
Springbett, Bruce, 2013
Stafford, Dave, 2013
Stonehouse, Don, 2013
Sturrock, Doug, 2007
Sutherland, Glinda, 2010
Taylor, Jim, 2006
Tobacco, Terry, 2007
Toynbee, Tom, 2007
Vallance, Margaret, 2007
Vernon, John, 2013
Wadley-Smith, Barry, 2013
Wadley-Smith, Jennifer, 2013
Warner, Charlie, 2007
Warren, Geoff, 2013
Williams, Audrey, 2008
Wilson, Bob, 2007
Young, Louise, 2007

FILM FOOTAGE

Archival

BC Sports Hall of Fame Archives, various
CBC Archives, various
National Film Board of Canada, various stock footage

Commercial Video & DVD

British Empire and Commonwealth Games Documentary, National Film Board of Canada, 1954.

Four Minutes, ESPN Original Entertainment, 2005.

Strength of Giants, CBC Telescope 67 television program, September 28, 1967.

The Miracle Mile: A 50th Anniversary Special, Canadian Broadcasting Corporation, 2004.

WRITTEN SOURCES

Journal Articles

Dawson, Michael. "Putting Cities 'on the map': the 1954 British Empire & Commonwealth Games in Comparative and Historical Perspective," *Urban Geography 32,* 6 (2011): 788-803.

Noakes, Timothy, Jackie Meklar, and Dan Pedoe. "Jim Peters' collapse in the 1954 Vancouver Empire Games marathon," SAMJ Forum, August 2008, Vol. 98, No. 8, pg 596-600.

Newspapers & Major Magazines

Auckland Weekly News, July–August 1954.
Chilliwack Progress, 1953–1954.
Evening Post (New Zealand) 1954.
Life, 17 May 1954–16 August 1954.
Maclean's, 1954–1955.
New York Times, August 1954.
New Zealand Herald, July-August 1954.
Sports Illustrated, 1954–1956.
The Globe and Mail (Toronto), 1953–1954.
The Province (Vancouver), 1938–1955.
The Ubyssey, 1953–1955.
The Weekly News, (New Zealand) 1954.
Vancouver News-Herald, 1938–1955.
Vancouver Sun, 1938–1955.
Victoria Daily Colonist, 1950–1955.
Victoria Daily Times, 1950–1955.

Newspapers/Periodicals for Selected Articles

BC Sport News
Brisbane Courier-Mail
CBC Times
East London Dispatch (South Africa)
Edmonton Journal
Georgia Straight
Glasgow Herald
London Guardian
London Observer
London Times
Melbourne Age
Melbourne Herald Sun
New Zealand Woman's Weekly
North Shore Outlook
Ottawa Citizen
New York Times Magazine
Scotland on Sunday
Sportwest
Sydney Morning Herald
The African Bulletin
The Independent (London)
The Runner
The Telegraph (London)
The Weekly News (Vancouver)
Time Magazine
Toronto Star
Vancouver Courier
World Sports

Photographs

BC Sports Hall of Fame Archives
Personal Collection (includes photograph gifts from various interviewees)
University of British Columbia Archives
Vancouver Public Library Special Collections
Vancouver Sun / Province Media Library

INDEX